The Power of Open-Book Management

Other books by John P. Schuster:

Hum-Drum to Hot-Diggity: Creating Everyday Greatness in the World of Work, Steadfast Publishers, 1993.

Advance Praise for *The Power of Open-Book Management*

"If we are going to thrive in this new world economic order, *everyone* must be a business person. If you want to know how, read this book. *The Power of Open-Book Management* is the essential guidebook for every organization that wants all its associates to understand how they make and lose money—and that should be *every* organization. The authors have gone way beyond the telling of success stories and given us the steps and tools for implementing what will prove to be the twentieth century's most important economic revolution."

Jim Kouzes, co-author *The Leadership Challenge* and *Credibility*
Chairman and CEO, TPG/Learning Systems

"Open-book management, coupled with caring leadership, is likely to become the norm in the twenty-first century. Schuster, Carpenter and Kane have authored a profound road map for fellow-travelers to follow into the next century. I highly recommend it."

Larry Spears, Executive Director
The Greenleaf Center for Servant-Leadership
Editor, *Reflections on Leadership*

"Enabling a large number of people in an organization to work together in a coordinated way requires they share an image and understanding of the system of which they are a part. This book offers a clear and pragmatic approach for doing just that."

Jeff Clanon, Executive Director
MIT Center for Organizational Learning

"If you want a learning organization, this is a must-read . . . the best combination of people and financial management rolled up onto one management approach anyone can imagine. It's refreshing to see people and companies working to make business and free enterprise a win-win, fully humanized endeavor."

Lori Bartel, Vice President of Operations
Excell Agent Services

"*The Power of Open-Book Management* shows how human values and sound business principles can work in harmony . . . before you open your books, open this one!"

Rob Zicaro
Employee-Owner, Web Industries

"Open-book management is the survival strategy of the twenty-first century. *The Power of Open-Book Management* is a must-read for those who want to adopt this ground-breaking technique for creating an empowered work force to grow their business."

> Richard H. Merrill, President
> Tyler Mountain Water Company

"Widespread use of open-book management as described in this publication is, in my opinion, absolutely essential as we move further away from the industrial to the information society and work in a global economy . . . It promotes responsible risk-taking and continuous learning as critical factors for both individual and organizational growth and effectiveness."

> Robert B. Rogers, Chairman and CEO
> The Kauffman Foundation
> (Formerly financial officer and member
> Board of Directors, Marion Laboratories)

". . . The twenty-first century is upon us, and this book will help make open-book management a permanent part of where business is headed."

> Jim Carter, Chief Operating Officer & Vice President, Operations
> Syncrude Canada Ltd.

"Open-book management is a remarkable from-the-ground-up movement that is transforming management. This book provides an easy-to-use, step-by-step guide to making it work for you."

> Corey Rosen, Executive Director
> National Center for Employee Ownership

"This book not only tells you why open-book management is a sound idea, but also it helps you put it into practice. The author's extensive experience and practical applications come through strongly and benefit anybody who wants to get started."

> Sven Atterhed
> The Foresight Group, Sweden

"The Power of Open-Book Management provides an answer to the age old question of 'how can I get all my employees to act and think like owners.' It is packed with insights and examples of what leaders must do to organize around information and customers. Those companies that learn to process information and adjust quicker than others will be the ones that prevail in the twenty-first century. It is a must read for anyone interested in how we will work in the future."

> Tom Corbo, CEO
> MANCO

The Power of Open-Book Management

Releasing the
True Potential of People's
Minds, Hearts, and Hands

John P. Schuster
and
Jill Carpenter

with

M. Patricia Kane

JOHN WILEY & SONS, INC.
New York • Chichester • Brisbane • Toronto • Singapore

Library of Congress Cataloging-in-Publication Data:

Schuster, John, 1948–
    The power of open-book management : releasing the true potential
of people's minds, hearts, and hands / John Schuster, Jill Carpenter,
Patricia Kane.
        p.   cm.
    Includes index.
    ISBN 0-471-13287-X (cloth : alk. paper)
    1. Organizational effectiveness.   2. Organizational learning.
    3. Management—Employee participation.   4. Incentives in industry.
    I. Carpenter, Jill.   II. Kane, Patricia.   III. Title.
    HD58.9.S384   1996
    658.3'14—dc20   95-42390

Printed in the United States of America

10   9   8   7   6   5   4   3   2   1

We hope this book will contribute to the lasting and loving union of ideas pioneered by Frederick Taylor and Mother Jones, two early 20th-century figures from the world of work, whose spirits live on. Frederick Taylor was the father of scientific management, the practice that relegated the worker to carrying out management orders and being subjected to time-and-motion studies. Mother Jones was a labor organizer, feared and loathed by industrialists for her radical views of employee rights. May the precision and utopia Taylor sought, and the fairness and decency Mother Jones fought for, find expression in an open-book world.

Foreword

After years of working with the partners at Capital Connection, I am deeply impressed with them as professionals and as human beings. We met while I was teaching innovation management and intrapreneurship to one of their clients. I am indebted to them for figuring out ways to present and use intrapreneuring without triggering the corporate immune system. Now they have used that same talent to spread one of the most liberating management tools of our times, open-book management.

In the decade ahead, open-book management may have as large an effect on how we do business as quality did in the decades just past. The wide acceptance of quality techniques spelled the end of the old bureaucratic systems of management which are the legacy of the seventeenth century. Quality empowered ordinary employees to cross the boundaries of the organization in search of the root causes of variation. This was a giant step away from bureaucracy toward systems based on the lateral coordination between peers. Lateral communication is the key to higher organizational intelligence.

But today, while essential, total quality is more the price of admission to today's highly competitive markets than a reliable source of competitive advantage. You need quality plus some of the next generation management tools. Open-book management is one of the most powerful and perhaps the most accessible of the next generation transformation tools.

Open-book management involves everyone in the language of the business, the language of finance. It gives every employee the training, the language, and the up-to-date information to make good decisions in their day-to-day work. Without widespread sharing of information with employees, organizations are flying blind.

There have always been some advantages to openness with employees and there will always be some advantages to secrecy. The balance between the two is changing. The advantages of openness are rapidly increasing while the advantages of secrecy are in many cases decreasing.

The advantages of openness are growing because the challenges organizations face are becoming much more complex. To respond to these new challenges, companies must digest huge volumes of new information and use it in creative ways before their competitors do.

Markets are segmenting into smaller and more demanding customer groups. Technologies change fast and are more complex. As we approach the limits of natural systems, the careless practices of the past become unacceptable, and the new practices require more ecological intelligence and care.

Companies today must be intelligent at both the global level of how it all fits together and the local level of how to satisfy a specific customer in a specific culture right now. This can only be achieved by using all the intelligence of the organization effectively. But the intelligence of an organization is widely distributed, one brain per person. Organizations can match the challenges of the day be finding ways to empower and align all the talents in the organization to solve problems and serve customers. It's hard to see how that could happen unless the employees know what is going on.

Open-book management is flourishing now because we are going through a change as profound as the change from the feudal empires of the agricultural era to the market-mediated societies of the industrial era. As the challenges humanity faces grow more complex, the form by which we organize societies and corporations changes. Nations hit the wall of complexity hundreds of years ago and those that advanced did so by abandoning the primitive forms for bringing order, namely systems based on a chain of command. Nations were able to create a more detailed and intelligent order by using self-organizing systems, such as the market economy and the peer judgment system in the science community.

The evolution of advanced societies toward market freedom and democracy illustrates a paradoxical principle that is just now emerging from the science of complexity and chaos: The greater complexity and chaos of the challenges, the more *freedom* is needed to create enough order to make an adequate response. In self-organizing systems, we create more order by finding ways to make freedom work. Good information widely distributed is one of the most basic tools for making freedom work.

When the more complex demands of the industrial revolution challenged nations in the seventeenth and eighteenth centuries, those nations flourished that abandoned the constrictions of feudalism and liberated their people. They used new mechanisms for bringing order without the domination of the many by a few feudal lords. Similarly, as companies hit the complexity of the information age and the global economy, those companies that are finding more effective ways to liberate the intrapreneural spirit of their employees from the bonds of bureaucracy are flourishing.

As we enter the third millennium, a vast transfer of learning is taking place. We are taking what we have learned about how to organize whole nations and applying bits and pieces of it to managing companies, not-for-profits and government agencies. The basic sources of order in the intelligent organizations that are emerging are choice and community. Open-book management serves both.

We cannot trust empowered employees to make good choices unless they are also well-informed. Educating employees on the basic figures of the business through the interactive process of the "intensive huddle system" gives employees a context that guides their imaginations and their intrapreneurial initiative in constructive directions. Empowering without first distributing knowledge doesn't produce good results. Thus empowerment without open-book management simply confirms all the old beliefs that reinforce hierarchy and ponderous systems of control.

Similarly, open-book management is a powerful tool for creating the spirit of community. Shared knowledge of the numbers creates a shared game, a common environment in which everyone's score rises and falls together. Inequality, not only of rank, but also of knowledge and understanding, will corrode community. Sharing the basic business information is a giant step toward greater equality. Sharing the numbers with everyone promotes full membership in the organizational community.

The evolution of systems capable of dealing with the challenges of the information age is only partially complete. The boring and routine tasks that once constituted the work of the average employee are vanishing as machines take over repetitious work. What is left for humans is increasingly work requiring a bit of imagination, caring, creativity, communication skills, or intelligence, and often a fair measure of all four. To be effective in the information age, we need to use the best thinking of all employees. But "garbage in, garbage out" applies to people as well as to computers. People's ability (and desire) to use their intelligence for the benefit of the organization is determined by the degree to which they are given good information.

I am willing to bet that once quality systems are in place, the next big step toward liberating the intelligence and capacity of organizations will prove to be open-book management. As explained by Schuster, Carpenter, and Kane, it seems so obvious it is hard to understand why everyone is not already doing it. Open-book management can transform organizations and give them a major advantage over any organization stuck in old ways of thinking, like keeping employees in the dark.

In *The Power of Open-Book Management*, Schuster, Carpenter, and Kane give a detailed explanation of how to make open-book management work. First, it shows how to sell open-book management to executives, managers, and individual contributors. Then comes the best part: The book explains the basic principles of open-book management and then shows that there are many ways to implement those principles through examples of companies that have done so in different ways.

Schuster, Carpenter, and Kane take on the tough issues, such as reward systems, with the wisdom of those who have learned from their mistakes as well as their victories. With each topic, they alert readers to the most common ways to fail and how to avoid them, as well as providing examples that illustrate a variety of ways to succeed. With the wisdom of both good and bad experiences, they show how to make open-book management work in any organization.

GIFFORD PINCHOT

Preface

❧❧ ❧❧ ❧❧ ❧❧

If you can measure what of which you speak and express it in numbers, you know something about your subject; but if you cannot measure it, your knowledge is of a very meager and unsatisfactory kind.

— Lord Kelvin

The academics, teamed with consultants on the developmental side of the business theory field, tend to write the books that are conceptually sound and descriptive. They live by the ringing truth in the old phrase: "There is nothing more practical than a good theory."

The business press shies away from theory and instead provides examples and some how-to's. It both inspires and provides advice for the small-business growth sector, demonstrating the learning experiments on the fast-moving fringe, and informs and teaches about developments in big companies in the major industries.

Both groups provide an invaluable service and influenced this book.

The purpose of this book is to incorporate sound theory, lots of practical how-to's, examples, and some inspiration, so that readers can both learn and expand their knowledge of open-book management and have enough detail to take some action. Theory without how-to's is impractical; how-to's without theory may work some of the time, but are often not replicable in settings when unexpected interference pops up that requires new applications of theory.

Our Background

We gathered the ideas and examples for this book by observing and working with companies that wanted to become better businesses through authentic employee participation, which involved making financial tools usable by all employees. We started our company Capital Connections, Inc., in 1990, after gaining extensive career experience in large and small companies, and in our own consulting and training practices.

Inc. magazine, a publication that focuses on small business, had captured our attention by writing articles about what became known as open-book management. Our early assessment was that while this set of practices may have started on the fringe, and was especially embodied in the Springfield Remanufacturing Company (a company 160 miles from our homes in Kansas City, Missouri), the practices would not stay on the fringe. Inc. had indeed been doing its job reporting on the worthwhile experiments in the growth sector. Open-book management had something fundamental to offer.

We got hooked on the promise and the practice of open-book management. We haven't been the same since we started to work with it, and this book is one result of the past six years' effort.

Fads and Fundamentals

Our strong belief is that open-book management is a sound, practical and results-enhancing way to run a business. When used well, it benefits all the participants in the business and narrows some of the age-old gaps between functions and levels, management and employees that have plagued business since its inception.

It is the best combination of management practices that we have seen. While fads come and go, we have evidence that this set of practices, under whatever name, is rock solid and points in new, sustainable directions.

If you have been involved in the organization improvement scene the past few decades, as we have, nothing much surprises you anymore. Although there have been inspiring breakthroughs in pockets of companies and not-for-profits and government everywhere, many of us are more than a little jaded by a marketplace of approaches that have produced hundreds of buzzwords and techniques, promising too much and delivering too little. Even the real gains brought by total quality and team-based systems tend to get little consideration because incompetent efforts have left a bad taste. There are many who salivated on delicious gourmet promises of empowerment, customer satisfaction, and profits but ended up with peanut butter and jelly on plain white bread.

The predictable stages for senior management teams who test new systems—becoming aware of the new method, getting interested and gaining knowledge, trying it out, having difficulty getting past "the low-hanging fruit," then getting tired and disillusioned—will occur for some with open-book management. Many will have interest, some will take action, and some of those experimenters will work to make the essence of it happen. We say it many times in this book: Competent, concerned, and deeply committed leaders are a key requirement to bring the power of open-book management into full bloom.

Some, sadly, will misuse the concepts or manipulate them to their own ends. They will publish company income statements, polish up the budgets, spread them around a little more to management, and claim to their customers, on the eighth green, that their company "has absorbed the principles of open-book management into our quality processes and we now have all our employees financially aware. Let's tee up."

But the real open-book movement will flourish and survive past these shallow applications. Why? Because it is sustainable and empowering; it can move a company and its people closer to their potential. The Malcolm Baldrige Award now includes business and financial performance in its criteria, indicating the shift toward open-book management concerns.

Those who embrace open-book management have a generosity of spirit and spread the word to help each other, in part because open-book management is not just about generating profits, cash, and wealth but also about distributing it for the good of society. Finally, as competition increases, managers will have no choice but to generate a workforce that is itself a sustainable competitive advantage, a team of business-smart entrepreneurs.

How to Read This Book

You can read this book your way, as stimulating evening reading at home, or with your team, a chapter a time, at weekly staff meetings. We receive continual questions of the "we want to go open-book, how do we get started?" variety. These questions, along with the consulting and training we've been doing, greatly influenced how we put together this book. Here is what you can expect.

Section I, "Open-Book Management: What Is It," which includes Chapters 1 through 5, describes open-book management and how it works. We have emphasized why it is needed, what systems and practices are at work with open-book companies, and what problems it addresses. We outline the main model for open-book systems, starting in Chapter 2, and end with a call to leadership, in Chapter 5 to set the tone for open-book management in your enterprise.

In Section II, "Open-Book Management: Getting It Started," Chapters 6 through 10 provide a detailed how-to-implement process. These chapters contain the best of what is currently known for a company or division that wants to start, but may not know where to begin, using the language of business and accounting in its day-to-day work.

Chapter 11 is for middle managers who want to move ahead with open-book management *without* having a companywide initiative. Middle managers will make best use of Chapter 11 if they first read the other chapters in Section II; they have lots of ideas and how-to's that are applicable.

Section III, "Keeping It Going," offers ideas on how to sustain open-book management for the long haul, allowing the company to reach high levels of employee business know-how. It addresses the all-important issues of planning in Chapter 12, information-sharing and decision-making in Chapter 13, and motivation in Chapter 14. We have observed companies that have gotten the initial early gains from open-book management, and then report a slowdown or lag time. While that is natural, Section III describes the disciplines that change a company culture permanently, that make open-book management a way to do business day in and day out.

Not for the Faint of Heart

Open-book management, like any worthwhile endeavor, is a challenge to do well. It requires real persistence, lots of business skill, and leadership to make it happen. It absolutely stimulates learning and a higher level of thinking for participants who use ever-changing data, focus on a goal, and exercise individual and team judgment.

With open-book management, some of our human frailties have to take a back seat—less blaming of others, less self-promotion at the expense of others, less glossing over the truth, less resentment and unproductive competition. It calls forth a commitment to do your best for yourself and the good of the team and enterprise. It takes honesty, risk-taking, open admission of mistakes, a love of feedback—good and bad—and a bent toward lifelong learning. Companies with open-book management do not rest on past laurels.

For all these reasons, this form of management is not for everybody, especially those who liked the old days of entitlement and are still looking for a free lunch, even if it's just a grilled cheese sandwich.

A Favor to Ask

While we are grateful to be offering this book, we also feel somewhat eager and anxious. For while we have researched, studied, applied, listened, rethought, and relearned, there is still so much more to learn, to test, and to discover. After several years of study and work, we can now appreciate the many nuances in open-book management practices that we couldn't hear or see at first. This is where the anxious comes in: We are anxious to learn more.

So we are going to ask you for a favor.

As you apply the methods and principles suggested in this book, call or write us and let us known what you learned at Capital Connections, Inc., 801 W. 47th Street, #411, Kansas City, Missouri 64112, (816) 561-662, (800) 833-4263, or E-Mail: 72163.1711@Compuserve.com. This is an evolving field and a work-in-progress. We want to know what you and other pioneers are doing to cut new pathways that others have yet to try.

JOHN SCHUSTER
JILL CARPENTER
PATRICIA KANE

September 1995

Acknowledgments

꒰꒱ ꒰꒱ ꒰꒱ ꒰꒱

There are many people to thank for the ideas, experiences, and examples that make up this book.

Our clients not only gave us the honor to serve them, but provided live learning laboratories for the ideas presented here. The pioneers in these companies represent every level and function, from CEOs to frontline champions. We thank them for their honesty, courage to move ahead against the barriers they faced, and most of all for their desire to improve their businesses by taking people into the uncharted waters of participation through the numbers.

Although space limitations will not allow us to mention all these innovators, we want especially to thank Ev Larson at the Corning Manufacturing complex for his early beliefs and convictions; Paul Davis at the Scanlon Plan companies, who wanted a financial learning experience for 500 people; the whole GSD gang at Sprint, especially Craig Carter, Pam Wagner, and the open-book team, and Chris Rooney, for the sponsorship; Bristol-Meyer's Anthony Casella for the training opportunity; Excell Agent Services and Lori Bartel for endless enthusiasm; Jeanette Hendrych at Intel for early experiments with our learning game; Mikael Lund and his Volvo compatriots, so eager to learn and dialogue; Don de Guerre at Syncrude, for the depth of knowledge in organizational development theory and its applications with open-book principles; Mary Lou Pernod and Judy Meyers at Reuben H. Donnelley, for all those energetic salespeople craving a higher level of business literacy; Bill Engler and Joe Bestor at Kaytee Products, for their serious study; the Tyler Mountain

Water believers, like Mark Gasparovich, who gets tough when the going gets that way.

A hundred thank-you's to our many friends and fellow practitioners who encouraged and supported us during many stages of Capital Connection's growth:

David Glassman, groundbreaker and networker, for the great Canadian connection and the partnership with Capital North Consulting, Ltd.

Jack Knuth and Anne Behrens, for walking the first steps with us.

Cyndi Rue, our woman of all trades, who kept the Capital Connections office together while writing preoccupied us and Julie Kottman, for joining the team.

Don Goldenbaum, whose creativity helped us make Profit & Cash™.

Lori Aiken, whose boundless spirit and open-book knowledge enriched us in the early years.

Sven Atterhed and ForeSight, whose global network and Swedish clients enrich our work.

Donna Ziegenhorn, for marketing know-how, business experience, writing skill, and encouragement.

Russell Brown, for patience and creative input.

Trevor Ralston and Jan Mercer Donaldson, for the "early days" and product ideas that will still happen.

Our associates Catherine Brooks, Kit Mair, Rebecca Kraft, Maureen McGuire, and Kelly Flynn, Mary Hansen, Tom McCoy, Bernie Novokowski, for joining the fray, and Mike Murray for spreading the word.

Cathy Kramer and the whole Association for Quality and Participation team for the education platform and the example of service.

Rick Surpin at Home Care Associates and Jay Harris at *Mother Jones* for pioneering open-book management in not-for-profit settings.

Lakewood and the Positive Employee Practices Institute (PEPI), for cosponsoring the first gathering of open-book practitioners.

Jim Kouzes, for taking an interest in our work from the beginning and steering good people our way.

Rockhurst College, for sponsoring the first open-book seminar in our hometown, Kansas City, Missouri.

Don Barkman for his skill in networking and training.

Above everybody and everything else, we owe an enormous debt of gratitude to the people at Springfield Remanufacturing Company (SRC), in Springfield, Missouri, so generous with their time and energy from 1990 into 1994. As our initial business partners, they had us play the Great Game of Business® (their unique version of open-book management) with them. The discipline, along with all the learning, stuck.

There are many heroes and "sheroes" at SRC. Instead of giving more mention to those already in the limelight, we want to thank the whole community; and in particular those behind the scenes, the frontline workers and team leaders at New Stream, Megavolt, Avatar, Engines Plus, Sequel, and Heavy Duty, who welcomed our questions and were eager learners in our pilots.

Inc. has provided leadership for open-book management and support for us, and author and editor John Case holds a special place in our hearts—for giving shape to the field and having so much class.

And thanks to Jim Childs, our editor at John Wiley, who saw the coming of the movement and guided us, quite gracefully—even when we were cranky with too much on our consulting plates—through the development of this book.

Contents

Wealth is achieved essentially by one's own efforts. It is earned, little by little, in an active market where goods, services, and ideas are exchanged and people are constantly learning and adjusting to each other's needs. Wealth comes from knowing how to use resources, not from owning them.

—Hernando de Soto
The Other Path

Section I

❧❧❧❧

Open-Book Management: What Is It?

Chapter 1

❧❧❧❧

Open-Book Management:
The Need and the Promise

*Quality control is one thing. People control is another. The first
we all need. The second nobody needs. We do need new structures and a new attitude that, I hope, will take us further toward using the talents and skills of everybody. Times have
simply gotten too tough for any company to allow even the
slightest amount of talent or skill or knowledge available to go
to waste.*

—Kerm Campbell
President
Herman Miller

Economics and Empowerment

A large number of businesspeople, managers, and academics realized in the early 1980s that many North American
companies were losing their competitive edge. At about
the same time that "Eat Your Import" bumper stickers started
showing up on cars and trucks across the United States, these
same people began to reexamine some of the traditional management methods. Despite several improvements in business
processes—the rise of information systems, management by
objectives, project planning, and a host of other evolutionary
systems—the environment was right, even desperate, for radical change, a business revolution.

3

The business community provided an ample number of signs:

- A compelling and frantic Tom Peters shouting about customers and employee involvement.
- The haunting story of quality gurus Demming and Juran who had to go to the land-of-the-sun to be heard and continue their teaching.
- Headlines about Milkens, Keatings, and Boeskys; their subsequent jail sentences; the S&L bailouts.
- The declining earning power of significant segments of the working classes in the U.S. and elsewhere.
- The announcement from General Motors of job cuts nearing 100,000, followed by similar layoffs at employed-for-life companies like IBM and Procter & Gamble.
- The skyrocketing cost of health care wreaking havoc with profits.
- The staggering cost of environmental accidents and cleanup.

It was time for Western businesses to change their collective mind-set in a significant way and to try something new. Two revolutionary notions emerged: Improve quality for the customer, and increase involvement and empowerment for the employees.

These ideas did not spring from altruistic motivations. Management's feeling the pain of weak financial and noncompetitive market performance forced their emergence. Team-based, quality-focused, employee-involved, empowered work settings became management's holy grail. The approaches that have emerged in this quest—TQM, high-performance systems, learning organizations, business process improvement, reengineering, sociotechnical systems—are by now too numerous to mention and too difficult to distinguish.

Leo Morton is a former AT&T microelectronics executive and Sloan Fellow, who is now at the fast-growth gas and electric international utility, Utilicorps. An observer and participant in many quality and employee-involvement efforts, he describes a cycle that sounds familiar to those who have tried to explain to all employees why changes and improvements are necessary: "Most managers," Morton says, "develop a four-phase approach to change, working their way backwards from poor financial results to the belief that empowered people will make the difference." Figure 1.1 illustrates his Four Phases of Reactive Empowerment—also known as "Oh, My God!"

Figure 1.1 The Four Phases of Reactive Empowerment

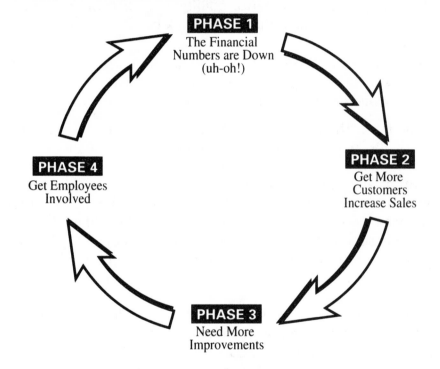

PHASE 1
The Financial
Numbers are Down
(uh-oh!)

PHASE 2
Get More
Customers
Increase Sales

PHASE 3
Need More
Improvements

PHASE 4
Get Employees
Involved

THE FOUR PHASES OF REACTIVE EMPOWERMENT

1- Less than healthy numbers leads to
2- The need for happier/more customers leads to
3- The need for quality and service improvements leads to
4- Involved employees doing the improvements.

Phase 1. "Profits are down and so is the price of our stock," management painfully admits. "That just can't continue into the next quarter."

Phase 2. "We have to increase sales and market share," say the managers. "We need to bring in new customers and delight them, so they will buy our products and services (and, uh-oh, we better cut costs too)."

Phase 3. "If we are going to do that," management figures, "then we need a whole series of new initiatives. We need customer focus, superior quality, new distribution, better delivery and much more teamwork between sales and operations."

Phase 4. "And, to do that," the managers correctly conclude, "we'll have to get our employees involved. Because we managers sure as hell can't do this all by ourselves."

For more than a decade, across the corporate landscape, companies pursued employee-involvement and quality strategies as magic keys to financial success. Success stories were plentiful and popular. Xerox, Motorola, and many others won awards. They described how their employee involvement programs had led them to greater profitability. The old work structures, these stories demonstrated, had held people in jobs they couldn't see out of, concealing from them how their small part fit into larger work processes. And these structures began to crumble.

When it became clear that a turned-on workforce was the key to financial success, employee involvement became the rage. In the late 1980s, Douglas McGregor must have turned, if not spun, in his grave. A quarter century earlier when he wrote *The Human Side of Enterprise,** he had postulated that the old "Theory X" assumptions of work would give way to a new set of management practices that would involve employees. And it did.

---

* McGregor, D. *The Human Side of Enterprise.* New York, NY: McGraw-Hill.

Many companies and even whole industries made progress. Entrepreneurs started new businesses at unprecedented rates. Self-directed teams emerged at many companies and took on new "intrapreneurial" responsibilities. The U.S. auto industry, in an amazing turnaround, won back market share previously lost to Japan.

Not Radical Enough

So the involving-people strategy for improving business worked. Well, it sort of worked—for some. The problem was that for every Xerox or other award-winning company, a thousand others were struggling to make the new vision of the workplace a reality. Getting started with training and team formation was the easy part of quality improvement and employee involvement, but it often did little to change the underlying processes, such as coordination between departments. It was like putting a Porsche body on a Yugo chassis. It might appear capable of traveling an autobahn at 150 mph, but still mostly just sat on the shoulder waiting for the tow truck. As with anything, the hard part was sustaining the effort—measuring financial results and keeping employees motivated to take the business to yet another level.

In the early 1990s, despite progress in some companies and industries, business and popular press articles on "why quality is failing" began to appear. The notable abandonment of employee-involvement processes at the McDonnell-Douglas West Coast facility, after two years of preparation and initial implementation, showed that the strategy of involving and empowering employees was more complicated than it had seemed on the surface.

Questions naturally arose about how to measure the financial impact of these initiatives. Though some companies could point to specific savings and new customers, the questions were never fully answered. Reengineering simplified many bureaucratic nightmares, but the drive for improvement never abated.

In the search for better answers, management considered every solution that was offered by anyone claiming to be a consultant. Some companies were willing to try anything. They made mistakes. Some of the more common approaches that did not work can serve as a kind of all-star list:

"We've Got to Try Something" for Improvement Initiatives

The Quick-Fix Fixation. Pray and hope for quick fixes. Reorganize again. Downsize. Lay off workers and fire key managers. Don't look for real work that needs to be done or new markets to explore. Trim costs, instead, by disposing of people. Try some accounting tricks, like selling off assets until you're in danger of disappearing up your own balance sheet. Use more glossy photographs and colorful charts in the annual report; investors love that.

The Go-Ye-Forth-without-Tools Tool. Involve employees all over the company—without educating them about the business. Encourage employees to "improve the operation" but provide no clue as to what "improvement" might mean or how it will be measured. Hold on tightly to financial controls. Underrate people's intelligence. Do not permit them to manage or, if possible, even to see, the financial statements. Ask them to improve, but provide no vision of what improvement looks like. Distribute jigsaw puzzles to all employees with no picture of the completed puzzle. Be sure to install suggestion boxes beside the time clocks.

The Smell-the-Meal Menu. Involve employees—up to a point. Solicit their suggestions, provide additional information upon demand. But don't, whatever you do, permit them to make any decisions. Invite them to an employee banquet, but tell them they may only smell, not eat, the food.

The Adjust-Their-Attitude Attitude. Do lots of training to "fix" attitudes. Invite motivational speakers to conduct pep-rally-like seminars in-house. Publish an internal newsletter chock-full of helpful hints on how to do a better job, and the importance of maintaining a positive, upbeat attitude.

Ignore the systems and environments that produced the unwanted attitudes. Recognize Employee(s)-of-the-Month on prominently displayed plaques (photos optional— hang 'em by the time clocks?).

The Teams-Run-Amuck Relay. Form oodles of teams. Form Total Quality Management teams, Process-Improvement teams, Cost Control, Customer Satisfaction, and Employee Motivation (see preceding initiative) teams, and any other teams you can persuade, cajole, or coerce your employees to join. Don't set shared goals or wed their performance to a common, bigger picture. Do not encourage cooperation between teams, but foster institutionalized competition. Buy new jerseys for the company's co-ed softball team.

In short, *companies involved employees in too many things that were not fundamental to the organization's business*, things that didn't add or create value. In spite of the best of intentions to involve and empower employees, management never really helped employees become part of the business.

Companies trained endlessly on the soft stuff, like communication skills, which are absolutely necessary—and altogether insufficient—to create high-involvement, high-responsibility cultures. Lacking the faith to fully inform and empower them, managers sold their people too short to ensure effectual participation. Management too often settled on approaches that *sounded* revolutionary, but really weren't radical at all. Employee-involvement strategies were never really *implemented*. Management just announced them or lauded their justifications.

The logic of involvement and empowerment for business is sound, but it hasn't been tried yet.

The *Economist* summarized all this in a recent article,* "Talk to managers in Europe and the United States and you will learn that they are all re-inventing the workplace. Visit those workplaces, and you often find that the changes are marginal, introduced out

---

* "New World Order," *The Economist*, April 9, 1994, p. 76.

of faddishness rather than conviction. Only a few . . . have implemented lasting changes, and they have usually done so because of a crisis."

Even so, the perceived need to deepen quality processes
opened the door, so to speak, for open-book management. Here
and there, a few savvy managers saw the necessity of tying quality and employee involvement directly to the financial side of
the business.

The financial part of a business and the people in that business are inextricably linked. They cannot be addressed, effectively, as separate entities. But most of the involvement, quality,
and empowerment efforts of the past decade missed that key
point. They separated the so-called soft people side from the
so-called hard financial know-how side of the business.

One source of power in open-book management is bridging
that gap. Open-book management plugs all the people of the
business into a readily available power supply—business and
financial information they can use to make daily decisions on
the job. Turning this information into knowledge allows them to
release more of their human potential, their heads and hands
and hearts, while advancing the business toward its goals.

Open-Book Management Means
Business Literacy

We are moving, now, toward more complete forms of employee
empowerment. You can see this in the shift in the words used for
"employees." At first, this shift was often corporate-speak eu-
phemisms, from "workers" or "job holders," to "team players," to
"business partners." But over time, this word shift has come to
signal a fundamental shift in the workplace paradigm. While not
new, this shift still needs time before it can be defined, named,
and matured into a widely accepted set of common practices.

The drive to engage all employees in the financial side of the
business by educating and promoting widespread accountability

is a newer trend within this overall shift. And it too has yet to congeal as a conveniently packaged, single-label movement. Some people call it *open-book management*, others, *business literacy*. We'll be using both terms in this book.

Literacy implies a command of language and refers here to *all* the languages of business including the dialects of the various generic business functions such as finance, marketing, sales, and customer service. It also includes whatever other terminology arises from the specific markets and industries the organization serves—engineering, manufacturing, health care, information, food service—whatever.

Business literacy is, implicitly, a broader term than open-book management. It specifically includes all the languages of business, rather than just the financials, and it implies a set of management practices: planning, involvement, rewards, and communication processes designed to involve all employees in creating, maintaining, and producing business goals.

One of the practices implied here is opening the books, as opposed to reserving financial information for managers and financial specialists. It just makes sense. But *simply sharing financial information with employees does not substantially increase their empowerment or accountability.* Employees in business-literate organizations must be able not only to understand the numbers, in real time, but to run the business. Opening the books is a good place to begin; but it will not, by itself, create more empowered work settings. For the purposes of readers who want to implement these business and empowerment practices, however, the terms open-book management and business literacy will be used interchangeably in this book.

Open-book management, as a term, has a specific history. *Inc.* magazine, in the person of senior editor John Case, started calling this approach to business "open-book management" around 1993. It's also the term that our firm, Capital Connections, used in cosponsoring, with Lakewood Publications' Positive Employment Practices Institute (PEPI), the first conference on open-book management, in June 1993.

PEPI's original executive director, Kathryn Collins, saw open-book methodology for the innovation it is. She invited *Inc.* editors to the conference, and George Gendron, *Inc.*'s publisher, was a featured speaker at one of the general sessions. *Inc.*'s roots are in small business. Lakewood's roots are in the Fortune 1500. A brochure went to both mailing lists bearing the label: "open-book management," and it seems to have stuck.

There is a term from poetry called *synecdoche* (rhymes with "where is the key"). It refers the way we often represent the whole of something by naming a part of that whole—a hundred head of cattle becomes a "hundred head," "nice wheels" means a sporty car, and "good-looking threads" describes sharp clothes. Open-book management and business literacy are becoming the parts by which we name the whole of empowered, entrepreneurial workplaces where all employees know and participate in the business.

In this book, as you read the terms open-book management and business literacy, we mean essentially the same thing.

One Problem, Two Approaches

Before looking at what open-book management is exactly, and how it can become a part of your business or department, let's see its effects.

The following companies, though fictitious, could be any number of medium-size to large companies facing a bad quarter with more changes to come. In the first scenario, traditional thinking prevails; in the second, the company has business literacy on its side.

Scenario 1 Monday, 7:30 A.M.: In the boardroom of a multimillion-dollar-a-year company, executives meet to discuss the company's disappointing financial performance in the final quarter of the fiscal year just ending. They're worried by the investment community's response to poor results already reported in the press. The price of the company's stock has fallen and likely will continue to fall if the fourth-quarter report is not accompanied by an announcement of some new and convincing initiative to improve performance in the next fiscal year. They've decided to act fast.

Ralph B., the chief financial officer, leads a discussion of their options for cutting costs. He recommends several measures to trim variable expenses as much as, and as quickly as, possible: freeze hiring; prohibit all travel below the VP level unless it is specifically approved; mandate cuts in all other expenses not directly related to fulfilling current orders or supporting immediate sales. The other executives accept his recommendations with little or no discussion.

Jim D., chief executive officer, takes it a step further. He puts a proposal to initiate another "rif" (reduction in force) at the top of the agenda for the next meeting. Everyone concurs. He recommends shelving "for the time being" several initiatives with long-term potential to generate new revenues. They require front-end investment. "We're not looking for new ways to spend money," he says. Again, the other executives concur.

The following Thursday, 7:00 A.M.: The various directors of the same company convene quick meetings in conference rooms scattered throughout the corporate headquarters with the managers they supervise. They pass the latest decisions along to their subordinates: All travel is canceled until further notice, except in cases of extreme emergency, which will require approval (several managers wince visibly); a hiring freeze is in effect immediately (several more wince, a few groan audibly); everyone is told to "cut all other expenses to the bone" (sighs all around).

"Sorry," the executives leading each meeting say, "that's just the way it is. We have no choice. This is all about the last quarter's poor performance," they say.

An intense discussion ensues: "How are we supposed to reach our first-quarter objectives (for the new fiscal year) if we no longer have the resources?" "You know, some of our best projects will grind to a halt. The resources we've already invested in them will be wasted." Some managers imagine the potential impact all this will have on customers. Others picture, in broad terms, the potential loss of business. The managers feel boxed in, with no effective way to express their concerns or apply their knowledge to the problem that generated the decisions they've just been handed. They leave these meetings to call still more meetings of their own, wondering how to present these decisions to their supervisors and project leaders.

The participants in both the Monday and the Thursday meetings shared the same problem. Their company had not performed up to the financial standards of their industry. And the executives of this company made the best possible decisions, given the information available to them. But the most current and detailed information in the company wasn't available to them. While they were making key decisions on Monday, it lay dormant in the heads of the people who would later be handed the decisions, after the fact, on Thursday.

A more creative response to the fourth quarter performance might have been fashioned if these managers and executives had forged it in unison. They might have found an approach that made better business sense. But they didn't know how to talk to each other. They didn't speak the same language. The executives were speaking—and *thinking*—market share, investors and stock price, EVA (economic value added), cash flow and profit before tax, while the management teams spoke and thought of product development, customer service, sales volume, price discounts, and budget. The politics of the budget, and the decision-making and communication practices that manage the company did not prepare these managers for big-picture thinking and coordinated action for tough times.

Managers in business, historically, have been caught up in the all too typical bureaucratic compulsion to spend all the money in the budgets at their disposal. If they didn't, that funding would disappear in the next fiscal year—and with it, the people and projects that provided status and higher pay for the manager in charge.

When this crisis arose, neither middle-level managers nor top executives seemed to realize that the other was looking at the same corporate elephant from the opposite side. The executives made cost-cutting calls from the vantage point of worried analysts and big shareholders, while the managers coped with the consequences from a perspective of trying to add value to projects, products, and service without spending money.

A typical mid-level staff meeting in a corporation like this one is not so much a system as it is an event. It may be anticipated. It may be dreaded, endured, or survived. It may be remembered fondly when the news is good or sadly when the news is bad, as it was on this occasion. But it's a one-time, here-it-comes, here-it-is, there-it-went kind of thing. Then it's time for everyone to get back to work.

Managers or team members get together, go over a few issues, often do a little posturing to look good for the boss, and then the participants leave. Some general coordination happens. If it is budget time, or near the end of the quarter or month, the boss or the financial specialist reports financials. Everyone is told what has happened since the last similar report. At companies like the one described in Scenario 1, the bad news is passed around and complaints are stifled or aired, depending on how open the boss is with team members and how skilled the boss is at generating honest dialogue. And in either case, the managers and their teams have little impact on the decisions or their outcome because they are looking at historical data—it's too little too late.

Open-book management, on the other hand, uses the language—and the thought processes—of business and finance to create a communication system that moves information as it evolves, not after the fact. Unlike the communication event described here, an open-book communication *system* can operate as a series of interlocking staff meetings and convey precise information upward, over and across the organization. It can close the gaps between executives and managers and frontline performers.

Everyone in an open-book system can be "in the know." Everyone knows which numbers they affect and how they affect them, because they've been a part of reporting those numbers. They know everyone else's numbers, too, because they've been shown what those numbers mean to them. A well-run meeting in a business like this isn't an interruption to the work schedule, it is a *part* of the work schedule.

Scenario 2　Once again, it's Thursday and 7:00 A.M., but today's meeting is a staff meeting in a conference room of a multimillion-dollar company that operates in a different way. The second month of the fourth quarter has just begun. Leaders of this company's customer service department have gathered for their regularly scheduled weekly meeting. It's not a typical business meeting. Each of the half-dozen team members brings a list of business issues they believe merit discussion and a performance scorecard that tracks the number of calls handled, hours worked, disgruntled customers satisfied, and so on for the people they supervise. The objective is to collect and consolidate these numbers and send this week's departmental forecast up to the next level of management.

Ellen J., the team leader, gets things started: "Let's do our numbers," she says, "and then we can get to our issues. Let's see if we were a bit too optimistic last week." Ellen is concerned that last week's forecast, which predicted exceeding their previous goal for "customers served" by 10 percent this month, was too ambitious. The team, however, had thought that without overtime or increased labor costs they could still fill orders and respond to the increasing numbers of calls for information on the new delivery service, thus fulfilling their target bonus goal.

Ellen records the statistics on a white-board as her team members report their labor estimates, length-of-call averages, and other information for those phone associates who had been monitored. The quality numbers measuring customer satisfaction with the phone associates are acceptable, the same as last week. And the length-of-call average is up slightly, with the understanding that the new delivery service takes some explaining. But a major concern arises as the overtime is calculated.

"How'd we accumulate so much overtime this month?" Ellen asks with some exasperation. "And why didn't we see this last week?" As the discussion continues, it becomes apparent that not only is overtime going to be far above the month's plan, it is going to hurt the department's quarterly number and negatively affect its chances of earning a performance bonus.

The explanations team members offer for the increased overtime are weak. There's no acceptable way to explain this bad news to upper management and the rest of the managers who'll be attending tomorrow's meeting. And there's no place to hide from the results. When these numbers get reported, the entire management team will know that customer service did not manage its overtime well.

"This won't be the first time I've had to report a number that has gone south," Ellen says. "But I never get used to it. Maybe everybody else will have great news, so our bad news won't seem too bad. But then we'll really stand out. At any rate, we have *got* to do a better job of controlling that cost next month. Any suggestions? What kind of help should we ask for from sales and marketing so this won't get any worse?"

As it happens, Ellen doesn't get her wish at the meeting with her peers. The purchasing and sales departments also have bad news to report: some big price increases came in without warning and the sales group has lost two sizable jobs it had included in its forecast. Instead of being overshadowed by good news from other departments, the customer service department's poor overtime number combines with other bad news and becomes part of a more general red alert. If the employees of this company can't turn the situation around in the next month, the whole quarter could be a wash. And that would make the investment community very uneasy, and nearly everyone in this business-literate company understands the implications of uneasy investors.

The numbers move systematically upward, in this company, to the executive team—and across to all the departments, and down to all employees—every two weeks. The bad news is quickly distributed and digested by employees throughout the company. A push begins almost immediately and at every level to turn the numbers around.

The purchasing and sales departments, along with Ellen's team in customer service, already had held brainstorming sessions to improve their numbers, so they are the first to implement cost-reduction and cash flow improvement plans in conjunction with other departments. Supervisors from both departments have already met with their colleagues in operations to find new ways to trim expenses. To improve cash flow, purchasing coordinates with accounts payable to stretch payments to some suppliers who owe the company a few favors. Sales works with the accounts receivable folks to identify a few customers whose payments could be expedited, given favorable terms.

But that's just the beginning: Human resources postpones some hires, training reschedules some classes for the next fiscal year, managers all over the company voluntarily curtail their travel—several of them stepping up their use of the company's newly installed electronic mail system to stay in touch with remote manufacturing sites. The continuous improvement teams keep working on their key measures to bring their work processes under control and hold a couple of special sessions to develop some short-term plans.

The game at this company has always been to contribute as much as possible to the bottom line at the lowest possible cost. During tight times like the current quarter, however, the game intensifies. They operate like a basketball team in the final minutes of a close game. It's time for the full-court press: exciting and exhausting, but not something that can, or should, be sustained for a whole game or season. They work at a level that would be impossible without a fully coordinated team effort. The results are impressive as the fourth quarter draws to a close.

Using a communications system like this doesn't mean that every staff meeting will be a pleasant one in which only good numbers are reported. It won't ensure that expenses will never need to be trimmed, hiring postponed, or travel curtailed. Nor will managing a financially literate workforce with an open-book approach guarantee that every challenge of the marketplace or downturn in the industry will be successfully countered *within* the same quarter in which it is identified. But open-book management *can* promise this much: Companies that employ it will have the opportunity to respond to whatever challenges and opportunities they confront, as quickly as they are identified, with the best information available throughout the organization. Systems such as these engender trust and increase overall organizational intelligence. They harness the thought-power of teams and individuals and encourage problem-solving across functions.

The Need and the Promise

The unique ability of open-book management to do two things—involve and motivate employees, and create better financial outcomes for companies challenged by changing marketplaces—makes it a management idea whose time, in many people's opinion, has come.

As this book goes to print in the mid-1990s, others proclaim that a political idea whose time has also come is to stop entitlements and balance the budget. It is too early to tell what changes will really come about from attempts to reduce welfare, get people into jobs, and to balance the budget. Free-enterprise solutions to big government are popular. And those solutions will have a better chance of working if there are more participants with real knowledge of that free enterprise system and the parts they play in it. This is what open-book management does—disseminate workable business knowledge.

Many adults Americans, the ones not so caught up in survival that they have had time to think, have either engaged or listened intently, or both, to the long-standing debate:

> Lower taxes, get government off the backs of people, let the economy generate wealth and the rising economic tide will raise all boats, argue the people on the right.

> Some people have leaky boats, or none at all, argue the traditional or neo-leftists. So government's job is to stimulate growth and maintain social programs and entitlements for the elderly, the poor, the young, and let that wealth get redistributed more fairly.

Many Americans know the debate too well, and long ago decided which approach they favored. What no one can debate is that, government or no government, a good economy generates the jobs that help create social well-being for families. And no one can debate whether it is a good idea to provide the economic and business education for participants in that economy who have jobs or aspire to get them. How can equipping wage earners and professionals, and all those with limited business education or know-how, with the tools to better do their jobs and improve their companies have any real detractors?

The need for open-book management as a set of business practices and a philosophy of management goes beyond what it can do for companies. It impacts the needs of society. It promotes responsible and involved citizenship from many who were told, and who thought, the companies and the industries they support in the making of a nation and world are too complex.

Open-book management and the business literacy it promotes is here to stay. Keeping people ignorant is not an option.

Chapter 2

Why Open the Books?

The problem with socialism is that so many people share in its misery; the problem with capitalism is that so few people share in its rewards.

—Winston Churchill

Change is no longer an occasional crisis. It is continual—without pause. Companies face a continuous stream of challenges brought on by global competition, new technology, and more demanding customers. The real challenge, these days, is managing surprise, not just predictable changes. The environment for modern business is permanent white water, and no one has shot this river before. Companies that can thrive on the unpredictable are the ones destined to grow. To do that, employees must be able to align themselves with common goals that everyone understands. Everyone has to grab a paddle and prepare for the next set of rapids, and the next.

Managing Surprise

Corporate survival now depends on the kind of coordinated efforts that can only come from people who are informed and motivated by a clear and encompassing vision and from a shared language that can transfer information clearly and rapidly. That's the only way they'll be able to shift priorities rapidly enough to remain customer-responsive and meet competitive challenges. External shifts with technology, customers, interest rates, or the competition need to be quickly

Figure 2.1 External Developments

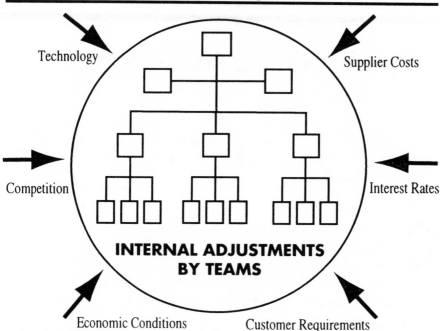

and thoroughly absorbed throughout the enterprise so teams can make the necessary internal adjustments (see Figure 2.1). The language of business, once a privileged dialect reserved for upper and middle management, will have to become the common tongue spoken broadly by all employees throughout the business.

The experiences of business-literate companies such as Syncrude in Canada and Springfield Remanufacturing Corporation and Chesapeake Packaging in the United States indicate that companywide learning is a prerequisite for sustainable growth. That, they will tell you, has made it possible for them to muster resources in new combinations to create new products while improving service, distribution, and quality.

■ Syncrude, Canada's largest oil producer, responded to explosive increases in worldwide production costs for crude with a companywide education program. Every employee is recruited and trained to participate in the organization's effort to bring the company's cost back down to a targeted $12 per barrel.

■ Springfield Remanufacturing Corporation (SRC) had an 89-to-1 debt-to-equity ratio and 119 hard-working employees when they started using open-book methods. Over 10 years later, with nearly 800 employees and a strong balance sheet, they proudly describe their highly educated workforce as their most powerful competitive advantage.

■ Chesapeake Packaging's Baltimore plant was in the usual pinch for the packaging and corrugated materials industry—rising material costs and plenty of competition. The need to do more with less increased as management looked for new solutions. Their 5-year journey into empowerment and quality led them to open-book management and several state and national awards—not to mention superior performance and quality for customers and high morale for employees.

When everyone in the organization can *think* business, then everyone can *do* business—by creating customer and market solutions, by generating cash, by producing strong balance sheets, and by generating wealth. Change can be accomplished intentionally and not just by instinctive reaction, if the enterprise thoughtfully and persistently builds training practices, communication systems, and methods for mobilizing talent and energy to meet customer needs. Then, when the inevitable occurs and surprises arise, the resources and systems will be there for managing them, pleasant and not so pleasant.

But if management wants employees to think and act like owners then a fundamental change must happen. *Management must treat their employees like owners.* That's precisely what open-book management, in its many budding versions, does: It involves employees in the basics of the business in many of the same ways that owners are involved. It asks everyone to create a plan. It spreads accountability, sharing the risks that can never be avoided and the rewards that often, but not always, come with hard work.

What's in It for Employees

The more that managers get excited about business literacy as both a mind-set and powerful set of tools with which to manage the business, the less excited some employees will become. And for good reason. They have had too many less-than-great experiences with the latest management trends to readily jump on bandwagons.

It is not hard to understand why some employees show a waning interest in employee involvement efforts or have a jaded view. Many an "involved" workforce improved quality measures with new ideas and hard work only to be rewarded with more stress, increasing demands, or worse, the surprise of unannounced and unforeseen downsizing layoffs (now called right-sizings, since even downsizing is a bit too graphic, for politically correct corporate-speak). The attempt to cut head count is not even veiled anymore by some of the consultants in process improvement/reengineering. It is only natural that employees now ask, "Why bother with open-book management? Isn't this just management's latest preoccupation, one that could lead to my job being eliminated, like the other fads?"

The old lifetime employment bargain had its benefits in bygone eras. Gold watches and pensions were guaranteed. But those days, and those guarantees, are gone. Given that—and that *is* a given—employees need to learn what makes a business viable and capable of sustaining a workforce.

Savvy employees will accept the cancellation of the lifetime employment guarantee and the end of automatic raises; they'll accept that career ladders have disappeared; they'll even accept the added responsibility of supervising themselves and managing their own numbers *if*:

- Through training and work experience, they become more skilled and more employable.
- The psychological and financial rewards for making the organization more profitable are shared with the employees who made them possible.
- Career advancement is still possible for those willing to take more responsibility by advancing their business knowledge.
- The fun and sense of achievement that comes with intrapreneuring, creating new value-added services within a company, becomes widespread in the new workplace.
- The mysteries of the free enterprise system (how capital is formed, how stock is valued, how investors keep score on companies) are demystified for those who have had jobs and drawn wages but have never "learned business."
- The new job responsibilities are accompanied by new authority in the workplace so that individuals and teams no longer have to wait for others to tell them what the problem is and are permitted instead to do real problem-solving.

Open-book management distributes the power to make decisions, and shares accountability. It fosters participation, taking management off false pedestals of power by making them teachers who share their knowledge and guide the business. The prerogative to decide, in open-book environments, will be earned and learned, not just accrued through appointment to a particular position. In this fashion, open-book management speaks directly to the traditionally painful paradox of running a business—how to balance the company's need to profit with its employees' basic human needs. Empowered business literacy proposes a fundamental shift from the old profits-versus-people paradigm to one that addresses profits *and* people. Indeed, it permits the people to pursue profit.

Fully and properly implemented, this newest agreement with the workforce has as much to offer employees as employers. People who have worked in open-book companies often chaff under the old system when they move to companies that have not yet made the shift. They know from previous experience that, whether their new boss is open with them or not, their security in their new job depends ultimately on their employer's fiscal well-being. But now, in a traditional environment, they can't tell if the business is really growing. To determine whether they want to stay with a new employer for the long term, business-literate employees need to see the same indicators a bank examines in considering a long-term loan. If they're going to invest—and working *is* a form of investment—they want to see the financials.

Open Books at Work: 1. Craving Financial Information

Physician Sales and Service (PSS) President Patrick Kelly visits his branch offices unannounced. As founder of the fast-growth $200 million company that supplies physicians in 24 hours, he wants a culture where individual initiative and team spirit replaces approval from the management hierarchy as the source for decisions. One of his practices is to share the income statement and key operating numbers of the company in detail so all employees understand the trends in profits, expenses, and service levels.

He'll ask precise questions at these unannounced "On the Spot" meetings like, "What was the percentage of transportation expense to total sales revenue for this month?" to his frontline packers. He gives $50 for a right answer to these exacting questions.

Employees like the $50. They like even more the sense of pride that comes with knowing about the company and being knowledgeable business thinkers. At PSS, which went public in 1994, employees ask their managers regularly for detailed financial data, a pleasant contrast to management forcing it down indifferent throats. They hunger for the information that helps them perform better, drives the value of their stock, and provides a sense of achievement and direction.

Integrate, Link, Connect

An underlying strength of open-book management is its integration of formerly separated key sets of business knowledge:

- The needs and unique values of the people.
- Current demands of the marketplace.
- Financial and environmental influences.
- The business's defined mission and goals.

Many businesses have started a confusing array of organizational development initiatives in these areas, often spearheaded by different departments such as human resources or quality or operations, and now face the challenge of integrating those efforts. As one Disney World manager put it, "We have to connect the dots for everybody around here." Open-book management for these companies is an extension of what is already in place.

Like any attempt to link separate components, this integration requires a system that provides ongoing interconnections. An effective system—in this context, open-book management—will blend with, enhance, and unify the programs it seeks to integrate. It provides repeatable processes that link the individual programs: Subsystems for educating, information-sharing, decision-making, rewarding, and coordinating.

The term "system" is used in the broadest context in this book as interconnected human/business processes and not computer-based information technology or management information systems. The natural world is a superior source of subjects to study the interaction of systems; for example, the weather, or the human body, which is a complete system with subsystems (e.g., the cardiovascular and endocrine systems). In thinking about open-book management, organizations can benefit from seeing themselves as a system with interacting subsystems.

The companies and professionals setting up these open-book management systems are guaranteed a collective learning experience. They will discover previously hidden capabilities and will find new ways of marshaling company resources to meet challenges and add value for customers. The power that emerges in this process will be both exhilarating and threatening. Employees at every level will delight in learning and facing new challenges, but they'll also tend to protect and defend the past, which has previously brought some success and comfort.

Much has been made of paradigm shifts in the past decade. *The paradigm shift in open-book management is from the tunnel vision of a specialty-specific perspective to an integrated view, or "big picture."*

One sign of personal growth is the realization that everyone, including you, has blind spots. Everyone can—and does, more easily than anyone likes to admit—get locked into a particular view of things and insist that it is *the* one and only way to look at the situation.

One sign of organizational growth in open-book management is employees, teams, and departments accepting the limitations of their specialty's viewpoint and integrating it into the larger view. Business literacy challenges all the employees to think differently and broadly about their company, their work, their responsibilities. Just how this new perspective manifests itself may be subtle, such as viewing the members of another department as colleagues with complementary responsibilities, rather than as career-path competitors with contrary goals. Employees may begin to consider, automatically, what the department next door needs from them. They may begin to offer that assistance routinely, instead of waiting for a formal request.

Bringing the enormously varied views and unique know-hows of individuals and units into a complete body, routinely capable of coordinated action, is an important goal of business literacy. The collective thinking and the operating paradigm that nurtures this complex coordination occurs when integration, not specialization, is at the heart of the system. Integration permeates every step of open-book management's planning, implementation, and practice; the paradigm has shifted; the change is permanent. Teamwork results.

Open Books at Work: 2. Polaroid Gives the Frontline Numbers Know-How

Polaroid's 20 percent employee ownership gave the company an opportunity to do something special with quality: It created a TQO, or total quality ownership, process. With the death of its founder creating a drift in direction, style, and purpose, Polaroid found itself floundering at a time when Fuji and others were pursuing and winning big pieces of their former market dominance. TQO became a rallying call to renew the culture, rekindle its entrepreneurial spirit, and grow beyond the shadow of its legendary founder, Dr. Edwin Land.

Employee-owners at Polaroid were trained in the business of the business—what the business goals were for Polaroid, not just the technological ones, and what their customers required. Jack Wilkins, marketing director, described the typical dilemma of companies wanting to increase business literacy: "The problem in most industries is that the financial system is set up for auditors and the executive board using consolidated financials in a language that the ordinary employee doesn't understand. Marketing information is something you talk about in whispers."

Polaroid has made bold decisions to restructure and move ahead with an empowered workforce. Business literacy is one of its key strategies, and its new plant allows the numbers to take on meaning where there was none. "All the marketing, financial, quality and schedule data, as well as all material information will be up on a network at every workstation in the plant. We intend to train folks to use the information so that coding operators will know how sales are doing and understand the financial implications of a decision . . . this will help empowered employee-owners obtain the information and the skill to make decisions managers made in the past."

Cultures become entrepreneurial when business knowledge is driven deeply into the organization and when that which has been separated gets integrated.*

---

* Internet: The Uniform Resource Locator for this document is: http://www.fed.org/fed/conf/utilize92/wilkens.html

Sprint's Chris Rooney, now head of Sprint International, was seeking to improve the performance of the 300-plus staff of the telecommunications giant's government services division. Through his directors, and the design team that they created, Rooney put open-book management in place.

One of those directors, Craig Carter, had gained considerable knowledge of quality and reengineering before the open-book effort. He saw its integrating and linking potential. "We needed a system," Carter recalls, "that would pull our efforts in training, quality, and business process improvement together, one that would have an immediate impact on our thinking about the business-a system that we could all have a part in. Open-book management fit that bill."

Systems Thinking and Learning Organizations

One reason open-book management fits comfortably with other business improvement processes like reengineering, improving customer service, and total quality management is that it looks at the business as a whole. Suppose management is trying to improve some part of the business, like customer service. Open-book management should help employees see that unsatisfied customers endanger sales projections and that new efforts to increase customer satisfaction usually involve increased expenses. Business literacy should help them understand those expenses and the cost of unsatisfied customers as a financial concern.

This big picture view is what the practitioners of systems thinking—the most popular of whom is Peter Senge—are all about. Systems thinking does not refer to data-transfer management on networked computers, the most common business use for the term "system." Rather, a systems thinking approach considers a set of repeatable practices and principles, or systems, that address the parts of the organization and how they relate.

Today's heightened interest in learning organizations uses the best of systems thinking for creating a new kind of organization.

Open-book management is an application of systems thinking that takes the parts of the business that in the past have been addressed separately, such as budgeting and employee involvement, and ties them together. It is a set of specific practices to promote systems thinking and grow learning organizations. As such, open-book management fits well into quality and team-directed practices by providing a new set of tools and by tying all efforts to financial outcomes.

The practitioners of systems thinking tell us it is a budding science, and Peter Senge and his colleagues admit they are still defining what constitutes a learning organization. However, companies that reach high degrees of business literacy using open-book practices are well on their way to instinctively or intentionally (or both), using a systems approach to raising the thinking and learning level of all employees.

A Language for Everyone

An inviting and refreshing feature of this new system is that practicing it does not require mastering a new set of terms or a new language. There are no conceptual gymnastics to accomplish prior to getting down to the business of improving business. Something is wrong when the term "quality functional deployment" starts appearing in the titles for breakout sessions at quality conferences. Some academics and consultants may fancy long words and obscure terms, but arcane vocabulary is a sign that the ideas behind the terms have lost touch with the direct give-and-take of employees and customers doing business on the front line.

As Jim Steffan, a financial manager at Sprint, puts it: "It's a necessity for all of us to review our performance against the plan in a common language. When we can identify variances, see the causes and take action, we can get better. This pressure to improve is enormous. People have to be more knowledgeable. Open-book management becomes a way of life."

Everyone has *something* new to learn, however. Those who know little about customer service will have to study that side of the business to become business literate, just as those who are unfamiliar with finance will have to learn a few things about the numbers. People who don't know how to get customers will have to learn about sales and marketing. Everyone has to learn, but not everyone in a business-literate organization has to become a CPA, or the salesperson, or a customer service representative.

The secret is to start simply. Begin with what people already know. Give the numbers context and meaning. Teach the basics of why people buy products and services. Demonstrate the fundamentals of customer service. Remove the mystery from *all* the formerly hidden and obscure work processes that comprise a business.

Once employees have learned the basics—the language of business—they will take charge of their own business literacy. They'll ask questions that take their learning to the next level, and they'll keep asking questions until they achieve the understanding they need.

Business literacy in an open-book environment consists of ordinary day-to-day talk about costs, finance, production, and service delivery. It is the stuff of which all business is made, what enterprise has been *about* right along. There are complexities in business that take years to learn, to be sure. But beginning open-book management doesn't require weeks of sitting in a classroom learning new terminology or concepts. You begin by talking about business and about people in that business: the plans they make, the obstacles they encounter, their successes, their failures, and the work that needs doing to satisfy a customer and generate cash.

To some, this ready, down-to-earth accessibility of open-book management gives it the appearance of being easy. It is not. The famous CEO Jack Stack, who created a company of business-literate people at Springfield Remanufacturing Corporation, talks about the difficulty of sticking to the program of planning, meeting, selling, informing, rewarding, celebrating, evaluating

— ❀ ❀ ❀ ❀ —

The following poem was written for the 1994 annual meeting of Scanlon Plan companies. It was read to 500 executives, middle managers, team leaders and frontline employees, many of whom have pioneered open-book practices for years:

Open Books and Open Minds

Capitalism has caused a great schism
    between those who know how to play
and those who work, but on the sidelines stay

Now we open the books,
    for everyone to take looks
So they can better do their part,
    taking the business and their work to a form of art

Serving customers, is a basic human privilege
The Good Book teaches that serving, not consuming,
    makes life worth the living
But for many, old business patterns kept people in the dark
    and profit for a few,
    not service, was the mark

Profit more than service, more than enhancing human life,
    Profit made at even the partial expense of others,
    employees inside or customers out,
    or nature's delicate environment,
was a blasphemy that shrunk our souls.

And even benevolent companies that cared
    treated employees like children
    who couldn't manage themselves or the company's wares.

At Scanlon companies, the veil has long been lifted.
Joe and Dr. Frost* built four principles
with which all stakeholders, employees too, benefited

The good word on the principles continues to move
And people come together to share learning and improve.
The lessons Scanlon folks can teach the business world are ample
Keep going, Scanlon friends, keep open-book truth at your core.
We need your courage and shining example.

---

* Joseph Scanlon, a former union member and officer, started original programs in participation and gain-sharing in the 1940s and 1950s; and his colleague Carl Frost continued this work at Michigan State University.

and then doing it all over again, year after year. "It is hard doing this all the time," he says. "Everything keeps changing, so we can never relax." People want to get it right and just keep it that way, he says. "But the challenges and the changes just keep coming. And then it's another year and we have to start all over and do even better."

Even after years of practicing open-book management and achieving high degrees of business literacy throughout the several small companies that make up SRC, it is still hard work. And it always will be. Like anything worthwhile—staying in shape, performing well in a choir, growing a great garden, running a lean and mean city government—open-book management demands continual effort. But it pays off, both for management and for employees.

Educating and empowering employees so that they can think and run the business as if they owned it takes sustained effort. And it takes a system, in fact, a system of systems like those described in the next chapter.

Chapter 3

The Sum of the Open-Book Parts Equals More than the Whole

To solve a problem, it is necessary to think at a higher level than at the level of thinking that created the problem.
—Albert Einstein (paraphrase)

Open-book management motivates employees by educating them on their part in their business's strategic direction and financial results and by involving them directly, for better or worse, in those results. They acquire both an understanding of and a stake in the business. With access to the right information in a timely fashion, individuals and teams in the organization will put that understanding to work to improve their stake in the enterprise.

Open-book management comprises four distinct systems linking business and financial education, cross-company communication, widespread leadership, and earned rewards (see Figure 3.1).

The arrows in Figure 3.1 diagram the following crucial aspects of open-book systems:

The dynamic nature of the systems. As business conditions change, numbers change, communication content shifts, rewards are easier or harder to achieve, leaders have new sets of decisions to make.

Figure 3.1 Business Literacy Model— Open-Book Systems

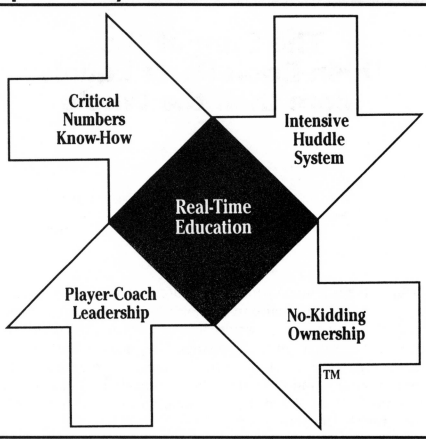

The continuity of the open-book structure. While conditions change, the annual cycle of business accounting provides a solid, repeatable, you-can-count-on-it rhythm to planning.

The interdependent nature of the systems. When employees understand their stake in the numbers, they want and need to see them as they are generated, not in hindsight. That creates a demand for leadership to develop and promote a forecasting method so employees may improve on their numbers as they develop. Achieving the right numbers generates rewards; and that, in turn, enhances the employees' understanding of their stake in the business, which makes them want and need to see the numbers—and so on.

In practice, all four systems interact constantly. They're inextricably connected in the workplace and separated here only for understanding the dynamic pieces that make up the greater whole.

In this chapter, we will look at the systems at the conceptual level. In Chapter 4, we will consider what they are in everyday practice.

But first, let's make a crucial distinction between a program and a system. True to the thinking that systems focus on relationships, the four open-book systems connect and contain programs, but not the other way around. A program usually works toward an easily defined outcome, a clean, crisp beginning and ending. A program's content can be uniformly communicated to all. It has fairly neat, linear, easy-to-follow steps. Most businesspeople recognize these characteristics in skill-based training programs of all types or, for example, in an initiative to drive out costs with a 90-day suggestion program.

Some training programs in open-book management seek to educate employees on the basics: how their company makes money, how it tracks its incoming and outgoing money, how it uses the money to provide appropriate resources, how it rewards those who contribute to goal achievement. Other training workshops can aim to help managers at all levels learn to teach and lead effectively. *These training programs may be useful and necessary in teaching people how to use the system, but they aren't the system.*

Systems are ongoing. Incorporated in the business's daily, weekly, monthly, and quarterly routines, they connect and coordinate the business's assorted departmental specialties and individual talents with the various features contained in a company's strategic plan. A program can't provide the vehicle for daily or weekly information flow, or for collaborative problem-solving.

A program can't offer a multilevel perspective on emerging challenges in the marketplace or accommodate interdepartmental give-and-take. A companywide system, or set of systems, can.

Characteristics of Programs versus Systems

PROGRAM	SYSTEM
Beginning/end	Ongoing
Influences one to few outcomes	Linked to multiple outcomes
Starts/stops	Evolves
Focused	Focused and widespread
Immediate impact	Immediate and long-term impact
Convergent	Divergent
Isolates	Connects
Aimed at changing behavior or attitudes	Aimed at changing the environment within which behavior and attitudes grow

---

The Four Interlocking Systems

The four systems of open-book management are at the heart of business practices. They are not new in and of themselves, but new applications of knowledge and practices already in place. For instance, financial knowledge is in the business, usually in the heads of a few. Business literacy puts it in the heads of many. Some up-down-and-across communication exists in all companies. Business literacy intensifies it and brings everyone into the business dialogue.

No-kidding ownership *motivates with recognition and financial rewards* that foster an ownership mentality while keeping the business exciting and fun. Player-coach leadership *distributes leadership responsibility and accountability throughout the enterprise.* Equipped with critical numbers know-how—*the working knowledge of numbers*—employees throughout the business can then share vital financial and operational information up, down, and across the organization, in an *intensive, closed-loop, communication system* called the intensive huddle system.

Critical Numbers Know-How

Critical numbers know-how is the working knowledge of the numbers related to finance, strategy, sales opportunities, costs, and customer satisfaction that all employees use to manage their part of the business. It addresses these common problems:

- ■ "We can't get everybody around here to work in the same direction. It seems like we're always at cross-purposes. You'd think we were working for different companies. The only things people around here care about are racking up overtime, getting big bonuses, or being promoted."
- ■ "Every three months, regular as clockwork, every employee in this place gets a copy of the quarterly report with their paycheck. And more people here get copies of the budget than anyplace else I've ever worked. But very few people bother to read them, and even fewer seem to understand them."
- ■ "We know the margins are shrinking. Anyone who works here can tell you that. But nobody seems to have a clue as to what we can do about it. The people around here just don't understand their impact on the business."

Although financial literacy has being getting more attention in the business press, it is still uncommon to see or hear financial terms bantered about the workplace in everyday talk. That terminology, at most companies, remains the private reserve of the financial specialists and the executive staff.

Most managers and other employees understand the day-to-day tasks that constitute their routine job responsibilities. Many can, and do, recite their job descriptions as if they were their favorite poems. But few can explain how the company stays financially healthy and in a position to require their services and pay their salaries. For too many employees, revenue and profit are "about the same"; and few appreciate the difference between profit and cash flow or comprehend financial ratios.

It isn't that people are generally numerically illiterate. We use numbers all the time. We watch our checkbooks and bank balances, calculate mortgage or rent payments, pay utility bills and stay current with credit card and auto loan payments. We monitor our cholesterol levels, gasoline mileage, weight, favorite teams' win-loss records, and our calorie intake. When we're away from work, we surround ourselves with critical numbers that hold meaning and are relevant to us as individuals—and we make decisions based on them.

Critical numbers know-how brings the same relevance to the numbers used in the workplace, where, again, all kinds of numbers, some more important than others, measure all types of processes.

Management has asked employees to track some numbers in the workplace for years, but only numbers that directly and obviously pertain to their narrowly defined job description or team task: the numbers measuring defects, rework, orders processed, product shipped, phone calls answered, sales calls made, scrap produced, and a host of others unique to the company and industry. Usually the supervisor, not the employees, has collected the numbers and passed them up somewhere to the next level, where decisions were made about what to do. Sometimes the totals were timely, other times not.

Individuals and teams sometimes received feedback on their numbers so they could gauge their performance. More often, they did not receive such data, especially if the numbers were satisfactory (within certain parameters that only "upper management" knew or understood). People were most likely to hear about unsatisfactory numbers, and more often than not, this negative feedback would be accompanied by an imposed, prescriptive solution dictated from above. Supervisors collected the numbers, passed them up, then waited for the feedback, which they would pass down in the form of a dictate that many workers didn't understand.

That process has changed somewhat in recent years, largely due to quality and continuous improvement programs. More and more numbers are in workers' hands at companies that take quality seriously. And the workers in these companies do the measuring now—with one critical exception.

Operating numbers like the ones previously listed may be everywhere, but not financial numbers. Worse, when the financial summaries and report cards are shared, workers don't understand them or have not been equipped to use the financial reports to make decisions. Few seem to see how what they do impacts all those 000's of the annual report numbers. The numbers are about past events leaving people feeling helpless and ineffective.

Because the company has yet to break the numbers down to a scale where employees can see how they make a difference, the significance of many financial numbers is lost.

Critical numbers know-how shows employees how the numbers they have always generated—phone calls answered, service calls, and quality variances—relate directly to the financial outcomes on which their jobs, bonuses, and sense of pride depend. They learn how to track in current time; how to team up with other departments and functions; how to think in terms of big-picture outcomes.

The Intensive Huddle System

An intensive huddle system moves vital financial and operational information up, down, and across the organization as it develops, in real time, so that teams and individuals throughout the enterprise can respond to emerging problems and opportunities as they emerge. These interlocking meetings do more than improve the company's responsiveness, however. They also generate trust because the huddle gives everyone facts—and the capacity to act on those facts. *This is closed-loop, intense, inclusive communication.*

The huddle system might be viewed as a main river that flows both ways and has many tributaries. The river consists of the financial numbers, but their meaning and significance come from the feeder streams. Keeping an eye on the flow and condition of each of the feeder streams is the responsibility of individual and team specialists. But everyone needs to know how the whole river system works and what happens when one of the tributaries gets jammed up with flotsam (e.g., service breaks down because of a computer glitch); or when one of the tributaries overflows (e.g., the sales department wins a huge number of unanticipated orders).

Common problems addressed by this system include:

■ "Every department in this place seems to speak its own language. We went down to account service [shipping, fulfillment, advertising, production, data processing] last week, to try and get things coordinated, but you'd have thought they were speaking Latin or something down there."

■ "I read the financial reports. I try to respond to the numbers, but by the time I see them, they're history. I never see anything until after the fact. We never get to work on the issues that affect costs as they come up."

■ "I honestly try to provide my employees with good incentives; but frankly, I have no idea if they're working or not." (And conversely, "The management of this place must think I'm a mushroom. They keep me in the dark and feed me . . ."—Well, you know the rest.)

■ "OK. My department tried to get with the program, and I thought we were doing well with it. But we couldn't get any cooperation from account service [shipping, fulfillment, advertising, production, data processing]. Coordination between departments around here is really spotty. Nobody around here has a big picture of what we're supposed to be up to."

- ■ "Don't look at me. These aren't *my* numbers in this business plan. Those were put together by people I've never even met. I had nothing to do with developing those numbers. Don't blame me if we don't hit 'em."

- ■ "If only I had known. We could have done something about that, but by the time we found out, the expense was already incurred and the customer didn't like us passing it on."

Gaps in perception and communication between departments and management exist everywhere. Not all gaps are bad, only the ones that can't be crossed and thus become barriers. People create gaps naturally as they set necessary boundaries to define responsibilities and functions.

Human resources became a separate department when the company got bigger and managers couldn't handle their own hiring. When more than five people were required to keep up with orders and a sixth person was hired to supervise and coordinate their efforts, shipping was born. Sales came into being when product offerings and potential market outgrew Harry, who used to sell the company's services between designing new software applications. And so on.

But while not all gaps are bad, they're certainly not all good either. They can pose certain problems. As gaps are institutionalized, bureaucracies form. The boundaries begin to inhibit communication. Disparate levels and functions within the organization cease to work well together. People, perhaps even unintentionally, begin to protect their turf and build fiefdoms. To remedy that, information must pass through the boundaries. Facts have to jump the gaps. Organizations establish and foster formal and informal information-sharing systems: vertical (up and down between levels) and horizontal (across departments) communication processes.

Open-book companies communicate through a vital, real-time system of interlocking meetings that puts critical numbers know-how to work building the big picture of the income statement from the bottom up. Hard as this may be for the financially indifferent to believe, numbers make a great companywide bottom-to-top medium of communication across *all* gaps. Numbers make it possible to follow the action as sales vary endlessly with customer trends and as expenses change daily because of improvements and goof-ups. Just as the Leading Economic Indicators follow the economy at large and the Big Board at the New York Stock Exchange follows stock prices, the income statement follows the microeconomy of the business.

Different companies will schedule their huddles with varying frequency, customizing the agenda and the roster of participants to suit their own cultures and missions. The key point here is that intensive huddles must be formally recognized as a medium for expressing the business's objectives and its progress toward those objectives in real time and in realistic financial terms.

Just as critical numbers know-how takes routine financials and gives meaning and power to them, the intensive huddle system takes staff meetings and transforms them into anything but routine events. It brings the team and the company together to set direction, to alert everyone to problems, to generate purpose and meaning, and to coordinate all the diverse activity necessary to get the job done. And when the goals are met, they provide the setting for pats on the back and a celebration of accomplishments before tackling the next challenges.

No-Kidding Ownership

No-kidding ownership mixes tangible financial rewards and recognition practices to keep the business exciting and fun. By providing every employee in the enterprise with a genuine mental and fiscal stake in the business, it spreads decision-making and fosters pride. Employees who believe they own and operate the business know a profound sense of achievement when it succeeds. It addresses these common problems:

■ "Did you see this morning's newspaper?!? Sales has a problem. Our chief competitor has just come out with a new product that's going to go head-to-head against our Model A1 Widget. I'm glad we're in customer service, where we can just do our jobs. We don't have to worry about competition like they do."

■ "Come on, let's reserve the suite. We can spend a little extra money on the hotel—and meals. It's not our money. This is business—it's on the company. We'll get reimbursed before it even shows up on the credit card."

■ "Heard anything about raises this year? I sure hope we get our usual cost of living adjustment—not that I'll see it. I've already spent mine on that new car. Company profits hardly went down at all, this year. We should get about the same raise, don't you think?"

■ "Of course, you and I get perks and have a bonus plan. We're management. Just think about how hard we've worked to get here. See, our frontline people, they aren't as willing to put in that kind of effort. They're used to 40 hours and overtime. Besides, they don't impact the bottom line like we do. We make the big decisions."

Sound familiar? People all over the world talk like that, and more importantly, feel like that. Whether they work in small or big businesses, for profit or for the not-for-profits, for the government, university, Army, Navy, Air Force, Marines—all too often, that's the sound of people at work—everywhere. Why people work, what they work for, how hard people will work, the physical and environmental factors that improve or diminish their capacity to work, the psychological and financial factors that motivate them to work; the whole working ball of wax has been examined, studied, and discussed for a long time. The results, generally, have been axiomatic:

- ■ A good job is its own reward.
- ■ Money is a motivator, but it's not everything.
- ■ After a certain level of pay is reached, pride is a bigger factor in motivating than a salary.
- ■ Bonuses are short term.
- ■ Employees want to feel like owners, but psychological equity—really owning their work—is not equated to financial equity.
- ■ Having fun at work is just as important as being well paid.

Well, OK. But given all that, how do you run a business? Open-book management adds an important perspective to the new models emerging for pay and reward systems. That is, the "feeling of ownership," without having a financial stake in the outcome is blue smoke. Without financial rewards, open-book management is a charade. It's the "smell the meal" process at work. Too much focus on the financial rewards, without addressing the other issues of psychic pay, like recognition and celebration, limits the motivating of financial incentives. But inadequate systems for sharing financial gain miss a fundamental tenet of open-book management.

No-kidding ownership gives employees a real stake in the business by providing incentives that focus attention and energy on whatever numbers are critical to the company. If those numbers already see frequent use in the halls of the enterprise, so much the better. If not, employees in open-book systems have a system of intensive huddles in which to discuss the questions raised by new incentives. They can readily increase their critical numbers know-how: "What's ROA? And do I do anything that makes that happen?" If the company's return on assets (ROA) matters enough to be part of an incentive package, its business literacy practices had better be prepared to define and demonstrate it. That's how no-kidding ownership educates, clarifies, and unifies efforts.

Player-Coach Leadership

Player-coach leadership is the thinking and behavior of leaders in open-book companies that promotes learning and business literacy; that designs the systems of numbers know-how, communication, and rewards; and that develops the leadership capacity of all employees to step up and be accountable for their part of the business. It is hands-on leadership. It addresses these common problems:

- "There is so much finger-pointing going on at the meetings over losing that customer, your eyes are in danger of getting poked out by a flying digit. Why is it everyone scrambles to take credit when something goes right but we have such a hard time accepting blame?"
- "These folks may be trying to keep us informed about what's going on around here, but it doesn't show much. When was the last time one of our managers really took an interest in one of our ideas, or explained what our customers are seeing in our competitors that we don't see?"
- "This management group gets another gold star in micromanaging—making sure we are counting nickels and dimes while the big opportunities keep getting little if any attention. If we continue to let our budget fixation keep us from thinking strategically, I'm afraid this company is going down the tubes."

Player-coach leadership, for our purposes, is as much a matrix of skills and practices as it is a system. This is the system that facilitates the systems described earlier in this chapter.

Player-coaches exhibit and share a firm understanding of the basics of the business; they become models for learning by learning themselves and passing along their knowledge. They grow and learn as the business grows and provides new opportunities. They know they can never know too much or give too much information to the teams they lead. They create other leaders within and around their group by mastering and exhibiting the art of storytelling with numbers.

Player-coaches bridge the gap between people and profits by linking personal potential to business goals. They embrace paradox: knowing when to lead, inspire, and rely on intuition; sensing when to manage, control, and employ analytical methods. Player-coaches create community by engendering in their teammates a sense of membership and shared purpose. By sharing a vision of the enterprise that is lofty enough for people to feel pride and down-to-earth enough to pay the mortgage, they help others create purpose for themselves.

These are people who have learned when to assert their power as coaches and when to restrain and defer to their fellow players. If they are not mature, emotionally and otherwise, they won't last. Open-book management creates corporate glasshouses; mistakes become apparent, and managers whose egos are easily bruised or who deny responsibility in creating mistakes probably won't make it.

Player-coach leaders serve the business, the customer, and those whom they lead in the best sense of servant leaders. Earning their position by their competence and trustworthiness, they don't hide behind a position or title. With their egos in check, they put themselves in service to the greater whole.

It is in and through these four systems that open-book management happens in big companies and small, across industries, in endless variation. The systems reinforce each other, providing structure and flexibility. Their inner logic helps companies' magnify their capacity to renew themselves in the face of external changes and demands. By providing structure with flexibility and principles with practices, the four systems of open-book management bring comprehensive thinking-and-doing tools to companies serious about serving customers and making money through educated employees.

The synergy between the systems dictates that the energy they release is about geometric and not linear progression. If a company employs two of the four systems, much less than half of the positive effects are captured and harnessed. With all four, the sum of the parts is much greater than the whole.

Of all the systems, player-coach leadership is the one which, if not in place, will kill the others. It sustains the others. A closer look at the leadership challenges in open-book management follows.

Chapter 4

᪥᪥᪥᪥

The Four Systems
in Practice

New ideas are not born in a conforming environment.
—Roger von Oech

In the practice of open-book management, different companies emphasize different systems. Each starts in a different place. One might begin with a new bonus system, another with financial training, still another with more comprehensive communications. But any company that wants to make a permanent shift to higher performance will need to develop and maintain all four systems. Many companies try to adopt or emphasize one system or two and are surprised when nothing much happens. Managers who do not develop a comprehensive view of how the systems create a synergistic effect will be disappointed in their attempts to create open-book systems. Let's look again at the Business Literacy Model (see Figure 4.1).

Start with the Basic Formulas

Open-book management creates a system for all employees to see how their individual or team numbers get added to others' numbers to achieve the companywide numbers that get printed in quarterly and annual reports. A simple profit and loss statement (or income statement) is a good place to begin tracking all departments' and teams' impact on the numbers. The increasing emphasis on cash flow metrics as the crucial financial

Figure 4.1 Business Literacy Model—Open-Book Systems

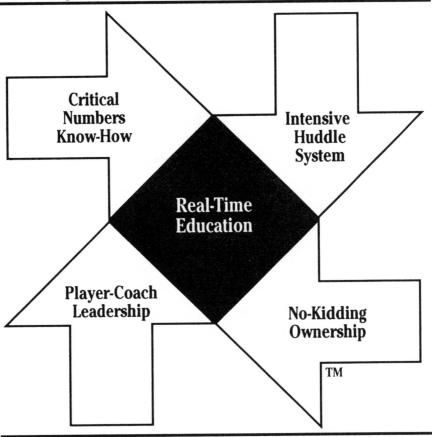

measures, doesnt diminish the income statement as a sound starting point.

The business of making money does not seem all that complicated. You produce a product or provide a service and people pay you for it. Right? Of course, you also spend a certain amount of money making the product or rendering the service, and you have to subtract that from what you've been paid, but still, it's really pretty simple, right?

Revenues − Expenses = Profit (or Loss)

Formulas don't get much simpler than that. But throw in a few twists: a "cost of goods sold" here, for instance, and a "purchase price variance" or two here and there; amalgamate a few departments; amortize a capital investment or two; and next thing you know, for most employees not accustomed to the lingo, you have produced a complicated, unintelligible blur of numbers and phrases.

Unintelligible, without meaning. To the point where it's as difficult to comprehend for anyone not trained in business finance as medical terminology would be for those not trained in medicine.

To those who have been trained, "cost of goods sold" or "purchase price variance" are common phrases on the income statements of manufacturing companies. They possess clear and simple meanings. To the first-time listener at a staff meeting, the phrases are specialized financial dialect that need translation.

Animating the Numbers, Accountings, and "Line of Sight"

In her novel, *Ceremony*,* Native American writer Leslie Marmon Silko writes, "You don't have anything, if you don't have the stories." The term accounting is sometimes used to mean story, as in "Give me an accounting of your experience." Accounting numbers tell the story of the business, the people in the business, and their efforts to satisfy customers and make money. In open-book management, accounting, far from lifelessly recounting the beans, describes what the blood and sweat of every person in the business have wrought. It animates the numbers. As simple as the formula is (Revenues − Expenses = Profit (or (Loss)), not all employees in the business know it because, remember, they haven't been asked to learn it and no

---

* Leslie Marmon Silko, *Ceremony*, New York: Viking Press, 1977.

one has ever taken the time to show them what they contribute to that formula. They have yet to hear their part of the story. They cannot see in it themselves or any of the people with whom they work, day in and day out. To them, it's a closed book.

For example, let's take a close look at an imaginary company. The *revenue* results of Acme Screw and Gear Company for this month come from:

- The human resources staff recruiting good salespeople.
- The marketing staff developing the right products.
- The direct sales force creating orders.
- The customer service staff taking orders.
- The shipping department having a great record of on-time delivery.

Acme *expenses* for this month come from direct expenses in making the product or delivering the service:

- The hourly wages of the service providers or factory workers.
- The costs of the materials used to make the service or product.
- The shipping costs of freight carriers and Federal Express.

And indirect expenses:

- The janitorial service contracts.
- The office personnel salaries.
- The customer service telephone calls.
- The computer cost/time to do billing.

Although several different departments affect the formula, when the role of each department is explained to the employees of that department, this simple formula begins to take on significance for them.

Even if there are hundreds of categories of expenses and many sources of revenue, employees start to see that the income statement is not a secretive blur of numbers and unintelligible phrases. It tells a story, their story. The more precisely these numbers are tracked directly back to each team, the sooner each team will see that story and will understand how all the parts of the business fit together. The income statement becomes a living document that describes what different departments and people in the company did for that given time period.

The same can be done with the balance sheet and the cash flow statement. With some practice and training, the value of a strong balance sheet, with appropriate debt levels, and a cash flow document that shows the all-important difference between profit and cash can also tell the story of their business and their work.

Open-book management creates a series of stories that are being told every day in the business. Doug Rothert, one of the original owners of Springfield Remanufacturing Company (SRC) and a financial teacher of the first order, talks about the power of stories. "It is getting at the stories in the numbers that brings it all together," he says. "Heck, all we do is try to bring the business to life and make it fun for everybody by teaching the numbers in such a way that no one is left out of the story. When we teach the numbers well, people start to realize that they are creating the story of the business as they go."

Animating the numbers makes open-book management much more than just teaching everyone financial terms and concepts by having them take "Financial Management for Nonfinancial Managers" classes. It is learning about their business and how to be an integral part of adding value to those financials. It means providing everyone in the company with a "line of sight" from what they do at their desk or workstation to the financial statements. Business literacy creates a connection between daily activity and the financial statement scorecard (see Figure 4.2).

The Practice of Bottom-Up Forecasting

Once critical numbers know-how permits employees to hear, in financial terms, the small tales that make up the big story

Figure 4.2 Line of Sight

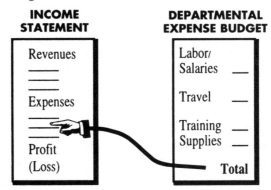

The Budget Is a Subset of the Income Statement

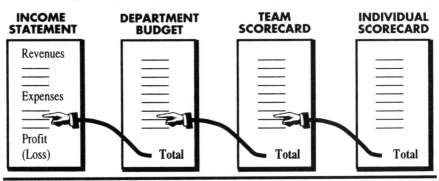

From Individual Work to the Income Statement

told by the income statement and the balance sheet, employees want to start telling those stories themselves, as they unfold. Given real-time information, employees who posses critical numbers know-how can help make the preferred story of the future, also called the business plan, become a reality by sharing their parts of that story. They share their stories in an intensive huddle system that conveys real-time information up, down, and across the organization.

The preferred outcome expressed in the company's overall business plan describes overall strategy and provides an honest assessment of its competitive advantages. Other plan components, for most companies, include a marketing plan, a human resource/employee involvement strategy, a new product development plan, a quality plan and, of course, a financial plan—with a balance sheet and the coming year's revenues, expenses, and cash flow projected month by month.

In business-literate companies, while the marketing department is primarily responsible for the marketing plan, the responsibilities for members of the department don't stop there. They work to achieve their marketing and sales objectives, as the human resource department focuses on its goals, and the quality team theirs. But all departments and functions also focus on company goals. They continually track, in regularly scheduled intensive huddles, how what they are doing is linked to the rest of the company.

In these huddles, their horizon expands beyond communication gaps. Their focus may remain local and departmental. But the view now includes the big picture. Surveying the financials—which constitute a landscape without gaps—employees, teams, and departments throughout the organization can see and take responsibility for the company objectives. The intensive huddle system keeps open-book management's unifying element, the business plan, in front of all the employees.

Each department's activities must be captured in the plan, and each team or department's critical numbers must be identified. Management's job is to charge each department with managing those numbers and its share of the activity, and to support them accordingly. When everyone does their part, the plan is successfully executed and its goals are achieved. Sounds simple, and it is—in principle. It just takes concerted effort to get all employees up to the task, and then ongoing coaching, as in any professional endeavor, to excel.

That's the essence of open-book management's paradigm shift and this is the communication breakthrough that business-literate companies pursue: The employees must know enough about the business and its finances, and their part in both, to manage their own activities. Finance will still verify the numbers historically, but employees will manage them futuristically (see Figure 4.3).

The Practice of a Common Language

Prevailing business paradigms say employees managing their own numbers and financial variances with a view to the future is impossible, probably because it has never previously been imagined. A typical reaction by CEOs to a description of open-book management resembles this actual reaction from a $200 million global manufacturer, "I can't get my VPs to explain a variance three weeks *after* it happens. It would be great if we could anticipate variances *before* they happen."

Even the great guru of quality J. M. Juran seems to accept that the language of finance should not be part of the front line's world when he writes:

> With any company there are multiple functions: finance, personnel, technology, operations. Each function exhibits its own dialect. The company also has multiple levels in the hierarchy and again there are multiple dialects. At the bottom of the company is the common language of things; at the top the common language of money. Those in the middle need to be bilingual.*

But nobody's right all the time. Business literacy doesn't require eradicating dialect or wiping out the differences between varying functions and levels. It does, however, increase the business knowledge of all employees across all functions and throughout all levels, making the language of money and finance the common vernacular.

The language of money is everywhere inside the business anyway, if looked for and highlighted. The budget touches everyone. Sales is committed to revenue numbers; the cost system puts a number on all activities; human resources knows

---

* *Juran on Planning for Quality*, New York: Free Press, 1988, p. 62.

Figure 4.3 Financial Information Flow

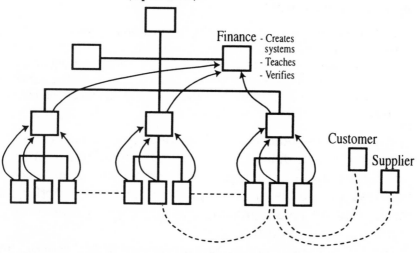

OLD MODEL

Finance collects data and sends down, historical performance numbers through chain of command

NEW MODEL
(Open-Book)

Finance - Creates systems
- Teaches
- Verifies

Customer
Supplier

Business-smart teams in concert with internal/external suppliers and customers, send current and forcasted numbers up to management and across to other units.

salaries and benefits; and anyone dealing with customers has to talk about prices. Open-book management capitalizes on the natural pervasiveness of numbers and gives everyone access to the syntax and meaning of financial language so all can use it and converse intelligently.

When all employees have embraced the business plan and its budget subsets, and have started using its numbers to communicate across departmental boundaries in a language that all understand, the paradigm in the organization has, for all practical purposes, shifted to permit empowerment in a business-literate enterprise. Critical numbers know-how and intensive huddles alone, however, will generally not persuade employees to make such a radical shift. Leadership, too, will be required, along with, in most companies, basic changes in the reward systems, both financial and psychological.

A Good Reward Will Get You Plenty

The design of bonus or incentive systems in open-book management companies is particularly crucial. Bonus systems that give back to employees some of the financial gain they have worked hard to create, through their willingness to take on more responsibility, provide a powerful feedback loop for learning and motivation. Good financially based incentives bring the power of critical numbers know-how and the intensive huddle system together to manage expenses and seize opportunities that add value for customers.

A good bonus system becomes a set of practices that should:

■ *Be a teaching tool.* When well structured and explained, a good profit-sharing or bonus plan teaches employees how they impact the financials. Usually, when a new bonus or profits plan is introduced, employees will ask, "What do we have to do to achieve that bonus?" They'll start seeking a "line of sight" to the budget to see where they can have the most

impact. They'll want to know what they need to do to produce which outputs. They'll discover a fresh new incentive to
learn what critical numbers they affect and how.

■ *Strengthen the financial status of the company.* An incentive system
that ties directly into a line of the income statement (or balance sheet or cash flow statement) that needs strengthening, tends to focus team efforts. If cash flow is the problem,
then a bonus program that reduces receivables for the year
might make the most sense.

■ *Unify a company.* Consider, again, the previously mentioned
cash flow problem. The accounts receivables people in finance, those charged with dunning customers, aren't the only
employees who can affect receivables. Sales personnel can
speed payments to the enterprise too, as they interact with
and provide terms to customers. Delivery people can remind
customers of how important it is to pay on time. Reducing receivables could, in other words, become a team effort, fostering the practice of cooperation across departments that
traditionally are at odds.

So many reward systems end up losing their impact over
time and actually fall into the category of one more entitle-
ment/benefit. When sound bonuses are at work, employees
become partners in the business, teaching their peers what
needs to be done to reach the financial goals, practicing systems thinking and focusing on the whole and not just their
part. And most of all, the reward will be earned or not earned
by what they do as a business in the marketplace, not because
of a benevolent CEO or a compensation system that gives out
arbitrary benefits.

No Leadership = No Business Literacy

Player-coach leadership makes or breaks open-book management. Good intentions are not enough to make it all happen—

Open Books at Work: 3. Dividing the Money Pools

President Jim Thompson of Electronic Controls Company in Boise, Idaho, has a 6-year history with an incentive system that works for the company. The profit-before-tax bonus pool of money is divided into three equal parts.

■ The first part is divided among all employees equally.

■ The second part is divided by seniority: The total number of months of all employees is divided by the total months of each employee at the company. The most senior employees make the most out of this pool.

■ The third part is divided by percentage of salary. The more money the employee makes in salary or wage the more money the person gets from this pool.

Says Thompson, "The reason we like this way of distributing the bonus is that it rewards us all for different criteria. "People really get jacked up at a monthly meeting when we get big bonuses because we held down scrap or handled a lot of volume due to good sales. We'll be cheering and celebrating those good months, and when the bad months happen we'll 'boo' and feel bad. We like our bonuses with a real tight feedback loop back to employees so we can see what we do everyday. It's really motivating."*

---

* *National Center for Employee Ownership,* National Conference, 1994.

real thinking and behavior and skill has to be at work daily. The following list provides leadership guidelines for upper, middle, and lower levels (for those in hierarchies that still have those distinctions). These qualities are for small and big businesses, for all the coaches and players accountable to their colleagues and customers in the special ways open-book management demands. Player-coach leaders must cultivate the following characteristics:

1. Master the basics of the business.
2. Create a learning model by learning themselves.

3. Tell stories that convey meaning.
4. Create other open-book leaders.
5. Embrace the people-and-profits paradox.
6. Stay both part of the team and in charge.
7. Lead and manage simultaneously.
8. Create community.
9. Use intuition and numbers know-how.
10. Create miracles by looking for them.

Not all leaders in business-literate companies have the same mix of these skills. With the usual bent for variety, open-book managers get the job done in their own way and style. But as a standard to follow, these 10 skills, many quite unique to open-book companies, are worth deeper descriptions.

Master the Basics of the Business

In open-book environments, managers and team leaders are responsible for transferring knowledge. As markets demand ever more informed decisions and flexibility, player-coach leaders are passionate about passing everything they know about their business—technology, customers, delivery and production processes, finance and costs, leadership, motivation, and teamwork—to everyone on their team. This transfer first requires that the manager knows the fundamentals inside and out to have something to pass on.

After the basics are transferred, then employees can work at surpassing their managers in knowledge and skill and achieving new levels of competence and performance.

Create a Learning Model by Learning Themselves

Open books make problems visible. Variances against a plan pop up all the time, and when a team doesn't meet its number, the team has to start questioning why: Was the plan ambitious, stupid? Did a process get out of control? How can we get it under control? What do we have to learn to do better next month, quarter, year? If we add this feature to the service, will it be worth the additional revenue?

Player-coach leaders are in the practice of asking questions for themselves and the team without having all the answers. They show their learning process to others, demonstrating the value of team thinking, making mistakes and soliciting feedback about their skills.

Tell Stories That Convey Meaning

Open-book environments are numbers-obsessed. But player-coach leaders aren't number crunchers with the personalities of calculators. The stories behind the numbers make the difference and convey the meaning, purpose, and teaching that make the numbers tools and worthwhile targets. When a customer service representative asks why revenue went up 10 percent this month, a natural time for storytelling occurs. Instead of explanations like "We sold more of the Acme deluxe product," or "We introduced the new product," the player-coach leader has a great opportunity to animate the number:

> Remember all the work in product development last year on the Acme deluxe? We even made some customer response calls out of here. Well, the product is looking good. Not only does the second month impact take our sales up, we've got more requests for next quarter than we can handle. The product development team is revved. Our engineer, Bill, put so much time in on this introduction in front of the customers, they're calling him "the sales master" now.

Create Other Open-Book Leaders

The ultimate act of leadership is to create more leaders. Open-book management creates a yeasty learning environment where people can push their learning in both job and business skills. Player-coach leaders use feedback/accountability/learning loops in the intensive huddle system and the day-to-day work to help their teams grow and exercise the leadership that comes with making judgments and assessing results.

Management has always been defined as getting work done through people. Player-coach leaders know that if they are doing their jobs well, *leadership is getting people done through work*. If one indicator of open-book management going well is better financial performance, then another equally important indicator is the development of ordinary employees into sound business thinkers.

Embrace the People-and-Profits Paradox

Business has long operated out of a hard versus soft metaphor. The metaphor describes the numbers as the hard and lasting and nitty-gritty stuff; and people as the airy-fairy, touchy-feely element of work.

Not true. While others have tried to say that soft is hard; that culture is the difference in whether numbers are met, few have believed and lived it. The human development folks and the finance folks occupy two separate worlds. Player-coach leaders use the environment to teach, develop, coach, and motivate the core soft stuff as a means of reaching the numbers and hard business objectives. They use the paradox to develop people and to make money, lots of it, at the same time. Making money is never the problem—what matters is how the money is made and what's done with it.

Player-coach leaders put soul in the numbers and they put numbers in peoples' souls, some of whom are even number haters and avoiders until their magic and the story they tell become clear.

Stay Both a Part of the Team and in Charge

Followers want their leaders to be a cut above them—sometimes. Followers also want their leaders to look and be competent, to command respect, represent them well, teach the business and excel in the numbers. To do this, leaders need to accept the status that comes with their competence or position, or both, and look the part.

But player-coaches are also players. They roll up their sleeves and get their hands dirty. They ask questions about the numbers, show their limitations, get advice, and follow it as part of the team they coach. When necessary, they can ignore their status and become part of the group.

This capacity to be both very human and a cut above is difficult for those managers who are afraid to be visible and take charge; and just as hard for those leaders who have spent their professional lives learning how to use status and its symbols.

Lead and Manage Simultaneously

The struggle between leadership and management is over for player-coach leaders. Those with natural leadership tendencies who inspire and create change, but who also excel at creating chaos in the doing, will be able to keep the house in order because open-book management relies on a plan, huddles and feedback, data and variances, the traditional tools of managers.

Those whose natural gifts are management and control will have to share information, empower their teams to plan, teach, motivate with recognition and bonuses, and most of all, animate the numbers with stories and meaning. These are the usual tools of leadership.

Leadership is not good and management bad, or vice versa. Player-coach leaders will combine and use both skills and all the tools in open-book systems.

Create Community

Open-book techniques are useful to the degree that they create purpose-filled, learning-driven, goal-committed companies. Individual accomplishment is valued by player-coach leaders but group accomplishment is valued more. From the bonus systems in no-kidding ownership to the inclusiveness of huddles and financial know-how, the power of the team and company as a whole is emphasized.

Common destiny is a hallmark of open-book companies, instead of the us versus them thinking that kills long-term superior performance by creating gaps, silos, and classes.

Use Intuition and Numbers Know-How

Fact-based, financially sound decisions drive open-book management. Intuition and hunches pick up where the numbers leave off. Good sports coaches play the percentages a lot, bring in left-handers to pitch to lefties, but they will also play their hunches and do the opposite once in a while. Getting whole companies to manage variances will spread the facts, unifying efforts and keeping outside business conditions and inside work processes continually connected. But all the facts in the world won't eliminate business risks. And changes in customers and environments mean making decisions for which the numbers have yet to indicate a trend.

Knowing when not to use the numbers, when to flip between decision-making modes, when to get facts and when to explore assumptions, is player-coach leadership at work. The human mind and heart know more than the mouth can explain and give voice to. At times logic chains are clear: if A then B, if B then C, and so on. Other times the mind jumps from A to Q, and it's a good decision.

Create Miracles by Looking for Them

Any human activity can become routine. Even two-term U.S. Presidents must wake up about year 7 and say, "Not much happening today—a few heads of state, a few billion dollars to sign into a bill. Oh well, maybe tomorrow will be more exciting."

Player-coach leaders look beyond the routine elements of work to what is marvelous, even miraculous in what goes on every day. Maslowe, the father of human potential thinking, commented on every day and its possibilities. "The people who look for miracles have it all wrong. When you look at something right, everything is miraculous."

Player-coach leaders create the little surprises that maintain peak interest; whether it's a refreshing way to recognize an accomplishment, a new insight into a customer, or a nephew's story about school and what it has to say about people and the way we learn.

Player-coach leaders see the latent miracles in the routine stuff of work. Financial reports and budgets become a series of promises between teams. Staff meetings become opportunities for learning and dialogue, commitments and covenants, celebration and growth. Normally just a way to make a living, work itself is also a way to connect to living, breathing, all-important customers, to create a right livelihood, and to change the planet with purpose and ennobling effort.

Seeing all these miracles requires an attitude—and player-coaches have one. It's the ability to recognize the amazing miracles in everyday life.

And upper managers have special responsibilities.

Chapter 5

ᴣᴇ ᴣᴇ ᴣᴇ ᴣᴇ

Leading the
Open-Book Effort

Indeed, if there is any single attribute of human beings, apart from language, which distinguishes them from all other creatures on earth, it is their insatiable, uncontrollable drive to learn things and then to exchange the information with others in the species. Learning is what we do, when you think about it. I cannot think of a human impulse more difficult to govern.
—Lewis Thomas, MD

The single biggest variable in whether open-book systems create a company of business thinkers lies in the quality of the leaders who make it happen. In its most fundamental sense, open-book management is nothing more than leaders empowering employees with the right and responsibility to use business tools that formerly were reserved for upper managers. Without leaders empowering and teaching, open-book management systems will not work.

But for many leaders in existing direct-and-control bureaucracies, much unlearning has to be done. Consultant and author James O'Toole says that 95 percent of leaders today say the right thing, but only 5 percent *do* the right thing. That is the crux of the matter, accuracy of O'Toole's percentages aside.

With sound leadership, even mediocre no-kidding ownership, critical numbers know-how, and intensive huddle systems will evolve and improve. The people themselves can improve and debug the systems as long as leadership provides the opportunity and the tools. With poor leadership, the best systems will die on the open-book vine and shrivel into one more bad memory of a program that didn't work and shouldn't have been tried.

Widespread business literacy puts new demands on the leaders. Their behavior, even their thinking, occurs in a glasshouse—for all to see, study, and critique. Open books give new meaning to the term *visibility*. Leaders in open-book systems are held accountable by their colleagues as they embrace their responsibilities. In low-information systems, managers had a place to hide themselves and some of their decisions. As one 27-year veteran of a large, low-risk management company put it, "I could disappear in the hallways around here if I wanted to."

In open-book environments, the fishbowl effect means leaders must be able to explain their decisions and be ready for the scrutiny the positions attract. They earn their leadership status everyday.

Accountability and Widespread Status

"Player-coach leadership" is a double-edged term. All the coaches have to be players, that is, stay close to the action. And all the players have to be coaches, that is, take responsibility for teaching others and for delivering service to their internal and external customers.

The emphasis in player-coach leadership is not on climbing to a formal managerial position. To be sure, humans create systems of status and dominance and submission everywhere, and business-literate companies are no exception. Humans seem to be wired that way. Open-book companies have positions of leadership, and hierarchies exist for good reason: No matter how business-literate the front line gets, some coordination from the top is good and necessary.

But in player-coach leadership, the real emphasis is on taking leadership for the position you have. The difference here is that from the floor sweeper to the CEO, every employee has a job to do that contributes measurably to the common good. All employees exercise leadership as soon as they seize responsibility for their part and tie their work to the good of the whole.

Leaders in the top positions define and communicate how they will deploy themselves and meet their responsibilities to the business. With that done, the leaders require each and every person and team in the enterprise to do the same defining and communicating. This practice allows mature, self-responsible behavior to spread. It allows the company to govern itself, network across departments, handle conflicts, resolve grievances, and design its future as an adult learning community.

Bob Argabright of Chesapeake Packaging describes his philosophy and approach: "I recently went through an exercise with all our people," he says.

"I asked them to define what a leader is. All the verbiage they used to define leaders—trust, knowledge, communicator, motivator, role model—I asked them, is there any of this that you don't have inside yourself? I want a company of businesspeople—I want 145 leaders within this company."*

Neurotic, bureaucratic organizations create dependence and victim thinking that is reflected in it's-not-my-job/finger-pointing/they-did-it patterns. Alfred Adler, the renowned psychologist, said, "The life lie of the neurotic person is failure to accept personal responsibility." Player-coach leadership fosters responsibility as a natural outcome of making commitments and sticking to them.

Recognition and feedback from huddle and no-kidding ownership practices provide status on the team and internal pride in accountable behavior. In this way, open-book companies take on the properties of sports teams. At the Olympics, a woman's volleyball team will have champion spikers who make the headlines and are the visible stars. These stars, however, are supported by the invaluable, less visible skills and energy of the

---

* Chris Lee, "Open-book Management," *Training*, July 1994, p. 25.

diggers and setters who create the opportunities for the stars. It is that way with football, with business, and with any group effort—some are in position to get the glory and enjoy the status and others are not. Blending the skills of all the players, including the diggers and setters, into a team effort is what creates excellence.

In open-book systems, player-coach leadership spreads status and pride in work liberally and as a matter of course, giving feedback in huddles to all the players on the importance of their part. Recognition is not reserved just for a few.

In sports, examples of widespread status abound. Coach Tom Landry, formerly of Dallas Cowboys fame, was instrumental in computerizing and quantifying the game of football. His scientific look at the game helped the Dallas Cowboys rise to prominence for many years.

As the story goes, the Cowboys had a mission of being a world-class entertainment organization (which explains the Cowgirls and a few other entertainment fringes that had little to do with football). Because successful entertainment rests on winning, exciting football, Landry then broke down the mission into a set of goals that would guarantee winning. For instance, Landry would give the offensive team a set of numbers to work toward; let's say, an average of 28 points a game. The defensive team then would also be given a set of numbers, 17 points a game. That 11-point spread would mean that the Cowboys would win 12 out of 16 games and be in the playoffs and the hunt for the Superbowl ring every year. Sound familiar? Cowboy haters and Cowboy lovers know what this is about.

If the team was going to score 28 points, every person had some responsibility: the offensive linemen, in relative obscurity; the wideouts, the running backs, and the quarterback, with all that visibility. Everyone in the offense knew exactly what was expected of him on every play.

The quarterback, the unforgettable Naval cadet Roger Staubach for several of Landry's years, was given a set of numbers to deliver. Complete 58 percent of the passes, for an average of 9 yards a pass, with only one interception for every three touchdowns, with only one interception for every 55 passes, and so on. At the end of the game, Roger could look at the numbers and see precisely how he had done.

But the quarterback wasn't the only one. Each obscure lineman, long ago forgotten except by avid hometown fans, had a set of numbers and received precise feedback. In this way, status and responsibility were widespread, and the stars knew who did the blocking while they threw and ran for touchdowns and headlines.

One sign of player-coach leadership in action is the widespread engagement of all levels and functions, the visible stars and the behind-the-scenes average performers. As Bear Bryant, Alabama's legendary football coach, described his team's success, "We win games not because the stars do well. They always do well. It's getting the more average players to rise to the occasion and make the big plays that makes the difference on a winning team."

In open-book management, a positive kind of office politics takes over. Instead of people hiding information and using it as a source of advantage, the books are opened. Personal value and social status are based on how well and how much information is shared. Instead of how much you know being the source of status and influence, it is how much you teach. A good teacher asks questions that stimulate learning in others.

Politics happens wherever there are people. But in well-led open-book companies, with information open instead of closed, power games between managers and team battles over turf fade into the background. Responsibility for your team's part in executing the overall company plan comes into the foreground. When the planning process necessary for the intensive huddle system kicks in, all players and teams commit to their set of numbers and outcomes. Responsibility emerges rather than power politics. How you can do your part becomes the goal.

❀ ❀ ❀ ❀

Open Books at Work: 4. Spreading Responsibility and Status

Bob Argabright, CEO at Chesapeake Packaging in Baltimore, not only runs the plant he was asked to lead in 1988; he turns out leaders. Another open-book company made famous by *INC.*, his plant has become a model against which other organizations have benchmarked. Here, leadership is a natural outcome.

Argabright took his assignment to manage the Baltimore plant to heart and decided that the way to turn employees onto the business was to open up all its systems. Argabright, as a player-coach, knew that sharing the numbers with employees—allowing them to make mistakes, learn from those mistakes, and push the business ahead—was the essence of empowerment and leadership development.

One of the systems that Argabright put in place was to create company "presidents" out of his department leaders. Understanding that all employees will do better when they understand the importance of their job, Argabright made "intracompanies" out of the administration group, the operations group, the purchasing group, and so forth. The president's job was to take on the role of running "the business" of each department: setting budgets, defining goals, and solving problems. After 6 months, new presidents were elected by the intracompany members.

Under this system, with ample freedom from Argabright, Chesapeake's employees became player-coach leaders. Says David Shanahan, Chesapeake's controller: "The outstanding characteristic about Bob is the trust he generates. He really gives people here the freedom to improve whatever they can. And we do."

Rises in the cost of their primary raw material, paper had threatened profitability. But employees voluntarily attacked other controllable costs—like water, maintenance, and supplies—and held those to record lows.

As someone close to the action (player-coaching), Argabright taught his employees the business (mastering the basics) and granted them the freedom to move ahead as a team and make the business run. Player-coach leadership creates a contagious environment that brings the team together (creating community and spreading accountability). "Until we learned to learn from our mistakes and not be afraid of them," said one manager at Chesapeake, "we had no idea how fast we could go. This place is humming now."

Dream-Weaver Manager-Leaders

In open-book environments, the difference between management and leadership gets blurred. Open-book systems take tools formerly reserved for managers and spread them around the workplace, leaving the question: Now what are the managers supposed to do? Everybody else has taken their tools, so the managers need to come up with new roles and tools—teaching and coaching, bringing in new resources, facilitating teams to challenge themselves, setting up new learning opportunities.

Hmmmm. That sure sounds like leadership, doesn't it? And that is what happens. Jack Stack, CEO of SRC, uses the phrase that when the bottom rises, the top also rises. In this instance, when the thinking of employees is raised through the tools and practices of business literacy, the managers are pushed to step up to the thinking and behavior of leaders. They grow into player-coach leaders.

But the line between leadership and management is still far too distinct in many companies. The research on leadership suggests that while employees understand the need for good management, they crave good leadership. Consultant and author John Kotter describes the distinction in A *Force for Change*:*

■ Management controls and solves problems.
■ Management minimizes deviations from plans, and thus helps produce predictable results on important dimensions.
■ Leadership motivates and inspires.
■ Leadership energizes people to overcome major obstacles toward achieving a vision, and thus to produce the change needed to cope with a changing environment.

Employees don't need or want more strong managers who don't also lead. They have tasted too much of that flavor. There seems to be no shortage of those who can set a direction with a

---

* John Kotter, A *Force for Change*, New York: Free Press.

plan and then work to control events so the plan is executed, a kind of working definition of management.

What employees responding to Kotter's surveys said loud and clear is that the kind of leadership capable of answering their unmet needs, which sometimes get buried with too many years in the bureaucracy, was indeed in short supply. Helping to satisfy the twin driving needs for *continual learning* and *making a difference* is where management leaves off and leadership steps in.

Take the need for learning. While leaders want to meet goals to the same degree as their manager counterparts, they want accomplishing the goals to stimulate natural learning and development. When the customer is served, the profit margin is made, or the product gets out the door, both managers and leaders say, "Look what we did!" Player-coach leaders take goal accomplishment to the next level, also proclaiming, "And look at what we've become in the process!"

The need to make a difference is just as strong. Leaders turn the goals of business into fully human, exciting, worthwhile aspirations—the stuff of legends, and not just more money for the company. In this way, leaders transform the goals of managers into the dreams employees want to pursue but are often too afraid to long for—because those dreams may be dashed—in their work lives.

Leaders are comfortable working in the arena of human dreams, where the financial variances can only point. Companies try to tap this aspiration level all the time, with a broad range of success and failure. The Body Shop and Ben and Jerry's capture one side of the success scale, and Drexel Burnham Lambert (does anyone remember them anymore?) exemplifies the other.

Most companies are somewhere in between.

But very few companies ignore this unmet human need to make a difference. Why else all the corporate credos and value statements on the walls of the foyers across the Western corporate world? Why does Hallmark Cards think of itself in the social expression industry and not as a card manufacturer? Why do insurance sales people offer financial security for families, instead of making quota pushing product?

This aspiration and dream dimension is fundamental to all leadership, business or otherwise.

What if Martin Luther King, Jr., in 1963, at the steps of the Washington monument, had shouted, "I have an objective!"

The moment would have lost a little something.

Open-book environments address at their roots human aspiration and dreams. The emphasis on control and variances that comes with critical numbers know-how is a manager's delight in spreading control and variance management throughout the company. But the emphasis on control of the numbers—and not the people—allows all to take responsibility, to dream well, to push their limits and do something extraordinary for themselves, their families, their customers, their colleagues, and society. Like the "Karate Kid" learning from the master, first practice the basic strokes waxing the car, then dream of the championship match.

Not all managers in business-literate companies are, or should be, inspirational leaders. But they are, at the least, coaches. If top management sets the tone for the business being a place where people can pursue the dreams they have, then middle and front-line managers and team leaders will have great models for developing their own talent as dream weavers.

The No-Choice Choice

Some of the companies who first experimented with open-book approaches had no choice. Springfield Remanufacturing Corporation (SRC), our initial partner in this work of business literacy, was a source of inspiration and a subject of research in our development of the tools and processes to implement widespread employee involvement that focuses on the business. When SRC tells the story of their buyout—of being leveraged 89 to 1—they usually get guffaws and gasps from the listening audience. But there is no question why they turned to open-book management to run their business: They couldn't afford a mistake.

Ricardo Semler tells a similar story of Semco in Brazil. The wild fluctuations and turns of the Brazilian economy led him to teach all employees how business runs. He too had no choice. He had taken it as far as he could. His company faced a crisis. He and his employees could not afford a mistake.*

Robert Frey, the CEO of Cin-Made, a small manufacturer in Cincinnati with a long history of increasing business literacy, puts it this way: "No company can change any faster than it can change the hearts and minds of its people, and the people who change fastest and best are the people who have no choice."†

Quality guru Phil Crosby has a similar view: "Very few companies make much money, very few have a reputation for quality, and very few deliberately incorporate changes without having to suffer a crisis first."‡

Player-coach leaders use the power of these no-choice times in a company's life cycle to create new approaches. They step into the fray and convince others that, if they can't manage their way out of their present fix, perhaps they can lead the way instead.

But after enough companies respond to crisis by empowerment with business literacy, others begin to respond to keep up with those who have innovated under duress. Leaders can also create change through their values and their vision, which, if strongly held, are the equivalent of a no-choice precipitating event. Quality and involvement started with many companies that were in major trouble and spread to those that wanted to improve. Good and bad leadership stories emerge.

---

* Ricardo Semler, *Maverick*, New York: Warner Books, 1993.
† Robert Fry, "Empowerment or Else," *Harvard Business Review*, September/October 1993.
‡ Phil Crosby, "Leaders and Learning," *Journal for Participation and Quality*, March 1994, p. 30.

---❄❄❄❄---

Open-Books Not Yet at Work: 1. No Urgency

The story of a large Fortune 100 manufacturing facility suggests that two circumstances can prevent the open-book processes from taking place:

1. Not having a precipitating no-choice set of circumstances to face.
2. Not having sufficient player-coach leadership.

With a huge market share and no real competitors in sight, the management of this firm voiced an interest in applying open-book management to their quality process as a progressive next step. Quality's dependence on employee involvement and an understanding of customer satisfaction work processes can create a good beginning for deepening business literacy.

The lack of numbers knowledge among employees of this firm was typical for this kind of setting. Purchasing and finance swam in numbers all day long, but most other employees and all but a few managers knew none of the intricacies of the income statement. The company's reward system included a return on equity portion that few understood and still fewer could influence. The information flow necessary to keep business facts in the hands of those who could make better business decisions was clearly in need of redesign. The 1,200 person operation was ripe for improvement.

But in the end—while some progress was made toward getting the employees to understand financial statements—margins and market share stayed fat. Management was too fat and happy to really go the distance. The company continued the way it always had, with functions that kept score on quality and production, but with employees not really understanding their connection to customers or the budgeting process or the costing system or what the numbers meant.

Management chose not to push too hard for change, suggesting that the entitlement mentality that comes with being too comfortable for too long is alive and well at every level of our society. There was no compelling need. It would require a great deal of hard work involving a redistribution of power.

❄ Continued

⊰ Continued

They'd have to get approval from headquarters. It was all just too formidable.

The tendency for leaders to stay overly busy, to not understand the power of beliefs, to underestimate the influence of their actions (especially those not in tune with their espoused beliefs) to attack the symptoms and not the causes, all conspire to create "programitis" out of even the most sincere change efforts, including efforts to move to open-book management.

Choosing to Choose

No-choice turning points can precipitate the thinking that either drives companies out of business or takes them to new heights. People in charge must create a compelling vision for the move to open-book methods to be truly substantial. Often, that sort of vision and commitment emerges only when leaders perceive themselves and their enterprise as facing the equivalent of a no-choice situation. But not always.

While many individual companies are now taking the values-and-vision approach to business literacy versus the no-choice up-against-the-wall approach, one group of companies is worth mentioning because they have maintained their player-coach leadership with open-book management for many years.

The Scanlon companies are a federation of organizations that pioneered employee involvement processes long before it dawned on the rest of the business world. They are a wide-ranging group of companies that include Beth Israel Hospital in Boston and Herman Miller in Michigan. Taking some of their initial inspiration for employee involvement from the ground-breaking work of Joseph Scanlon in the steel industry in the 1940s and 1950s, many of the companies are in Michigan and were influenced by the work of Scanlon's contemporary Dr. Carl Frost, at Michigan State University.

--- ❆ ❆ ❆ ❆ ---

Open Books at Work: 5. Leading from the Middle

In an open-book manufacturing plant in the Midwest, the costs of shipping product on small pallets represented a significant factor in the budget. As the materials manager looked over these costs, he noticed that they had a significant impact on profitability, which was less than 5 percent, even in good years. And there had been some bad ones.

If the company had to buy a more expensive batch of pallets, if they had to use extraordinary shipping means, frequently they failed to meet these narrow margins despite their hard work. This supervisor's job was to come up with ways to attack the shipping costs. His manager turned over the "business" of shipping to him and taught him financials—instead of just working on shipping dates and quality. He, in turn, started generating ideas with his team to improve the numbers.

They came up with several ideas, two of which were implemented because, after running the numbers and doing some figuring, the payoffs were significant.

The first was leasing a new truck, instead of using other carriers. Finding a reliable driver was part of the challenge (his first one lasted only three weeks), but over 12 months, the company saved $60,000 a year, straight to the bottom line.

The second idea was making pallets out of new, less expensive, but just as durable, material. By replacing the former supply of pallets with a cheaper wood from a local source, each of the pallets that went out by the hundreds every week was three dollars cheaper. This savings of $25,000 dollars a year also went straight to the bottom line. Said the supervisor, "I was just doing my job. Without the financial information, though, we wouldn't have seen the opportunity. We've got to come up with more ideas next year."

He believes they will.

Paul Davis, the executive director of Scanlon Plan Associates, the association for Scanlon Plan companies, describes how practitioners shared business knowledge for many years and created high degrees of business literacy throughout many of their organizations. The by-product, says Davis, is that "we've created a whole level of flexibility and adaptability in our work forces that acts as a key asset in these times of rapid changes."

With Scanlon companies and some employee-owned companies, the continuing push toward business literacy by player-coach leaders stems from a profoundly felt need for improved performance. Fierce competition and rapid change have convinced management that the groups of employees they used to manage had better become organizations of self-managing business-people where everyone is responsible for the desired outcomes.

To make that happen, management will have to become player-coach leaders and help others do the same.

Keepers of Visions, Values, and Beliefs

More than any other task, player-coach leaders at all levels need to nurture the beliefs and values of their teammates and extend them into the world of possibilities.

We have all seen individuals who have not made the most of their talent. And we have all seen those who make the most of what they have because of the beliefs they hold. Whether athlete or musician, parent or engineer, any field of human endeavor provides examples of the drama of humans achieving, underachieving, and overachieving.

Player-coach leaders see that in every situation there is latent potential, and they work to actualize that potential through appealing to their employees' highest level of thinking and being. They work on the dream:

Cynics appeal to what we are at our worst.

Realists appeal to what we are.

Player-coach leaders appeal to what we most want to become.

Player-coach leaders see the same events as everyone else, they just think something different. They believe that we can do better. They are potential-seers.

What if Martin Luther King, Jr. hadn't seen the potential and the principle in Rosa Parks not wanting to sit at the back of the bus? What if Joyce Hall, founder of Hallmark Cards, hadn't seen the potential in sending greetings on postcards? What if Sandra Day O'Connor had not seen law as a noble career, which set her on the path to becoming the first woman on the Supreme Court?

Many a stellar athlete or student or team or company never lives up to its potential. The scholars of human achievement will forever debate and describe the factors that make the difference, but one factor they regularly agree on is belief. Those with beliefs that encourage and allow individuals and teams and companies to exceed their expectations find ways of doing so. Those with beliefs and attitudes that constrain their talent and gifts find ways to limit their accomplishments, and find great excuses for doing so.

The entire premise behind open-book systems is that the old beliefs of how businesses should be run are in question. The power of open-book management, when it releases the minds, hearts, and hands of all employees, is in the belief that there is no limit to what businesses and the people in them can accomplish. When player-coach leaders remove the constraints on information and knowledge from the old business belief systems, all things are possible.

Beliefs, Then a System, Then Practices and Tools

Open-book management is built on a set of beliefs. While it requires a set of tools and interlocking systems, the description of which forms the core of this book, the heart of the issue, is that open-book management refers to a set of beliefs about human beings and free enterprise, about work and people. It is a stance about human nature and how we go about adding value in the world through our collective efforts. If an organization lacks these beliefs and attitudes, then the fundamental benefits of pursuing business literacy will be lost.

Without the commitment that comes with belief, sometimes belief without evidence, the whole process just won't work. It takes a certain amount of (dare we say?) faith to make open-book systems and tools work. And this, and perhaps this alone, must come from the top down. Leaders have a special responsibility in shaping the enabling (or limiting) beliefs of an organization. Their most important contribution to the business is the creation of its collective attitude and beliefs. They bring these beliefs to bear on daily decisions so that employees and customers feel their impact. This responsibility takes precedence over all their other admittedly important executive duties.

While many see the techniques and practices of open-book management, fewer see the principles and beliefs that make the practices possible. That set of beliefs, or creed, starts, but does not end, with the following:

- All workers, even those not trained in business, can learn finance and other complex business systems.
- When managers create the conditions for learning and performing, informed workers naturally organize themselves into productive units that will serve customers.
- Sharing vital information and measures of organizational performance will automatically assist all employees of the system to play their individual parts better, to form the required teams, and to develop the necessary teamwork with other teams.
- Free enterprise is a great idea and more people can make it work than ever before imagined.

- If the organization is to acquire a real and lasting capacity for renewal, then each person in it must be able to think in terms of the overall direction and success factors of the business, even if that person's immediate role is limited.
- People can do their jobs and at the same time work for the health of the whole organization.

The failure, or limited success, of many of the change efforts in organizations is in part due to their not addressing the level of beliefs. Paul Davis, executive director of the Scanlon companies, a group with a long-standing philosophy of full employee participation, puts it clearly: "Don't increase business literacy if you are not going to let folks do anything significant with their knowledge. You have to believe that the intelligence of the organization is invested in everyone."

An organization must cling to that set of beliefs tenaciously, as if its life depended on it, for it does. Nothing else is sacred. Everything else it must be willing to change: decision-making procedures, information-sharing systems, compensation methods, product lines, service delivery, everything.

In adopting a set of beliefs that fosters business literacy, the organization recommits itself to people and their potential.

Section II

꓀꓀ ꓀꓀ ꓀꓀ ꓀꓀

Open-Book Management: Getting It Started

Among the newer companies on the Inc. 500, opening the books is no longer a very radical idea. . . . When asked how many shared financials with their employees, about half those present (at the Inc. 500 conference) raised their hands. . . . Then we asked how many thought employees understood the information. One person raised her hand. All of which strengthens our belief that, while growth leaders have lost faith in the traditional ways of managing and motivating people, they haven't yet figured out how to use the new ones.

Inc.*

---

* Editorial comment, *Inc.*, August 1994, p. 11.

There is no simple cookbook recipe for implementing open-book management so all will be perfect; no other companies to mimic; no gurus to follow you around and give you all the answers (although consultants may be coming out of the walls soon with "business literacy" on their cards, having just pitched their "quality expert" cards, which were preceded by their "expert on all new trends" cards).

But the good news is there are lots of examples to learn from, and the numbers are increasing all the time. And there are principles to follow that are at the core of making it work.

This section of the book explores those principles in depth. The principles are drawn from three pools of knowledge:

1. Business management and leadership theory.
2. Organization development and change theory.
3. The early adopters of open-book methods and what they know.

These pools have favorite, and sometimes conflicting, theories and principles. What was the previous decade's business holy grail, such as management by objectives for those of you old enough to remember, is this decade's forgotten set of practices, belonging to the Lenin school of discredited political, business, and social theories.

This section on getting open-book management started is laid out sequentially: It details four of the six phases to follow, (the last two are in Section III) from the first step of the journey, picking up this book at your favorite bookstore and reading it over a cup of cappuccino at the espresso bar, to the last step some three years later, of hosting visiting companies to your department because you have become a world-class example of an open-book success.

The six phases represent the best thoughts and actions of what the three pools of knowledge point to when an enterprise takes on open-book management. Preparation is heavily emphasized because, frankly, the messes that happen when the company doesn't prepare aren't pretty. Actual setbacks occur with faulty preparation by the leaders. Don't be surprised if you start sharing financial information, and employees think there is another set of books somewhere else. And, without good training to accompany the sharing of financial information, there is often *less* employee interest at the second monthly all-employee meeting to look at numbers than at the first—"Nothing changed since the last meeting and the numbers are pretty boring because I can't influence 'em anyway."

The last chapter of the section, Chapter 11, is specifically for middle managers implementing what they can of open-book management without a company or divisionwide initiative driven from higher in the organization. The same six phases apply, but with modifications, scaled down for those in the middle with fewer resources and less support (e.g., a company that doesn't want to share the strategic plan) for business literacy and its practices.

The level of cynicism and distrust in companies today from the failed implementation of many other types of change efforts sobers any writing team about to put down one more implementation scheme, including this one. But simply a description of what open-book management is without an attempt to describe how to do it in some detail was neither enough of a challenge, or a service. It felt better to be detailed, informative, and in places perhaps incorrect, than to be general, inspirational perhaps, and very correct because not enough opportunities to be wrong were included.

Unique Formats and Common Open-Book Principles

Companies implement open-book management with their own style and pace. Open-book management cannot be imposed from the outside. It must grow and be nurtured from within to have meaning and to enhance the goals and develop the people of each particular business. How an organization starts business literacy depends on its current situation: its mission, leadership strengths, values and philosophy, financial health, competitive environment, and training resources.

While every business is singular, there are common elements in successful implementations. This section outlines the framework for those elements, with lots of specifics. Most everyone is attracted to a phased-in plan with a known beginning and a worthwhile end which, when built on principles and targeted toward a worthy goal, gets a team or a company started down a path. But most everyone also knows that, once started, plans don't happen in a sequential and linear way, that all paths have unknown turns and rocky patches, that life and work is always at least a little, and sometimes a lot, sloppy and confusing.

This is where leadership and determination, and sticking to the principles while flexing the plan, are all important. Plans chart the overall path, and then the reality of implementation takes over. The six phases overlap each other. What one company puts first, others put later in the process. Instantaneous and unplanned actions are necessary, often bringing new insights and fresh energy to the implementation that are better than the original plan.

In football, coaches call each play to respond to current game conditions, only some of which can be anticipated even with the best pregame plan. The team misses opportunities if the coaches don't update the plays frequently. In most sports, developing a good game plan is critical. But the execution of that plan in game conditions may bear little resemblance to the tidy paper version. The goal line is always the objective. But the players' discipline and adaptability win games.

Two well-known American football stories, affectionately named for their seeming divine intervention, exemplify the power of the unplanned: the "immaculate reception," Franco Harris's catch-off-the-helmet deflection for the touchdown for the 1970s Steelers, and the "Hail, Mary," Boston College's last-minute prayer touchdown by Doug Flutie in the mid-1980s. Both are cited as two of the greatest plays of all time. As their titles imply, they were spontaneous, but game-saving plays.

Open-book management implementation efforts have these kind of surprises, good and bad—the turns no one expects. The good ones become the "Hail Mary" stories, told and retold inside companies: the unexpected sale that saved the year-end results, the sharp eye of a truck driver noticing unloaded packages that saved a customer.

Realistically, the planning and execution of any endeavor is regularly influenced by luck, both good and bad, and by unplanned events and outcomes. A key for open-book implementers is to ride this paradox: Plan rigorously and stay flexible; exercise the discipline of planning and be ready to move quickly and to improvise. They need to guide and to coach, without over controlling the implementation.

As business educator Harlan Cleveland says: "Planning is improvisation upon a theme." Implementing change may be more like a creative jazz ensemble than a perfectly conducted classical symphony. Introducing business literacy is such a powerful process that, even with a planned introduction, it often takes on a life of its own, growing simultaneously in multiple directions. The leaders and coaches need to be thoroughly prepared, and planning is the most important part of preparation. By being rooted in the principles of participation and shared business learning, each open-book implementation is a company's unique, creative act.

Learning Differs from Teaching

The success of open-book management is based, in large measure, on continuous and rapid learning. It shifts managers and employees from the old paradigm of having answers and using them over and over, to one that, by raising questions, stimulates new information to put to use. Attitudes shift from reaction ("Why doesn't this work anymore?") to active inquiry for new answers that continuously find application.

A bias for action over thinking, in which learning is not viewed as legitimate work, has created frenetic work cultures in many companies. Warren Buffet describes this "lust for activity" as one of the factors that creates lemming-like nonthoughtful management and investment decisions. In these environments, hyperactivity takes the place of real learning and value-added steps. Faster cycle times, ironically, are based on continuous learning and taking the time, not to stay frenetic, but to institutionalize team and organizational learning as a strategic advantage.

Old patterns of education, with teachers as disseminators of information, funneling knowledge into the heads of students, create passive learners without the capacity or active curiosity for learning how and what to learn. Critical and creative thinking processes lie dormant in employees who were first schooled as youngsters to spout back answers, while letting the smart kids get the A's, and then, as adults, introduced to work settings with bosses holding all the answers.

Open-book management flies in the face of such passivity: It encourages all employees to become learners again, and to take responsibility for learning how and what to master. Starting with effective involvement-driven classroom training, and following with the vigorous information flows of intensive huddles, open-book practices stimulate the accountability and curiosity to learn and do the business. The classroom is a good place to start: It can lay down the concepts and provide the original framework. Then the annual business planning and the bonus and huddles take over; they provide the action learning laboratory and the feedback and motivational conditions that feed learning.

From Apprentice to Mastery: Open-Book Learning Takes Time

Shifts in language and thinking are the hallmark of the journey into open-book management. They indicate learning milestones and levels of accountability for owning the work. In the following manufacturing example, for instance, where setup times are a critical process to handle quickly, note the difference:

- *Prebusiness literacy thinking*—"We had bad setup times this month. We'll have to work faster. You know how the customer puts our sales folks under pressure if we don't get it out right on time."
- *Postbusiness literacy thinking*—"The problems in setup cost us 28 additional hours. Our labor effectiveness number went to 84 percent and we didn't absorb the burden we normally do. That nicks away at our bonus. And the customer needs the product now. We promise them fast delivery, and our sales team uses our speed as a competitive edge."

This increased and more precise knowledge, plus shift in attitude toward teaming with the customer and sales, does not happen overnight. But with good initial training, coaching by team leaders, and the power of repetition in the huddle meetings where the numbers are gathered and explained, the learning seeps in, deeply and permanently. Better thinking and a richer business context in the minds of the employees allows their performance to take on more responsible and mature dimensions, serving the many stakeholders in the business.

As you use the steps in this section on how to get open-book management started, look for language shifts and the level of employee questions that indicate permanent shifts in thinking and attitudes. Keep in mind that the following business literacy learning cycle takes years of maturing, like the mastering of any body of knowledge or profession. Companies seeking true open-book management realize that a few seminars on how to read financial statements won't be enough.

The Learning Cycle

1. Awareness	1 to 6 months
2. Apprentice	6 months to 1 year
3. Journeyperson	1 to 3 years
4. Mastery	3 years and beyond

---

1. Awareness (1 to 6 months)
   Classroom training on the business, as represented by financial statements:
   — The economic and industry environment.
   — The company's competitive strategy and how the financials reflect that strategy.
   — The company's financial statements.
   — The costing system and pricing strategy.
   — Customers and how and what they buy.

2. Apprentice (6 months to 1 year)
   Huddle system rolled out. Employees get assigned or volunteer to take ownership for their specific numbers in the budget. Initial questions arise revealing the level of learning taking place. Incentive system shows how financial results impact pay and company health. With time and practice, the questions get more advanced. At first, employees seek simple facts:
   — What is this expense category in the budget?
   — What goes into travel that it costs that much?
   — Is this salary budget inclusive of temporary help?
   — What do we have to do to earn the bonus?

   Then, judgments and complex tie-ins are included in the questions:
   — How much influence do we really have over the cost of those supplies?
   — How does our bonus tie into this budget number?
   — Do our salaries always net out to 60 percent of our total costs?
   — Shouldn't we get a different allocation expense for Information Services since we didn't use them nearly as much this year?
   — If we lower our supply costs, but no other teams do, we won't get our bonus anyway and all we did is make it harder on ourselves, right?

— Shouldn't management know that our costs have really gone up for graphic support this year and we're needing to make up that price increase somewhere else?

3. Journeyperson (1 to three years)
   Huddles sustained week in and week out for several years. Employees send their numbers weekly from the prehuddle and receive numbers from the rest of the company at the posthuddle:
   — The questions continue and move to a higher level indicating a more comprehensive understanding of many aspects of business and finance.
   — Employees understand what it takes to deliver their number and how they influence others in the company.
   — Monthly and quarterly financial statements by the company are reviewed and analyzed. Spontaneous discussion of company performance is widespread.
   — The stories behind the numbers start popping up and making sense. The numbers are human now, with the income and cash flow statements telling the big picture on profits and cash and the balance sheet displaying the health of the enterprise.

4. Mastery (3 years and beyond)
   Several years of business planning and the disciplines of open-book management have driven the learning deeply into the consciousness and daily procedures of individuals, teams, departments, and the entire company. The yearly plan is a participative event with opportunity for input. All employees bring their expertise and their knowledge of the business to the forum for deciding company direction. The long-term plan creates scenario thinking with all employees engaged at some level in building their collective business future:
   — Questions about improvements tie to value-added services and entrepreneurial attitudes for expanding markets and gaining new customers.
   — Business literacy is deep and economic cycles, product life cycles, interest rates, global trends, the customers'

customers, and advanced questions on measures are discussed and debated.

— Long- and short-term rewards are designed yearly to keep short-term performance focused and to make strategic moves for the long-term viability of the company.

— Acquiring new core competencies is the key to long-term success.

— Entrepreneurial opportunities emerge as teams anticipate their internal and external customers' needs, and build business plans to pursue new offerings.

Chapter 6

꞊ꙭ꞊ꙭ꞊ꙭ꞊ꙭ

The Open-Book Platform

Open-book management doesn't simply mean that a company can hand employees the profit and loss statement each quarter, and expect them to care about the information it holds and to understand how their efforts affect it. Teaching employees to understand the numbers is integral. So is giving them a piece of action . . . open-book management does entail a major cultural change in most organizations.*

—Chris Lee
Training Magazine

usinesses go through six phases on the open-book journey. How you take the journey, how much learning you do, how much fun you have, and how many challenges you meet along the way will be strictly up to you, your company, and its people. The discipline of implementing these steps, when coupled with the business and people practices the company seeks to implement, builds the platform on which open-book management can stand.

The six phases hold true across industries and company size. They are fundamental. But smaller companies, with less than 100 employees (there is no hard rule; this is only a guideline)

---

* Chris Lee, "Open-Book Management," *Training Magazine*, July 1994, p. 22.

95

and few layers of management, can expect to go through the phases more quickly, and with less need for the intense preparation to get all the functions and levels of the business on board. As is natural, scale affects much in implementing open-book management. A yacht turns more quickly than an ocean liner, but the ocean liner *can* turn. In any case, even the smallest of companies can learn from the phases as outlined. They won't skip them, but have fewer people and less time involved in the doing because their size allows for simplicity and speed.

The first three phases are:

1. Determining Level of Readiness.
2. Defining Goals.
3. Building the Open-Book Implementation Team.

During these phases, the company—its leaders and a designated design team, usually a multifunctional team responsible for the detailed implementation of open-book training and systems—study open-book management and craft the goals along with the strategies and the methods their organization will use to reach business literacy.

The other three phases are:

4. Crafting the Plan.
5. Implementation and Rollout.
6. Ongoing Improvement.

The implementation planning, the basic training and learning, and the initial rollout of the four systems take place during the fourth and fifth phases. In the final phase—Ongoing Improvement—the systems are debugged and improved, and advanced learning and performance takes place.

The following overview of each phase provides a broad perspective, and Figure 6.1 charts this basic information. The details and examples of each phase are covered in subsequent chapters.

Six Implementation Phases

Phase 1. Determining Level of Readiness

There is a twofold objective in this initial phase:

1. To comprehend what open-book management is about and the potential it holds for strengthening the business.
2. To establish a baseline by assessing the company's current level of competency in the four dimensions that make up open-book management.

To accomplish the first objective, the senior managers lead the way. They study and learn by reading (see the articles and books recommended in the Bibliography), by holding an on-site briefing conducted by a knowledgeable open-book management consultant/practitioner, and by making on-site visits to open-book companies. Discussing their insights leads to speculating about specific benefits, and the senior managers decide, if the benefits speak loudly enough to them, to obtain the resources to begin working toward the second objective, understanding how well they are currently doing.

Establishing the specific level of open-book competencies that already exist within the company sets an all-important baseline against which to measure future progress. When this phase is completed, management should have a clear picture of what open-book management is and what, if any, open-book practices are already at work. It's a reality check with the goal of knowing what really is happening, not what management thought was happening, which are most often two different things.

Setting the baseline does one more important thing: It involves employees and helps to heighten all employees' awareness of open-book management. It starts to create anticipation and excitement for those who see the promise of what can come ("We'll have more information and do better work") while injecting the reality of how far the company will have to go ("We'll all

Figure 6.1 Six Implementation Phases of Open-Book Management

Phases	Objectives	Participants	Activities	Resources Needed	Time Required	Common Pitfalls
1.A. Awareness (Chapter 7)	Comprehend OBM and what it offers	Senior Managers	Read articles and books; Visit practitioners; On-site briefing	OBM* literature; OBM coach	4–6 hours; 1–2 days	Sound simple; Easy to "tell" vs. providing leadership
1.B. Determine Level of Readiness (Chapter 7)	Assess current levels of competency	Task force; OBM consultant	Survey; Interviews	Set of standard practices; Coordination and planning	Over course of 1–2 months	Seen as unimportant; Rushed; Too small a sample in data gathering
2. Define Goals (Chapter 7)	Articulate direction for company with OBM; Specify goals —Critical Numbers —No-Kidding Ownership —Huddle System —Leadership Practice	Senior Managers with input from those involved in Phase I task force	Workshop Think Tank; Review and analyze data of the Readiness report; Designate Design Team members	OBM facilitator; Readiness report; Strategic and business plans; Evaluation of current initiatives	1–2 day workshop; Individual preparation time: approx. 2 hours	Lack of individual preparation and buy-in; Turf and politics; Minimal big-picture thinking
3. Establish and Educate the Team Implementation (Chapter 8)	Deep learning; Identify best connections for linking OBM to current company strengths and goals	Implementation Team —Mid-Managers —Functional experts	OBM training; Study OBM materials; Share learning; Site visits to OBM companies; Trial applications; Identify barriers	Meeting time; OBM materials; OBM coach; Direction from senior management	Weekly learning and application meetings for 1–2 months; Individual reading/study	Canceled meetings; Unprepared team members; Overwhelmed by other demands; Lack of management support

GETTING (phase 1.A/1.B); STARTED (phase 2/3)

Phase	Goal	Who	Activities	Resources	Time	Pitfalls
4.A. Crafting the plan (Chapter 9)	Craft implementation plan	Implementation Team; Sub-teams design bows and Huddle System	Planning Workshop; Set Milestones	Workshop facilitator; Readiness report from Phase II	1–2 day workshop; Subteam meeting time	Lack of leadership support; Failure to reschedule canceled meetings
4.B. Design and Conduct Training (Chapter 10)	Develop and pilot basic OBM and Critical Numbers training	Sub-teams to develop specific training components	Recruit sub-teams; Gather resources; Develop and write training; Initiate training	Employees with financial and business know-how; OBM coach and trainer	6–10 development and planning sessions; Schedule for training	Lack of training resources
5. Implementation and Rollout (Introduction to Section III) (Chapters 12, 13, 14)	Initiate use of OBM practices through the company; Reinforce business thinking and real time education in Huddle System	All managers and employees of the company	Create or refine scorecards; Start huddles and practices; Flag opportunities for learning; Celebrate small victories; Coach huddle leaders; Conduct training; Align reward/bonus program	Scorecards; Current data on customers, operations, etc.; Managers who coach and run huddles	Weekly Huddles; 40-minute prehuddle; 60–90-minute main huddle; 30-minute posthuddle; Continue basic business finance classes	Form over substance in huddles; Impatience for perfection; Missing opportunities; Bonus not working; Impatience
6. Ongoing Improvement (Chapters 12, 13, 14)	Improve business results by mastering OBM practices	All in the company	Ongoing huddles; Frequent recognition; Develop new leaders	Semiannual evaluation by design team	Time enough to continue the learning and educating	Lack of consistent accountability; Lack of vision

KEEP IT GOING

*OBM = open-book management.

have to understand return on assets and forecast expenses?") to achieve competency.

In many companies, data gathering, assessment, and gap analysis in this baselining phase are done in concert with external consultants, and for good reason. It is very difficult for a company to study itself. To really know where you are starting from, it is advisable to use an objective, experienced resource. The company, through an assessment task force, gathers data about itself and makes assessments against a standard of practices in each of the four dimensions of open-book management.

Using written surveys, interviews, and focus groups the task force of four to six middle managers and consultants obtains the information needed, summarizes it, and organizes the data in a readiness report. The senior management team uses this report to guide their decisions in Phase 2 and beyond. The options for managers to choose from, based on the data in the assessment report may include:

- Doing nothing.
- Offering financial education.
- Extending TQM effectiveness with open-book management.
- Carefully planning and instituting a new way to run the business and plan for its future.

The last option, a new way to run the business, is the deepest application of open-book management. It amounts to reinventing the business, or reforming its culture, so that daily practices, interactions with customers, and the thinking, decisions, and ways people go about their work are different because of heightened business literacy. The other options, including financial education and doing nothing (e.g., because it is the wrong time), are still worthwhile choices to make as a result of the assessment. If the decision is to proceed, the company needs to tackle the work of Phase 2.

Phase 2. Defining Goals

The objective in this phase is to use the best thinking of the senior management team and the assessment task force to clearly articulate the direction the company will take with open-book management. At the end of Phase 2, management, with the help and the input of the assessment task force, specifies and declares for all in the company the goals it wants to achieve through open-book management. Rolls Royce's 6 years of what British CEO Charles Matthews calls "business appreciation" training, after a downsizing that saved the company and a quality process that involves everyone, is very different from Manco's CEO Jack Kahl's obsession with innovation for customers. A workshop in which the managers and task force members have an opportunity to interact with each other, to listen and bounce around various scenarios, is a useful forum for this phase. The workshop becomes a think tank for considering the range of options available, in light of the company's strategic plan and growth cycle.

During this workshop, managers answer this fundamental question: *Short- and long-term, how will this company be better as a result of becoming a company of business-literate employees using open-book systems?*

The executives also complete a number of specific tasks. They:

■ Identify the critical numbers and other key performance indicators on which employees will need to be educated.

■ Speculate on how the various employees contribute to these numbers.

■ Define the first several short-term achievements, or milestones, by which the company will measure its progress toward its long-term goals for critical numbers know-how.

■ Contrast and compare the intensive huddle system with current communication systems.

■ Discuss current reward and recognition programs relative to no-kidding ownership standards.

■ Give serious thought to reformulating norms and standards for leaders and managers based on the practices described in the player-coach leadership system.

When the direction and goals are in place, Phase 3 of the implementation process can proceed.

Phase 3. Establishing and Educating the Implementation Team

Most of the work in this phase and the next belongs to an implementation team composed of a cross section of managers and supervisors, from sales and operations, for example, and functional experts, like finance. The transition between Phase 2 and Phase 3 is a precise and smooth handoff from the senior management team that sets direction to a design team that plans and executes the implement in full.

A separate implementation team is not absolutely necessary. Line management, especially in small to medium-size companies, can do all the implementation work themselves through their own immediate teams. In general, the senior managers have little time or understanding to do the kind of detailed work that installing open-book management takes. Many of the changes that open-book management brings about have to do with teams and departments coordinating with other teams across the organization, action that is often far removed from the executive offices. Make no mistake, senior managers sponsor the change across the organization, but middle managers and key frontliners and supervisors, those close to the detailed work that makes huddles and numbers know-how work, can best design the training and implementation plans that suit them.

The emerging technologies in large group learning and participative design and planning could greatly aid the introduction of open-book management. The so-called Large Group Methods, being pioneered by many consultants and company practitioners, can quickly expand the internal vision and planning for open-book well beyond a multifunctional design team. From 50 to 500 people come together in the same room to solve problems, begin change efforts, and design new ways of working. No specific large group events are mentioned in the open-book implementation phases as outlined, but imaginative practitioners and implementation teams will no doubt use these large group tools to accelerate business literacy within enterprises of all types.

Putting several of those who assisted in the first two phases on the implementation team ensures that the lessons already learned will be put to good use. An external guide and coach can enhance the quality, continuity, and speed of implementation.

The makeup of this team ideally consists of people from operations, sales, finance, administration, customer service, and other key functions in the business. If every level in the organization is on the team, the resulting rich set of perspectives will help the team do its work and create buy-in at every level in the organization. This includes the front-line performers, who often have the most learning to do in open-book management implementation. When the frontliners hear why they are learning, because their peers on the implementation team have the complete story of business literacy, the implementation will go more quickly. On one team, the clerical support person in the legal department and a customer service representative had significant impact on the final training on financials, and saved the team from significant design errors of making the financials too complicated.

At least three criteria are important for team membership:

■ Do they know the organization? (*Frontliners who are long term employees are an exceptional resource.*)
■ Do they have the time to be a consistent contributor? This looks obvious, but in today's lean and leaner work settings, it is a big question.

■ Do they believe in the power of open-book principles such as ongoing learning, full participation, and communication?

Building the team is a necessary preparation to carry out the subsequent phases successfully. In Phase 3, implementation team members:

■ Learn as much as they can about open-book management.
■ Explore further the opportunities cited in the readiness report.
■ Identify connections between the practices of business literacy and the business goals of their company.

The team meetings initially focus on learning and, again, it is useful to have an open-book management coach during this process to lead and draw out the important insights on the workings and the promise of business literacy. The team delves into the specific outcomes management has outlined. They bring to bear their own detailed knowledge of the cost and production and service delivery systems. Interacting with other team members, they raise their own level of thinking, taking on the perspective of the business as a whole and not just their function. The team members need to think like business owners who can coach their colleagues into business literacy.

As the implementation team solidifies its leadership for the rollout effort, other employees, often those who were part of or heard about the assessment, ask what the team is up to. This in turn leads to insights and small initiatives by those who are excited about the prospects of being a "real" business player in an open-book company. *Do not overlook these sparks of interest. Companies can begin to reap returns early through those who recognize the low-hanging fruit and turn it into extra profits.*

The implementation team's education, assuming they are not full time on the team and have lots of other work they are doing, can take four to eight weeks, depending mostly on what they already know. When the team members agree that they know enough, and are ready to create a plan that maps the way for the rest of the company, Phase 3 concludes.

Phase 4. Crafting the Plan

The preparation is over—now the team gets down to the all-important task of planning.

This planning phase has three objectives.

The team first crafts an implementation plan that maps the way for their company to get to their destination, defined in Phase 1 when the senior managers set the direction. This means taking into account the demands of the day-to-day business, the resources available, like time and money, the gaps between what is and what the company wants to be that were identified in the readiness report (Phase 1) and all other factors that affect the implementation.

The second objective is the development of the basic training in finance and leading the huddles, the structuring of the huddle system and the initial design of a reward and recognition system for creating the no-kidding ownership mentality. The plan marks each stage of progress by a specific milestone and with a celebration of the achievements, a no-kidding ownership practice to put in place immediately.

The third objective is integrating the open-book management practices into your company's current culture, norms, and practices, including your planning/budgeting process, quality improvement and reengineering initiatives, training, and meeting format.

At Syncrude Canada Limited, the assessment and subsequent planning guided their overall effort. Don de Guerre, head of organizational development and a member on their start-up committee, explains how tying open-book management to what was already going on was crucial:

> At Syncrude, the Business Literacy Start-Up Committee developed a plan to integrate the development of Critical Numbers Know-how and . . . an Intensive Huddle System with ongoing companywide team and leadership development activities. They planned to help

━━━ 🕸 🕸 🕸 🕸 ━━━

Middle Managers Jump-Start Their Departments

At this point the implementation often loses some of its sequential, step-by-step nature. Middle managers who have
tended to share all information and coach employees about the
business see open-book management as something they have
wanted to do all along. After reading an open-book article, or
talking to an old college sorority sister in an open-book company, or going to the one-day open-book management seminar
offered by the Association for Quality and Participation (head-
quartered in Cincinnati), these managers know they want to get
going with business literacy and not necessarily wait for a companywide initiative.

They'll try little experiments. They send themselves and others off to financial training sessions. They teach the cost system
or spread the budgets to everyone.

It's not just early-adopting middle managers who experiment
at this stage. Implementation team members may make "trial
runs" at applying parts of what they are discovering, influencing others and peaking their interest. One implementation team
member took it on herself to go the annual stockholders' meeting, to get the strategy of her Fortune 100 corporation from the
top and to hear shareholder concerns directly. Her report back
to the team gave them a sense of a missing piece in their own
business-literacy/investor relations.

These experiments may seem uncoordinated or a hodge-
podge waste of time, but the opposite is closer to the truth.
These many and various changes in the way departments
run can add up and be very beneficial. And, if the company as a
whole is implementing greater business literacy, taking on
changes in incentive pay, and designing information-intense
huddles, *the experiments can emerge spontaneously while the
implementation remains orderly.* The team still operates with a
big picture and sets the long-term milestones.

In Sprint's division for providing telecommunications service
to the deaf, open-book advocate Peggy Fields, after hearing
about open-book management in another Sprint division, con-
tracted for a business literacy seminar for her team. She subse-
quently educated hundreds of operators in the service centers

🕸 *Continued*

🔹 *Continued*

the budget. After a year of providing formerly missing information, and teaching what it tells, the benefits are obvious: "We have created a capacity for managing change that just didn't exist before," says one of Fields's Sacramento managers. "When we explained how overall expenses added up in the budget, employees opted to do all kinds of things to keep expenses in line, including days away from work."

Open-book management creates open learning environments, allowing those outside the team and the overall change effort to "plug in" and learn in their own way. The little experiments are the beginning of "new and improved" education and need to be recognized as a part of bringing open-book management to the organization.

---

teams and customers identify critical numbers through an ongoing participative redesign process (involving employees in the creation of their own scorecards and changes in workflow). The plan was to train teams and leaders in finance through the regular team and leader development process. They developed a line of sight between teams, through their customers to unit cost as the first critical number for the teams to focus on.

Much like the think-tank workshop in Phase 4, the collective learning and experience from the previous phases can be best applied to creation of a plan at a workshop or planning retreat setting. Careful planning will put in place an important principle—the more closely and carefully the open-book rollout is tied to current business objectives, the more likely early successes will appear.

Output from a planning retreat workshop includes several important documents and decisions:

- Three-year action plan.
- Supporting 12- to 18-month detailed implementation schedule.
- Designation of resources to develop and provide business finance understanding for all employees.

If the company or division is large, the implementation team may also need to form subteams to handle three very important areas for the plan:

1. Framework for the pilot huddle system.
2. Recommendations for reward and recognition practices.
3. Player-coach leader training and development.

The implementation team oversees and coordinates the subteams, whose work comes after the planning retreat. Senior managers and external coaches and consultants are useful as resources to the subteams in defining expectations and providing experience. The consultants bring the view and lessons learned at other companies, and the senior managers bring depth, experience, and direction.

When the planning workshop is completed, the work of this phase shifts to developing and conducting the required finance and business training, introducing employees to the huddle system and the other three systems of open-book management and their practices. Open-book management is not a classroom experience, remember. Real-time education happens on the job, in the day-to-day huddles in real, not classroom, time as problems and opportunities happen. But the end of Phase 4 is the training phase that will be classroom-driven. *Employees need good training classes where the financial lessons are fun and engaging so they can see what the shift to business literacy will look and feel like.* If the training is well designed, eager anticipation will help the implementation. If it is poorly done, the whole effort can suffer a setback.

The amount of time allotted for Phase 4 depends on business activity and demands, available resources, and the size of the organization. Through all the phases, momentum is crucial. Progress, even if slowed by unexpected events, needs to continue. The commitment required to press on is a key success factor. If trust levels are low when the company starts, everything goes more slowly. Often, employees won't believe the financials at first. They will question the intentions behind increasing business literacy. Strong, committed, persistent leadership is the only antidote for these companies. As with any change, timing and momentum issues are critical. A rule of thumb is to pace the implementation of changes fast enough for them to be seen and felt, but slow enough for them to be absorbed.

Phase 5. Implementation and Rollout

The objectives of this phase are to establish the practice of open-book management systems and thinking, and to promote real-time education through the use of the huddle system and no-kidding ownership.

The bell rings in open-book management when the huddles begin. The finance and business training classes may still be in progress or complete when the huddles start. That is up to each company. But the conclusion of the classes and huddle start-up need to be close in time because without the huddles' repetitive use of scorecards that lead to the income statement, much of what was taught in the classes will be lost. It's a use-it-or-lose-it proposition.

The first 6 months of the huddle system are only a beginning, full of trial runs and initial practice. The design team, upper management, and external coaches coach the huddle leaders. They guide and evaluate and answer questions that those not used to financial information naturally ask. They can help huddle leaders improve their practice by providing additional learning resources and improving the linkage between small team scorecards (see Chapter 13) and the company's income and cash flow statements.

As the huddles begin, the changes in rewards and recognition recommended by the no-kidding ownership subteam kick in. Again, timing is important. New bonuses can start simultaneously with huddles, if they are well considered and the company has some practice with variable pay based on performance. Or the company can wait until the huddles and training increase financial knowledge, so that employees know what the new financial target means. *Introducing bonuses too early, without teaching, will create motivated ignorance. Introducing them too late will yield knowledgeable but turned-off workers.*

Six months of huddle system practice completes this phase. The design team summarizes its recommendations for ongoing improvements, highlights the key accomplishments and important insights from the huddle and training and reward experiences, and notes the challenges that lie ahead for the leadership.

Phase 6. Ongoing Improvement

The objective of Phase 6 is to master the open-book management practices while improving business results. All employees, from top to bottom are involved.

Open-book practices require and encourage ongoing improvement, and each huddle is a real-time business learning opportunity. Consistent reforecasting and repeated discussions about events and challenges in the business environment keep the improvement phase going.

The implementation team is done with its work in the lead role and now supports the huddle leaders, teams, and senior managers who seek continuously to improve the company's open-book practices. It phases out its regular meetings as open-book practices take root and the leadership adopts a business-literate mentality in its daily practices.

Members of the implementation team and senior management convene every 3 to 6 months to reflect on the progress and decide if additional support or action is needed. After 3 years of practice have embedded the practices and the mind-set of open-book management, these evaluations sessions can be held every 6 to 12 months.

Phase 6 is never really over, but on the proud day when your company hosts representatives from other companies who want to see how an open-book company works, your company can say it has become an open-book company of empowered business-literate people serving customers with high-value products, and having fun in the process.

As Ye Go Forth: Some Tips and Thoughts

Typically, the introduction of open-book management stirs up interest and creates excitement. When financial statements are shared and accompanied by good financial training, when management asks employees to start managing the numbers, people want to learn and know more. They'll work to grasp the financial meaning and its implications more thoroughly so they can make better decisions. They'll want to meet the numbers in the business plan. The release of energy that comes with learning, with making progress, gives people a new set of business-smart eyes and ears.

Seeing the business in terms of its financial performance accelerates learning. More and more employees talk about their new insights and share their excitement. They discuss everything—from prospecting for customers to depositing the checks—in terms of the effects those actions have on financial performance. This encourages others to experience the empowerment of connecting with the big picture.

Open-book management has real impact when each person can proudly point to an item on the income statement or cash flow forecast and say, "That's my line! I help create that number." Such statements bring a whole new valid and valuable meaning to the term *accountability*. As the numbers become animated with the stories of their personal efforts, the contributors are motivated.

A company won't really experience the fullness of these open-book benefits until it has a huddle system that incorporates current financial data against a plan and reforecasts its performance consistently. On the journey to the full process, the primary visible benefit of implementation is the ongoing education in every phase of implementation. The education guarantees continuous learning about the business and how to make it better.

Chapter 7

⅜ ⅜ ⅜ ⅜

How Ready Are Ya?

Frenetic people are those who redouble their efforts once they have lost sight of their objectives.

Anonymous

Creating Awareness

Two executives are flying to their next destination, emptying out the contents of their briefcases and occasionally chatting over in-flight peanuts.

"I just read another article about a company that shares all its financial information with all the employees," says one.

"A company that does *what*?" replies the other, doing a double take.

"You know," says the first, "shares the financials of the business real regularlike."

"Well, why would a company wanna do that, I wonder," says the other, not having heard anything about business literacy.

"What I hear about it is. . . ."

And so it goes, awareness-building at 35,000 feet.

Typically, business leaders gain awareness of open-book management by reading about it and conferring with practitioners and consultants. By holding on-site briefings and visiting the operations that are using the principles and methods, a management team can start to understand what business literacy entails.

The Bibliography at the end of this book lists articles in business magazines and select books on the subject that we recommend to create the initial awareness. Reading the first five chapters of this book, coupled with an on-site briefing, also would be a good first step.

Bob Argabright, head of the Chesapeake Packaging operation in Baltimore, provides an excellent model of the leadership role in developing a company of businesspeople. The Scanlon Companies, among them Herman Miller and Beth Israel Hospital, and many others geographically concentrated in Michigan, have a strong base of participation and business literacy. Employee-owned companies, such as Physician Sales and Service (CEO Patrick Kelly), are also worthwhile studies.* CEO Jack Stack's case study of his company, Springfield Remanufacturing Company (see Bibliography), provides a good example of the leadership needed to shepherd open-book in the real world.

Looking at other companies' open-book approaches and studying their failures and successes is a great help for those that want to begin. Management teams considering open-book management can learn much by analyzing the principles and systems other companies have used, as well as their leadership and company history. But *beware the cookie-cutter approach*. Ultimately, each company needs to define its own approach, process, outcomes. People aren't happy when they borrow a life. Similarly, companies aren't successful blindly copying what others do. The term "blind-sided benchmarking" has started to emerge for good reason. Learning from others' best practices accelerates the learning curve, but trying to run one company with a system built by another won't work.

A unique and exciting aspect of open-book management is that it has been discovered and introduced by many different people within the organizations: presidents of divisions,

---

* "Case Study: Physician Sales and Service," *Employee Ownership Report*, from the National Center for Employee Ownership, January–February 1995.

organization development professionals, VPs of operations, CEOs, CFOs, customer-service executives. We receive calls and requests for information from just about anyone in the organization, but all the callers have some beliefs in common. They intuitively know that their business, or their part of it, will be more successful if everyone thoroughly understands the big picture, if they can think and make decisions utilizing financial data and if each person can trust others—regardless of their position or status—to work toward common business objectives. Helping others on their team come to that understanding is the first job of these introducers. Reading and briefings are a great place to start.

As the books and the articles move through the team, initial understanding grows. A whole host of additional questions will naturally emerge about how your company with its particular challenges, resources, style, and culture can make open-book work for you:

What is open-book management really all about?

What makes it different from our current management approach?

What problems does it solve?

What promises does it make for the future?

How would it fit or compliment what we believe in?

Who is currently using this approach and what kind of results are they getting?

People want to figure out if and how it can bring benefits to their particular way of doing business. To be sure, crafting your own open-book management journey can be challenging and at the same time satisfying.

Derrick Kershaw, general manager of Syncrude Canada, Ltd., used his key leadership role to introduce business literacy into their quest of continuously improving their business results: "We had known that our direction with reengineering and empowerment were taking us ever farther into business literacy and considering the total system—accountability for everyone and better decision-making in shorter time frames. Our team development processes, helping the supervisor/leaders gain the required skills in coaching, and ensuring that rewards and recognition supported the new way of working needed all of us behind the effort."

Kershaw and his team devoted time and energy to studying the benefits of business literacy and answering all the questions that arose. Management can handle these questions informally, or set aside time at weekly staff meetings to discuss different aspects of business literacy they are interested in.

The Work Begins: Establishing the Baseline of Readiness

The second task in Phase 1, establishing your baseline and assessing your company's readiness, provides the necessary data and information to put your open-book management initiative on solid ground. The following five-step overview describes the work, and the rest of the chapter provides more depth on each subtask.

The five steps for establishing the baseline are:

1. Determine data-gathering methods, sample size, introduction protocol, and time frame.
2. Identify and prepare a task force to collect, summarize, and analyze the data.
3. Gather the data.
4. Summarize and analyze data and formulate preliminary recommendations for a readiness report.
5. Deliver the readiness report to the company's senior managers.

The core work of baseline establishing is having employees and managers fill out surveys, and participate in focus groups during which current practices of the company are assessed against the standards and practices contained in each of the four systems of the open-book management. The time required to complete this process is influenced by the number of employees (as we will say often as a reminder for big and small companies), the size of the task force membership, and the amount of time the internal and external people can devote to this project. As a rule of thumb, small- to medium-sized companies can gather their data, analyze, and prepare a report in approximately 2 months. It takes large companies longer unless they introduce the work in a small unit.

At this point, while some expectations are forming and early visions are taking shape, it is easy and tempting for leaders to skip the data-gathering and jump into action. Several companies that we have worked with have bypassed much of this awareness and baseline-setting work. They did not want to spend the resources, mainly the time and effort. In our experience, the understanding, participation, and cooperation that grow out of the data-gathering, analysis, recommendations, and senior managers' discussions sustain open-book management results in several ways.

First, a great deal of education goes on. This critical preparation step exposes others in the organization to the ideas that the senior managers have been studying. It is impossible to use the tools of business literacy well without knowing them very well. Second, the process helps create buy-in, a principle that will come up often in the implementation steps. The principle here is simple yet profound: People support that which they help create. Data-gathering involves key stakeholders.

But perhaps most importantly, knowing where you are is essential to determining how to get to where you want to go. If your destination is London, getting there from Scotland means heading south, and the time and resources required are minimal. If you want to go to London and you're originating in New York, you have quite a different trip ahead, demanding more resources, and going south is not an option. Knowing where you are brings up the right questions.

How well prepared are those who are taking the journey?

What steps can be taken to prevent getting lost?

What previous experiences have shaped the travelers' expectations?

What resources are necessary to complete the trip in the time frame allowed?

In what kind of shape are the resources—training, management, information systems, financial data, trust—that you'll be using?

Do any of them need to be repaired and supplemented for a safe and efficient journey?

The knowledge and perspective gained during this first phase are necessary to the effectiveness of the subsequent phases. Grounding the goal setting—planning, training, and educating for open-book management on the current reality—makes it possible to measure progress from a baseline. The education will be tailored to address the actual knowledge shortfalls in finance and business that exist, and the rollout will draw on the expertise and strengths that are already in the workplace. This careful approach takes into account current capabilities, and discovers the show-stopping barriers to open-book practices in each company.

Identify and Prepare the Assessment Task Force

Employees from different functions and levels of the organization make up the task force. Six to eight is a common size, but it can be larger if the size of the company should warrant.

Teams of two people—one with open-book management background (the open-book coach) and one with thorough knowledge of the company, its business and its finances—conduct the one-on-one interviews and focus groups. They prepare by learning as much as possible about the principles and practices of open-book management.

External open-book management coaches can provide the business literacy knowledge and help to moderate the natural bias of the internal employees of the company. They also guide the overall process and prepare the task force members to use the data-gathering methods and to administer the written surveys. The open-book management coaches often take a lead role in the interviews and focus groups, while the internal task force member takes notes and asks operation-specific questions.

The coach brings a needed external perspective to the listening and analysis, both fresh to the specifics of the company and seasoned about open-book practices. At the same time, the data-gathering grooms the members of the task force in player-coach leadership competencies. They start to see firsthand the gaps in knowledge and communication that are limiting the people and the business.

Professionals in business, like professionals in sports and the arts, benefit from coaching assistance that points out blind spots, issues challenges, and provides additional resources. They get results more quickly. But remember, as important as the coaches are, they don't hit the tennis ball or play the concerto at the recital. In a similar vein, the team members execute large segments of the data-gathering process, and all the later steps, since implementation rests on their shoulders.

Fact-Finding Methods: Digging for the Data

Three methods are used to gather information and assess the current level of open-book management readiness:

1. Written surveys.
2. Focus groups with employees.
3. One-on-one interviews with executives and by managers.

The Survey. A comprehensive written assessment is a great place to start. It should have descriptions of the varying levels of practice for the standards of open-book management. How many employees need to be surveyed? A 20-percent cross-section sample of the population yields substantial data. However, some companies decide to include a larger sample mainly for the participation and educational benefits. The descriptors should be specific enough to evoke quantitative as well as attitudinal data.

A written survey using a quantifiable scale (1 to 6, for example, or a Rikert scale) makes it possible to measure the degree to which specific open-book practices are in place. The same survey is then used periodically to check the progress. The standards and practices that provide the benchmark for assessing your baseline and for developing progressive milestones are specific to each of the four dimensions.

Below is a sample of specific open-book practices applied to the four dimensions:

1. Critical Numbers Know-How

   Levels of employees who know the numbers.

   Current, accurate numbers and financial statements.

   Shared responsibility for the numbers.

   Animated numbers that are understood in relationship to daily, weekly activities of real teams and people, not distant functions.

2. Intensive Huddle System

   Communication as a priority.

   Numbers shared quickly and thoroughly.

   Good participation at the meetings (business review and reforecasting).

   Weekly and regular huddle sessions.

3. No-Kidding Ownership

   Shared decision-making.

   Feedback on decisions.

   Sharing the rewards.

   Customer contact.

4. Player-Coach Leadership

   Influence of status and perks.

   Sharing information as top priority.

   Recognition and cheerleading.

   Opportunities for leaders to learn.

A quantifiable scale for each item in the survey stems from descriptions of how far along the company is in its open-book practice. Here's an example.

The descriptors for the first item of critical numbers know-how—levels of employees who know the numbers—are shown in Figure 7.1.

A sample of an actual survey for this question may look like Figure 7.2. It indicates the managers' estimate of the current level of employees who know the numbers.

Figure 7.1 Survey Example

Level 1	Level 3	Level 6
Senior executives know where the business stands: The chief financial officer shares information with owners and the top executive team.	Most managers are fully informed on the numbers, see the financial strengths and weaknesses of the company, and understand financial goals. Middle managers are invited to participate in developing strategies to improve the numbers.	All employees are fully aware of the financial status of the organization. Revenues and expenses are itemized. Employees know the expenses they are responsible for. Employees work to improve the numbers on the cost reports.

Figure 7.2 Compiled Survey Example

COMPILED SURVEY EXAMPLE

Level 1	Level 3	Level 6
Senior executives know where the business stands: the chief financial officer shares information with owners and the top executive team.	Most managers are fully informed on the numbers; see the financial strengths and weaknesses of the company and understand financial goals. Middle managers are invited to participate in developing strategies to improve the numbers.	All employees are fully aware of the financial status of the organization. Revenues and expenses are itemized. Employees know the expenses they are responsible for. Employees work to improve the numbers on the cost reports.

This information identifies the baseline of strengths (in this case, the middle managers knowing the financial numbers well), and how far the nonmanagers have to go in learning the financial issues. In this example, financial information stops with middle managers, which is a common finding.

Often, very influential managers have a skewed view of how far down in the organization financial information flows. Data can keep individual biases from entering the picture and will encourage everyone to sing from the same open-book songsheet. Demming promoted "management by facts" for good reason.

In the subsequent phases, the results obtained from the survey and from the other data will be used to guide the effort, establish milestones as progress markers, and customize the education to the level that is actually needed.

Focus Groups. Focus groups of four to six employees are conducted for about 45 minutes each. The purposes are:

1. To see whether there is different and/or corroborating evidence for the data that the written survey yields.

2. To gain specific examples of the strengths, gaps, and opportunities.

3. To hear the experiences and opinions of those closest to the work and to the customers.

Enough focus groups should be conducted to provide a depth of understanding.

The Interview: Live Data Shape the Implementation. Starting with an introduction of the purpose of the focus group, an assurance of anonymity, and a request for candid responses, the open-book management coach (the external consultant if used), explains that all the questions will focus on the business, their knowledge of how it runs, and their involvement in it. While the coach asks the questions, the internal team member takes notes and asks supplemental questions that reveal more fully the specifics of their business operation. In the 45 minutes, questions that focus on the following topics stimulate the focus group discussions:

- Primary goals of their company—short and long term.
- The most important numbers.
- Their department's contribution to the achievement of those numbers.
- The individual's contribution to the achievement of the goals.
- How they know whether they are successful or not—how they follow the action.
- Their sense of job, department, company ownership—their stake in the outcome.
- How communication between department, teams, top, middle, and bottom, flows; how frequently, how timely, how accurately.
- The effectiveness of the current communication and information systems—accuracy, timeliness; how it is utilized.
- What people need to know about, or more of, to be more effective in their jobs.

One-on-Ones. One-on-one interviews with executives, managers, and team leaders also supply valuable insight and data. Using the preceding interview protocol as a guide, each person contributes his or her experience and perspective of the business, use of financial data, the effectiveness of the current communication systems, coaching and teaching practices, recognition and reward practices. That's right—for continuity and the best results, always use the four systems as the framework.

Gather the Data

If both the written and interview methods are used, then begin with the written survey. Compile the results in bar or pie charts to show the level of competence in each standard practice in the four systems of open-book management, as in Figure 7.2.

The task force uses the data as background reference for exploring specific areas in the interviews and focus groups.

Using the interview protocol as a guide, the interviewing pairs gather information from employees and managers. Listen and probe for examples of competency that can be further developed, for gaps and shortfalls that reveal opportunities for improvement, and for barriers that might threaten successful implementation.

Because humans are highly social and emotional beings, the data-gathering will naturally uncover many employees' feelings at all levels, the quality of working relationships, and the extent to which the organization's energy is focused on both political and turf concerns and business goals. If significant issues in any of these areas surface, they can be noted as themes or potential barriers in the organization's environment affecting and influencing the conduct of business. A number of companies use attitude or climate surveys annually. The team should use existing survey data to further evaluate the data it gathers directly.

To the extent possible, the members of the assessment task force interpreting the data need to identify and take account of their own biases in the mix of facts and feelings being scrutinized. For example, middle mangers frequently are selected to be on the task force. They naturally hear and view circumstances from a middle manager's perspective. If they are not careful to listen for the different views of the top and bottom perspectives, important contributions can be lost. For example, a work system that serves middle mangers well, such as expense approval, may be a tremendous chore for lower levels, who have to work around the system to get their jobs done.

The social sciences attest to how difficult it is for the human to objectively view itself as a unit of study. Providing for both depth and breadth of participation in the surveys and interviews as well as using set criteria for comparison of the findings, will bring a measure of objectivity to the assessment.

What a Focus Group Reveals

An example of discovering an open-book practice at work emerged during a focus group with technicians of the mine mobile division of Syncrude Canada, Ltd., where oil sands mining equipment is overhauled and repaired. This division, like all others in the company, had been expected to contribute to cutting costs and substantially lowering the overall cost of producing a barrel of oil. This cost per barrel is a critical number for the company, and it was shown to be widely known on the written survey. The interviewing pairs were in search of specific examples in the everyday world of work.

During the focus group, in response to the question about individual contributions to the big picture, a technician proudly explained the accomplishment of the training team that he was a part of. This team of frontliners had been given responsibility for the training budget two years earlier. It was explained to them that every department was being asked to cut costs to work for the overall goal of reducing the cost for producing a barrel of oil. After receiving education and coaching that prepared them for the new challenge, they began to schedule workers for technical training based on priorities: what they needed to know when working on costly and time-consuming repair jobs. They also decided to use the training dollars only for those who would be able to use it immediately: "We saw lots of ways to save money and still get the job done," one team member said, "It just took some good problem-solving."

These workers understood the goal, and took ownership of the project. And they felt immensely proud of their accomplishment, significantly reducing the cost of training. They didn't need a financial reward, but they did need, deserve, and receive lots of recognition. The player-coach leadership practice of recognition and telling stories of successes behind the numbers was at work as well. Their story was repeated again and again, reinforcing their accomplishment, providing a good example for their peers, and demonstrating a strength in that operating unit which could be leveraged in the future. The story was eventually repeated to the executive team during review of the readiness report and became an example for teams working to uncover additional cost-saving gems.

This example shows how data-gathering surfaces early forms of business literacy, so that further training and work can build on it.

Analyzing the Findings: What Does This Mean for Us?

The four dimensions and systems of the open-book management model provide the framework for categorizing and summarizing the collected data.

The analysis is delivered in the readiness report. It involves studying the gathered data and identifying the key strengths and opportunities for improvement in each dimension along with the supporting evidence or curious contradictions found in the written survey. The assessment cites themes and key points for leveraging improvements and changes. The task force also makes preliminary recommendations for possible next steps that highlight linkages to current initiatives such as reengineering.

The analysis sheds light on existing issues that haven't been attended to for any variety of reasons. It can be immediately useful and can generate fast action. For example, data collected in a medium-size company identified a threat to the ongoing success of their best performing plant due to a wide communication gap between managers and frontline workers.

The communication issues surfaced when frontline workers were asked in the focus groups about the information they received regarding production and business goals and how they used this information. Many workers couldn't "hear" the provided information, that is, really absorb it, let alone make use of it, because they were intimidated by their production managers.

Further exploration revealed it wasn't just the messenger's style that created the gap, it was the timing and frequency of the communication. Questions in the data-gathering interviews about their system of meetings revealed a fast-paced, intense work environment with no regular time set aside to pass on or think about information, or to discuss problems. Communication from managers to frontline supervisors and workers happened only when something went wrong—"How did this schedule slip so badly?" such communications were packaged in urgency and angst.

The communication gaps between management and the front line and the analysis of its impact on the conduct of business appeared *in the intensive huddle system section of the readiness report.* This company gave the gap immediate attention since it was highlighted and all knew the cost they were incurring for this broken process.

In the dimension of critical numbers know-how, many opportunities and weaknesses open up. Financial analysis plays a big role in this step. What critical numbers aren't being met that employees may not be able to compute or understand? Could employees impact a key ratio, like return on assets, or increase cash flow, if they understood the business better? The task force keeps these thoughts foremost as they study the data they have gathered, looking for the ties between financial performance and the systems that they just assessed. The assessment group may need to recruit the help of people who thoroughly understand the finances of the business (usually senior managers), to conduct this part of the analysis.

Quite often, questions aimed at identifying the employees' specific knowledge about the business reveal that each department has fragmented, narrow bits of information and myopic understandings that represent a specialist or one-dimensional view of the business. These views are not totally wrong, just incomplete. But the fragments are used as if they are the whole picture, which results in poor decisions and internal conflicts.

The classic example is the sales staff whose goal is volume sales, thinking the business will be healthier and stronger the more they sell. Sales reps often don't have the financial information to think in terms of the gross profit of their sales, or what makes up the cost of the sale or the sales impact on cash flow.

Identifying these gaps in business and financial knowledge thus reveals the leverage points, the education opportunities, and the advantages that will come with increased accountability and business know-how.

Analyzing the data on the no-kidding ownership practices brings to the foreground the effectiveness of the current financial rewards and risk-sharing program, as well as the quality of the psychological ownership in the various levels and departments. This dimension includes the level of decision-making and shared accountability. To assess this arena, it is necessary to understand the distribution of the rewards and risks and whether that distribution is supporting the achievement of the business goals. For example, a host of factors can contribute to persistent quality or customer satisfaction problems. The interview data may show that those most able to control the outcome see themselves working harder and smarter so that others (e.g., the top managers on a bonus program) can reap the benefits of their efforts. These gaps in psychological ownership are not unusual.

Employee comments like this are typical:

> Oh, I know we could do better, but good is good enough. Getting two more pallets shipped may mean my boss gets a bigger bonus, but we sure don't. Besides, the customer gives us false alarms on the ship dates all the time.

Or, for a dealer . . .

> Corporate may want us to institute a user's chapter. And chapters aren't all bad—we get some sales that way. But it's a lot of work, and the main benefits go to corporate for the membership fee.

And they are deadly for creating a high-performance company. Opening the books will have little effect until this lack of alignment is fixed.

Analyzing the level of player-coach leadership practices means looking at the data to see how much business coaching and teaching is going on, who is doing it, and how business focused it is.

At Springfield Remanufacturing Company (SRC), especially in the Heavy Duty Division where there is a very high level of business literacy and where player-coach leadership practices abound, frontline supervisors often spend one-on-one time with a worker who wants to better understand their standard cost system; this information helps the individual see the amount of overhead burden that is absorbed each hour of work, and how that is calculated. At staff meetings, where the income

❀ ❀ ❀ ❀

Management Cleans Up Its Act

Sometimes senior mangers put considerable focus on their own issues and concerns and lose sight of how they are influencing the rest of the company. The following example of a player-coach leadership gap illustrates just how critical leaders are to the day-to-day effectiveness of a company.

Comments in the one-on-one interviews included:

Those guys in Sales and Marketing having no understanding of what it really takes to run this business.

—VP of Purchasing

Purchasing hasn't kept up with the changes. They're out of step and don't support the new direction. We work around them.

—VP of Sales/Marketing

I think we all knew that the leadership here wasn't acting as a team, but I don't think we stopped to consider the negative impact it is having on our business results.

VP of Customer Service

During the employee focus groups, many individuals had talked about the day-to-day stress and lack of direction they experienced. The survey data in the intensive huddle section showed evidence of low levels of cross-departmental communication and lower levels of cooperative efforts to reach common goals.

When reviewing the readiness report, which included the assessment that the leadership of the senior managers was essential for open-book management to be successful, the leaders recognized their emotional differences and criticism of each other as the bottleneck. With the data in their face, this team did not resort to denial, but realized they were at the heart of the problem.

⊰ Continued

≅ Continued

They began to look at the business goals as their shared destination and the financials as the common language that could unify the needs of the entire company and help them to bridge their differences. This growing leadership awareness and appreciation of the positive power that they could release to meet the challenges in their business provided the needed catalyst. They committed to reinvest as a team. They decided to work on themselves first as a prerequisite to asking the rest of the organization to follow their call for open-book management improvements.

It is not unusual for leadership teams to experience tension and disagreements that negatively affect their company's performance. It is, sadly, uncommon for leaders to do something about it. For 4 months at this company, the CEO, president, and vice presidents met to consider the quality of their relationships relative to the functioning of the business. Each person came to grips with the part he or she played in tying up and blocking the business know-how in the political and emotional tensions that existed among themselves. "We got caught up in turf issues," one said. "We'll probably always have some of that, but we can't let it hurt us."

The knowledge that already existed on the team was freed up, which naturally released the energy in their people to want to learn and contribute more.

---

statement and cash flow analysis are used weekly, predictions about production and financial variances are made, and it is common to hear workers explaining to peers specific outcomes in manufacturing variances. At this company, when an employee has the knowledge and the know-how, the expectation is that he or she will teach and coach others. How much of this kind of business coaching is going on in your company?

Assessing the accessibility of those in key positions—and the amount of time they spend coaching—not only sheds light on that leader's teaching and coaching contributions but also indicates how much the accountability the leaders feel toward people lower in the hierarchy. Many senior leaders have fallen into the trap of relating only to direct reports and to the important stakeholders, especially financial sources, outside the organization. Business literacy standards and practices contend that senior managers have a responsibility to communicate, teach, and coach, and to generally steward the business intelligence of the company.

Not all companies recognize the importance of the assessment and planning phase. It is a time of individual and team reflection and evaluation. For some teams it means coming to grips with issues that have blocked progress for a long time. Conducting business, in most cases, does not have to be complicated or painful. In fact, it can be fun if everyone is on a level playing field working as a team toward the same goal.

Phase 2: Define Goals

Whereas Phase 1, establishing company readiness and baselining, is often rich with learning and opportunities for real improvements, its value is sustained only with a well-prepared and executed plan that leads to consistent learning and action. The data and the recommendations make for a smart, well-grounded means to putting open-book management to work.

Establishing the direction, strategies and goals is the next phase of implementation. It begins when the readiness report is completed and delivered to the senior management team.

The objective of Phase 2 in setting direction is to use the best thinking of the senior management team and the assessment task force to articulate the direction the company will take with open-book management. Does management want to:

Improve gross margins and improve motivation with good bonuses?

Change the company to be more participative?

Make more money for all the shareholders?

Become more competitive by getting all employees to attack costs?

Become more entrepreneurial, and customer oriented?

Have better teamwork?

Continue with next steps into quality?

Maybe they want to do something as simple as have more fun at work, but regardless, they have to know where it is they are going.

Phase 2 is decision-making time. Senior management charged the task force to assess how ready the organization is for open-book management and now it's time for management to study the findings and to react to and act on their recommendations.

In Phase 2:

- Senior managers read the readiness report and prepare questions and thoughts for their peers.
- The senior management team attends a workshop, or think tank, in which it deliberates about both the findings and recommendations of the readiness report and their own reactions to those findings and recommendations.
- Senior managers attending the workshop, at its conclusion, set direction and define specific goals.
- If they decide to proceed with open-book practices, senior managers assign a design team to map the way for the organization.

As simple as reading a report sounds, a few guidelines about how to read the readiness report can improve the quality of and set the tone for the think tank. Some findings in the report will challenge the senior managers, causing natural defensiveness, whereas others will confirm what they already know. The suggestion is for each individual to read first for understanding, and then think about the implications, concerns, and opportunities.

This approach will assist the quality of the team's dialogue about issues. Managers maintain their objectivity and a spirit of honest inquiry as they read the report.

It is best for managers to view the report in terms of the whole business and not just their individual function. The shift in this approach is to get away from the usual approach of managers coming to meetings with answers and fixed opinions and instead to approach the think tank with questions and an openness to learning and listening.

This is where dialogue enters the picture. Much has been made recently about the differences between discussion, which has the same root word origin as percussion and concussion, and dialogue, which has more to do with shared understanding. The think tank is meant for both: deep thinking with real listening and open minds, and pointed decision times for moving ahead with action.

The Think Tank

The process of getting all the senior managers together to go over the readiness report is crucial. The think tank sets the direction of open-book management for the company for years to come, so ensuring the meeting elicits the senior team's best work makes sense.

The assessment task force can begin the meeting with a brief presentation of its findings. Since the report has already been digested by the senior team, the meeting quickly evolves into a dialogue between the senior team and the task force, including the open-book management coach. The senior team digs into the findings of the report on which they want more clarity. An example may be that the readiness report says many employees find the current reward system confusing. Employees can't figure out how what they do influences the financial rewards they get. Management asks exactly at what level of management that confusion starts to set in, and the assessment task force responds with what they know. A written report with all the nuances of all the findings would be too long, so the dialogue expands the readers' understanding of the findings.

During the dialogue, the executives draw on the experience of the assessment task force and mindfully consider which aspects of the data are most significant to running the business successfully and in a manner that supports the company's values.

This is the point at which the senior managers can first apply the open-book management principles and systems they studied during the first step of Phase 1. As in most improvement processes, it is important to identify the leverage opportunities: those actions that can get the most output for the least resources. Leverage has both a fulcrum effect, which can create large changes with small moves, and a ripple effect, by changing one element that can spread effects to many others. Using their experience and intuition, coupled with their knowledge of the business and the marketplace, the managers set the direction for open-book advancements.

While managers explore the options (e.g., whether to start with a companywide effort or in one division), "what if" scenarios allow the participants to add individual thoughts on the potential value added of each option.

The senior managers of a start-up telecommunications company in Phoenix, Arizona, were in the unusual position of starting completely fresh. While they didn't have a report with specific findings to deliberate, each had previous work experience to draw on. As they considered their learning from their former companies, they could begin to form a picture of "what if we had a company that . . ."

The following statement defines the direction they set for their company based on open-book management, as well as their values and beliefs:

> To become the leader in providing world class agent services in today's marketplace, it takes more than good equipment and good intentions. Excell Agent Services combines its "best-in-class" equipment and technology with a workforce that is made up of skilled and motivated businesspeople, capable of taking on responsibility and making decisions. During the 20th century, a company's task was to organize work so it could be carried out by wage labor, by pairs of hands that could be replaced at a moment's notice. The changing marketplace has made that approach obsolete.

A 21st-century company's task will be to organize work so it can be carried out by businesspeople—by men and women who take responsibility and who share in the risks and rewards of an enterprise.

The challenge we are meeting at Excell is to eliminate the employee mentality and create a company of businesspeople. It's more than just a new management philosophy, it's a whole new approach. It's not just a set of techniques, it's a way of thinking. For a company to create businesspeople out of their employees, a different type of business structure must be put in place. Excell has studied today's successful companies to learn from their strategies. . . .

From these companies, we've learned the importance of a company mission statement that is clearly communicated throughout the organization, creating empowered employees who understand the importance of customer satisfaction. We've taken these techniques and combined them with our own experiences in building Sprint Services. The result is a business structure at Excell that combines the importance of a single vision with employee-owners |who| are educated and empowered to take the responsibility necessary to achieve our vision. Each employee is rewarded based on our company's success in meeting our vision.*

This declaration, an open-book manifesto for superior performance that drives Excell into its future, is the work of the think tank.

After the managers agree on key leverage opportunities, they further articulate the direction and goals by exploring strategies for adopting open-book management practices. Addressing the question "what will we have to do differently to be a company where everyone is informed and makes smart business decisions daily?" helps to focus the discussion.

A manufacturing company saw leverage in strengthening teamwork around the specific knowledge of the company's financial goals. They zeroed in on education about the details of what goes into the cost of manufacturing and distributing each of their products. They also saw an enormous upside in having all employees understand the importance of cash flow and how they could impact it.

---

* Printed with permission from Excel Agent Services, Spring 1995.

At the think tank, they imagined a bonus program strongly motivating their employees because they truly understood how their daily decisions and activities could help both the company and themselves make more money. They then envisioned the pride in the achievement that could result. The direction these managers set included fundamental, thorough education on:

- Their industry and business.
- How their financials told the story of their efforts.
- How the company's performance ranked in their industry.

They determined all employees should know how they specifically impacted the operating and financial performance of their company. They wanted a bonus system that would reward, educate, and build individual and team pride.

An important part of the think tank discussion for this management team and for others included the effect this direction would have on the company's customers, the energy and insights it could bring to innovation, and what weaknesses it could drive out of the business. For example, the company saw that the weakness of too much employee overtime could be favorably affected without management mandates. They could see that the levers of business finance education, and team bonus tied to bottom line results, could motivate the teams to control their own overtime without senior managers having to intervene.

In the think tank, the team also looks at the resources needed to start and accomplish the desired outcomes. Roadblocks that may need to be removed are also listed, as well as business issues such as regulations or competition that can influence the pace of the education and development of open-book management practices. Not all these concerns are addressed in detail by the senior mangers. Rather, they communicate them to the implementation team they select to lead the next steps.

Chapter 8

❧❧ ❧❧ ❧❧ ❧❧

Building the
Open-Book Team

*What we call the contagious force of an idea is the force of the
people who have embraced it.*

—George Santayana

I n small companies, many executives will want to be members
of the implementation team. The company size means that
the executives are closer to the daily business actions, and
have lots to offer. They need to keep from dominating the team,
however.

The president and vice president of sales for a $30 million
distribution company participated in every aspect of establishing readiness and setting direction, Phases 1 and 2, concentrat-
ing on the line-of-sight issues for plant employees. It wasn't
easy for them—they were located in the East and the plant was
in the Midwest. Keeping momentum in the implementation
didn't always go smoothly—rescheduling of meetings occurred
as business demands in other plants distracted them and the
rest of the team, causing the tension of balancing short-term
emergencies with long-term culture change.

But top management's commitment and team involvement
stayed constant. Their knowledge was invaluable for the rest of
the team. The plant managers and supervisors created the
specifics in the plan. And the top executives' detailed knowledge of the available resources and capacity of the company to
absorb additional expenses for team development and business training needs helped put a realistic and ambitious plan in

place. The most active champion on this team, the one with dogged determination for those distracting times, was the plant manager. His persistence kept the whole effort on track, even when the timetable was shifted again and again.

In large companies, senior managers may choose to actively participate on the open-book implementation team (also called by other titles, such as "team of champions," design team, team of teams), but it is not a requirement for team success. If senior managers are not on the design team, however, it is absolutely critical that they sponsor the effort, keeping themselves informed about the implementation they've put in motion.

Sponsoring includes many important roles: providing needed information, suggestions, and thoughts; participating in issue discussion when appropriate; volunteering to coach; playing devil's advocate where necessary; garnering resources the team can't get for itself, such as time or travel money. Chris Rooney's initial sponsorship at Sprint's Government Systems Division made all the difference in implementation. Even as he and other executives moved to other positions, the work pushed on through his successor and the implementation team.

The job of the implementation team is to become early adopters. There are pathbreakers in every organization, and this team needs to have several of them. As their knowledge about open-book practices grows, they need to get a "fire in the belly," an excitement and long-term commitment to do what it takes to bring on the innovative practices of business literacy. Because open-book management being is so inextricably tied to what the business is all about, members of this team must also know their business and its operations very well. Innovations stem from the yeasty brew of business and operations know-how with business-literate practices and principles.

The mind's-eye picture the team members develop how their company will look, act, and perform when it is business-literate will become a blueprint for the whole effort. The team, with sound sponsorship from management, and with the help of the employees they recruit into needed subteams with "right stuff," champion the effort.

The implementation of a successful plan is only as good as the teams of people who implement it. The entire open-book structure is based on the role of team members who assume responsibility for themselves and their job in the workplace, and who teach other teams to do the same. Developing the trust and respect of peers, and coordinating with them, is the heart of the business-literate culture. The ability of the team of champions to model high performance sets the tone for the entire implementation.

Selection Criteria

The first question is so fundamental that it looks easy—who should be on the team? But as simple as that sounds, it is the most important question to address. Just as venture capitalists have learned that the entrepreneurial team is as important to success, if not more so, as the entrepreneurial idea, those comprising the design team can make or break the open-book management rollout.

The first rule is to create an interdepartmental team—All the functions should be well represented (see Figure 8.1). At a minimum, finance, sales, operations (or line functions that make up the heart of the business, whether service or manufacturing), and human resources should be on the team. Any functions with a significant number of employees and an important role should be included (e.g., engineering, research and development). We have had teams with customer service representatives, machinists, the vice president of marketing, information services specialists, director of finance, trainers, organization development, legal counsel, and more. The goal is breadth, so the whole organization is thinking at the team meetings, and no function's perspective is left out.

Figure 8.1 Multifunctional Implementation Team

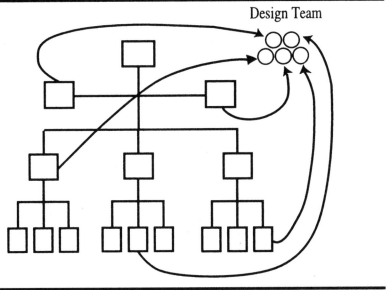

Design Team

Once breadth is covered, the criteria for selecting individuals with the right stuff kick in. The following list provides an initial screen for forming a successful design team. The members need to bring with them:

■ Knowledge of the key functions of the business they represent and an interest in the others.

■ Knowledge of the strategic and business plans.

■ A balance of members who have a long term of service and others who are relatively new (1–2 years).

■ People who think and speak for themselves and can hear and accept different points of view.

■ A balance between detail-oriented, concrete thinkers and those who generate and live in the world of the big-picture strategy and ideas.

These teams work well with 6 to 12 members, but it's wise to start with more members because unforeseen demands often cause one or two to drop out, or significantly pull back, their contribution.

This team's work opens the remaining phases of implementation. They will break the first ground, do some of the work, act as general contractors at other times, but most importantly, they'll lead the way. To manage the challenges associated with successfully forming and implementing a plan in the first year, the members of this initial team will need skills, practices, and attitudes that are up to the task. Each company will have challenges unique to its situation. In general, these challenges will require all or most of these abilities and characteristics:

Eager Learning. Members need to seek out learning opportunities as well as embrace individual learning challenges.

Critical Thinking. Members need to think through the many aspects and implications of issues and concerns, sort through what needs to be done, set priorities for effective implementation and create ways to move ahead that make sense to others.

Creative Thinking. Members need to generate fresh approaches, new options, and different frames of reference.

Improvisation Skills. Members need to evaluate and modify and create as they go. Like drivers making a pit stop during the Daytona 500, members must check out the performance dials, make adjustments and repairs, and quickly return to action.

Reflective Thinking and a Capacity for Dialogue. These individuals will be consistently challenged to clarify their own thinking and reactions and share them with other team members to build greater insight and understanding.

Maintaining Connections. Members need to stay well connected to colleagues outside the team. It's necessary for team members to maintain the contacts from their day-to-day responsibilities, even if open-book management becomes a full-time duty for an allotted time. They will provide information about the team's work to others. One-on-one or small group communications are very effective means the team members can engage in that naturally supplement announcements at large meetings or formal newsletters. Keeping connections opens another way for members to identify the ways that open-book practices can complement and strengthen other processes like quality, or reengineering, as well as overall business practices.

Listening. As members go about their work developing a plan and informing others about the team's work, it is critical to their education and long-term success that they do lots of listening—plain, simple, and powerful listening. Other employees may resist business literacy at this early stage, before their training. They may react with thoughts and feelings that can build into a barrier to implementation. Listening to these concerns, treating them as important without attempting to convert, convince, or preach the open-book philosophy, will do much to keep minds open.

Decision-Making. Team members make many different judgment calls. Members need to be good deliberators who can process ideas and move the team toward the core issues and decisions.

Understanding and Managing Change. Members need to educate themselves, if they haven't already, on what to expect when changes are introduced. Even with a goal to make open-book management a seamless extension of quality or team development, some employees will resist—and with valid and legitimate reasons. Even if training and communication are excellent, new information and methods will be coming into their workplace, and team members can assist in the adoption of the new requirements if they anticipate and assist the change.

Development of Tools and Resources. The team has the task of finding and developing good education tools. This takes the form of designing learning modules, creating scorecards for work teams, or crafting a huddle system to fit the communication and work-flow needs. Members need to identify internal and/or external resources for these development projects. This ability ties into those of eager learning, listening, and creative thinking. As members go about the implementation, naturally absorbing co-workers' thoughts and ideas, they get the required insight into what specific training and tools will be the most useful.

Getting Started

Individuals selected for a team need to go through the basic team formation steps to ready themselves for the challenge of their important responsibilities. Many companies use steps learned during a quality or team development program. If an external open-book coach is on the team, this person's role and expectations should be clearly defined. The roles of teacher, facilitator, coach, expert, and guide are the common ones, and they should know how to get the team off to a good start.

For those companies without familiar team formation guidelines, the following steps will provide an overview. A strong and healthy beginning will have big payoffs throughout the whole implementation, so don't shortcut this step. The trust and the foundation in communication are fundamental for handling the rough spots in implementation that will inevitably emerge:

- Get to know each other; the knowledge and talent each member brings, other current work priorities, and work history. Have members tell the stories of their work triumphs and scars.
- Given their initial level of understanding, discuss individual hopes and concerns about knitting open-book management into the way of doing business.
- Identify the personal benefit each member expects to gain— this can range from learning, to networking, to getting out of a stale job, to doing something important for the company.

■ Determine how you will conduct meetings; how leadership responsibility will be handled, who will coordinate details and organization needs, how frequently and how long you will meet.

■ Discuss how the team will deal with members who can't attend a meeting, last-minute or otherwise.

■ Determine the norms of conduct: on-time starts, speaking honestly, and following through on commitments.

■ Set the meeting schedule for the next 3 months.

■ Distribute open-book management materials for initial learning and review.

■ Make an early assessment of the team: Are all the functions represented, is there enough financial know-how, is there someone missing that management overlooked and who should be on the team?

The preceding tasks can be accomplished in the first meeting and should take 2 to 3 hours, depending on the number of people on the team. At the first meeting, it is worthwhile to encourage the team to choose a group name ("open bookies" usually gets considered and discarded in the name of corporate decency) that feels comfortable and pinpoints the team's targeted goal. It goes a long way toward making members feel team responsibility and ownership from the start.

Common Team Tasks

Once the team has formed, the work begins in earnest. All teams will need to do the following tasks in preparation for Phases 3 through 6:

■ Put themselves through an intensive learning and study process.

■ Review assessment data and recommendations.

- Decide whether the assessment data and recommendations indicate key first-year leverage opportunities for player-coach-leadership development.
- Clarify the vision and the desired end results.
- Map out the first-year actions necessary to achieve the milestones and support them with an implementation schedule.
- Determine the initial level of financial/business education needed by everyone in the company to start running the huddle system.
- Decide who will develop and deliver the company-specific financial and business education and customize the huddle system.
- Determine when huddles will start and how the huddle leaders will be prepared.
- Determine whether the company will modify or introduce a new reward system in the first year and who will need to be involved in designing it.
- Create new practices of recognition and celebration.
- Evaluate the program and modify the implementation as needed during the first year.
- Determine, at the conclusion of Year 1, whether to replace some team members on the design team so that other employees can take a turn. This is an outstanding learning and leadership grooming opportunity.
- Conduct a year-end review and prepare the action plan and implementation schedule for Year 2. The achievements and lessons from Year 1 will be the stepping stones to Year 2. Both outgoing and incoming members should participate in this event.

If the team members are assigned to the business-literacy work full time, all of this can go quite quickly. Many teams, however, keep their old jobs, and devote part of their time to the team, and so planning, design, and implementation will take more elapsed time, several months in most instances. Based on

special circumstances—union or not, size and number of locations, and the like—each company needs to adjust the tasks to its particular situation. And they will add in other elements that make sense for specific needs and goals.

Intensive Study: Doing Your Homework

The first three to four meetings are well used as open-book management study periods. Each team member needs to read case examples, books, and articles and to prepare notes and questions for the team meetings. If everyone does their homework, the study periods will be rewarding and fruitful. If not, they'll feel like a waste of time. It is, in a way, the first test of team accountability and commitment.

The purpose of these study sessions is to learn, imagine, and integrate the principles and potential possibilities of business literacy. Through dialogue, listening, and articulation of new insights, individual team members will begin to push the horizons and expand their own thinking of what could be. "What if" scenarios will begin to emerge. The vision articulated by the first executive who made the open-book management decision will begin to have meaning. Questions like "What will you be doing differently?" will be answered with specific activities. Conversations will be animated and enthusiastic. Added knowledge will inspire and provide the necessary energy to plow through the hard work that lies ahead.

Pam Wagner of Sprint relates that her primary education experience with open-book management was through the team study sessions.

"We learned so much from each other," she says. "The coaching from peers, the 'thoughts and learnings' sessions at the beginning of each meeting when we shared [what we had learned]—that's when it all clicked. The study sessions helped me prepare for really seeing my team's behavior change once I gave each person a line item in the budget to control. Then I could help other

supervisors look for those same changes in owning the financial results of their work."

A suggested format for the study sessions starts with each person taking a few minutes to share thoughts about the reading assignment and how it relates to his or her own company practices, and names key issues. This is the "thoughts and learnings" session Wagner mentioned earlier. There is no conversation yet: Just begin with a period for each person to make an initial contribution. A facilitator can note the key issues on a flip chart.

After the initial go-round, a facilitator-coach probes with a series of questions such as the following to develop the team's knowledge and learning capacity:

- What stood out and most captured your attention?
- What surprised you? Confused you?
- What made you smile? Sad? Mad?
- What points challenged your thinking?
- What would you say the key implications are?
- How do they apply to our company?
- What areas do we need to examine and explore further?

The facilitator makes notes and feeds back to the team what they are learning—asking, when useful, for further dialogue on specific points. This learning-and-thinking activity will not only teach the team about open-book management and prepare them to serve their colleagues as champions, it will establish the important practice of thinking and reflecting before planning and acting.

Benefits of Intensive Study: Learning to Hang Tough

Many things will result as the team gets into deeper understanding of open-book approaches. The first is that team members will learn many things about the business—its numbers and practices—that they only vaguely understood before. This

increased knowledge of the business and its financials will inform the rest of their work.

Second, intensive study allows the team to construct a belief and develop the commitment to sustain setbacks as the implementation proceeds—understanding that the job ahead is not easy, but is worth every bit of the effort.

Stay Connected

An important initial and ongoing task for the team is to communicate and build connections with those not on the team.

The focus groups and interviews from Phase 1 (establishing readiness) expose many employees to the basic ideas. Management will have announced the team's formation and people will know something is happening. Early on, team members should think of a way to thank those who helped in the assessment. A note of thanks, a promise of feedback, a card from the open-book team declaring the contributor's input was invaluable and may help change the way business will be done—anything clever and sincere and humorous will make a little positive memory to build on later.

The purpose is to keep channels open and to let the employees know that the team is working on their behalf. Some teams hold open meetings so that people can observe the issues that are being tackled. The team should request ideas and feedback often to heighten interest, test ideas, and create buy-in.

Beyond this level of connection, the team also tends to the important task of staying in touch with the key stakeholders and sponsors of open-book management. The team should identify the key internal stakeholders: top management and key staff (e.g., training and financial departments), and line personnel, and assign specific team members to each group. Staying connected means keeping these people informed, giving each articles to read, soliciting their ideas, and when appropriate, asking for their support and involvement. *As a rule of thumb, plan to overdo connection activity, and it will likely turn out to be the right amount.*

Staying at It

The champions on one implementation team had completed their planning and were in the middle of facilitator training when the corporate call came for a reduction in force across the board. The team lost two of its own members. The impact, predictably, was negative. The natural instinct was to grieve the loss of friends, resenting their loss of livelihood and the increased workloads for those remaining. But an interesting turn had already occurred. The team was now equipped, especially after seeing the company numbers and being more business smart, to discuss this loss in business terms as well as in personal terms. The discussion was more balanced; the emotional intensity, also known as moaning and groaning and "ain't it awful," was far less than with a previous layoff. There was room for laid-off employees to disagree, express regrets and, at the same time, acknowledge that this decision made good business sense.

The team regrouped, continuing its leadership with even more tenacity; recognizing that their journey was a long way from over and that they had just weathered their first serious storm. More storms quickly followed: key customer complaints, serious delivery delays, and additional budget cutbacks all took attention from designing the training and starting the huddles. These were setbacks and changes in the business that this team had said it would need to prepare for. Of course, they had no crystal ball and hadn't predicted the specific challenges their division would face, but they *had* articulated how important understanding financial facts would be in managing the unexpected, uncontrollable, unforgiving negatives that, like lightning, score direct hits from time to time.

It was a lonely journey for this team at times. Their colleagues were not yet deeply committed to business literacy and their leadership, while still sponsoring, was quite distracted by the business challenges. Without this team's thorough preparation, which started with the intensive study, open-book management would never have happened.

Continued

⇛ *Continued*

A third benefit of intensive study preparation also emerged as team members faced the adversity of losing members and resources. The loss restimulated the curiosity team members had developed during study sessions. They went back to their early notes and initial ideas. A fresh focal point emerged as a research team began digging to discover new methods of accomplishing the implementation. They redesigned the training to get more done with less, they sought new sponsorship from top management including the vice president of sales, and they pushed back the introduction of the huddles a few months, a minor delay that they used for more preparation.

In addition to keeping in touch with their assigned key stakeholder, members of one team talked about their new knowledge in each of their regular department meetings. They were surprised to get lots of feedback and questions: some skeptical, some eager to learn more, some challenging. The dialogues at these meetings offered useful data for constructing the implementation plan.

Another team asked each senior manager to videotape his or her views of open-book management. They got enthusiastic responses. In a 10-minute "talking head" summary tape, the upper management's collective resolve to use open-book methods came through very strongly. Trainers used the tapes during the business education workshops to set the tone and squelch any skepticism.

Tending to these connections with colleagues builds a cadre of believers who will begin to feed the team important information. When the going gets tough, their support will be important. Finally, staying connected stabilizes the organization, helping the new systems find their natural place without upsetting normal business routines or stirring up people's resistance to change.

Implementation Team Challenges

At a 4,000-employee company in Canada, the data-gathering and assessment work of Phase 1 was done in three pilot divisions. The management teams in each division discussed the summary report and preliminary recommendations for implementation and questions naturally surfaced. One of the management teams was particularly concerned about a recommendation to form a "team of champions."

They agreed that some designated group would need to focus time and attention on the other recommendations (creating a vision, an implementation plan, and a base of financial knowledge), if they were to move forward. But there was strong objection to the term team of champions. Given the number of new programs and initiatives that had been introduced in the previous 5 years, management was extremely leery of anything that might convey "another program, another change." Their fears were confirmed by a Phase 1 baseline finding that many employees, in both the front line and management ranks, were burned-out on new programs and "just want to do my job."

This was a first hurdle for this division. Before they could make their way into open-book practices, they needed to address a sensitivity to the very formation of the team meant to lead the way. Fortunately, this company had several strengths that offset the "new program" problem.

■ They valued and used excellent dialogue, listening, and group decision-making methods to raise and work through issues. This gave them the confidence to address this issue, and others they would have, knowing they could still take action on an improvement effort.

■ Through a redesign/reengineering change (one of many in the preceding 5 years) in the finance groups, finance people had been repositioned as a part of each operating team.

■ As noted in the recommendations on their summary report, there were a number of "good fits" between open-book management and initiatives of the past 5 years; most specifically with their team development, organizational redesign and, the favorite of the CEO, development of a culture where everyone thinks and acts like an owner.

At this point, they concluded that the managers, the finance people assigned to their department, and several supervisors should make up a task force. They called it the Business Literacy Start-up Task Force. Two other decisions were also made:

1. To have the task force members immediately address how to best position this team's efforts with the current team development and redesign activities.
2. To think through how to link, in the least disruptive way, with other operating groups and departments that weren't involved in this open-book effort.

In a telecommunications company, the cross-functional team of middle managers and professionals, recognized as bright go-getters, had the same concern that open-book management might be perceived as another "program of the month." But they too had a strength they could use: the wide spread practices of their quality program. The team knew if they could tie open-book to the familiar quality program in some manner, it would likely receive immediate recognition and acceptance. They formed a "Challenge Team" to undertake the open-book effort because all employees were familiar with challenge teams previously formed to take on specific quality issues.

The team later named itself the Bottom Line Challenge Team. Like a hologram containing the entire picture in every piece of the picture, this team quickly figured out that what they had to learn and apply to their positions would be what others in the division needed. Their ignorance of the business when they joined the team—almost totally lacking a line of sight and financial information—was remarkable to themselves as they looked back. They realized that the team charter required expansion of, and roles beyond, what most quality challenge teams had done previously, extending their roles to that of teachers-coaches for their colleagues.

Year Two and Beyond

The implementation team will shift roles in the second year, to become more of a team of coaches, problem solvers, and resources, to guide ongoing development. The work changes for the team over time. Most of the real rough spots in implementation will be smoothed out in Year 2, but there will be many more refinements to work on in Year 3 and beyond. The team will help keep actions on track when the unexpected happens— when things get temporarily derailed or when employees feel overwhelmed or discouraged.

In many companies, implementation teams disband after they have gotten open-book management started, so that management and employees completely take over at a point. If the team remains intact with an overview function like a steering committee, members scan the work environment for improvement opportunities and better applications of adding value for customers. They identify ever more creative ways to solve business dilemmas; to get results coming from more widespread employee involvement; to recognize opportunities as well as problems; to make a company of businesspeople.

Chapter 9

Crafting the Plan: Mapping the Open-Book Path

A good plan executed now is better than a perfect plan executed
10 minutes too late.

— General Patton

Copying the Sizzle, Missing the Substance

A manufacturing firm in the Midwest has heard about open-book management. Management is attracted to the concept because margins are low, motivation is not what it should be, and the future of its government contracts looks weak with lower defense budgets. The management team visits several companies, including a division of Honeywell, Springfield Remanufacturing Company, and several Baldrige winners.

The leadership team decides that a weekly huddle with the financials is the key for tying people together. "We've got to get people into the numbers," says the general manager. "If we can cut costs, we can improve our margins and we can find other customers."

The supervisors receive no training on the numbers ahead of time. Rather, leadership decides that the main huddle with all management employees going over the income statement is the best technique for educating and empowering employees. The financial officer reads the numbers to the group weekly. The income statement is projected onto a screen, and the CFO's numbers are penciled in by the CEO's secretary for all to read.

This process goes on for 6 months. Some discussion at the huddle ensues, but no business practices really change. The top management hopes for a positive impact. But after 6 months, supervisors aren't so sure. "Getting the numbers is OK," says one, "but we're still not focused on doing much with them." Because of the communication gap between top and middle managers, middle manager and supervisor concerns never get to the general manager.

Company performance stays flat. The numbers are not fully understood by those in attendance at the meeting, mainly floor supervisors. And because the CFO is still owning the numbers and floor supervisors don't have line of sight, no team or collective drive exists to manage to the numbers that someone else created.

Leadership missed the call. They had the best of intentions to open up their company to their employees and to get the business literacy ball rolling. Instead, their meetings became a communications gesture around financial numbers that did little to change the culture, make the business stronger, or engage employees.

Most managers know the power of good planning and the necessity of even mediocre planning. When it is not done well, planning can kill open-book efforts. Poor planning, and little understanding about how lasting change takes significant effort, killed open-book management at this company after 6 months.

Phase 4: The Implementation Plan

The crucial next step in mapping your way is creating an implementation plan that provides others both a way to learn and a means of incorporating new practices into daily work habits. When this phase is done well, the combination of education and new skills increases organizational learning speed. The learning path started by the implementation team is ready for others to travel, widening into a well-traveled learning road.

Several steps need to be taken in separate preparatory meetings so the design team will be ready for a 2-day planning event:

1. The findings from the interviews and focus groups conducted in Phase 1, need to be reviewed and discussed. Since the implementation team's understanding will have deepened through study, it will have a sharper, more precise ability to use the data than the assessment task force. Many of the assessment task force's recommendations will still ring true, but the implementation team will elaborate, modify, or add cohesion to the earlier work.

2. The design team needs to discuss the direction formed by the executive team in Phase 2 at the think tank. As conversations and study of open-book concepts take place, understanding deepens. Implications of the practices come into awareness. A crisper articulation of the direction helps the team set definitive milestones and put a process in motion. The interaction with the executives who initiated open-book processes will enhance understanding and commitment for all involved.

3. The implementation teams need to stay continually oriented to the external business conditions and the latest thinking of the executive team. If upper management has brought in a new team executive team member, or started thinking in new directions, the design team needs to know exactly what those changes are. Many times, change efforts in companies suffer from just this kind of shifting because of lack of communication. The implementation team's imperative to stay connected prevents unnecessary barriers in execution.

The executives' keen sense of how open-book management strengthens the company's core capability, acting as a constant beacon for the design team. Jim Carter, chief operating officer at

Syncrude Canada Ltd. attended a preparatory meeting of the implementation team and recommended that the company's 10-year business plan and process should be thoroughly understood by all his managers. Since the company relies on capital investment and technological advances, Carter knows the value of this knowledge for good decision-making and planning. His perspective provided direction for the implementation team to work with in shaping the Syncrude business literacy plan.

Briefing All Employees: Providing an Open-Book "Heads Up" Call

While these preparatory discussions are taking place, the team can start an open-book awareness series of briefings in the organization. One natural and nondisruptive way to accomplish this is through a brown-bag lunch series. Using videotapes, articles, and other discussion stimulators, facilitators can introduce co-workers to open-book concepts and benefits. These, or similar sessions, "bring people on board"; they invite employees to begin to think with the others who have already gained some open-book awareness.

Having two facilitators share the workload develops more trainers and broadens the exposure of the employees. One facilitator can be a implementation team member who explains his or her own learning over the past several months. The other facilitator can be an executive, a trainer, or human resource person, or any knowledgeable employee who has an expressed interest and can do a good job of presenting and fielding questions.

An internal or external coach can help organize the series of briefings to accomplish the objectives of stimulating awareness and curiosity throughout the company. This is also a timely opportunity to inform co-workers of the results of the data-gathering and of the design team's upcoming implementation plan workshop.

The same kind of brown-bag lunch series can be held after the plan is outlined to share the steps, answer questions, and respond to concerns. The following sample plan outline shows typical steps:

Activities and Steps for Year 1:

Quarter 1

Create baseline through assessment task force.

Set the business direction.

Implementation team starts planning.

Tie open-book to other company initiatives and practices.

Quarter 2

Financial education designed.

Huddle system training for managers begins.

Financial education conducted.

Pilot the huddle system and introduce use of score cards with performance drivers and financial targets.

Quarter 3

Refine huddles and develop measures and scorecards.

Redesign bonus programs.

Begin participative business planning.

Quarter 4

Provide more financial training.

Evaluate first-year effort.

Bonus implemented.

Use business planning process to educate.

Celebrate first year learnings and accomplishments.

This low-key approach keeps everyone informed and connected. Large operations with multiple locations can use video communications as the next best thing to being there. Whatever all-hands meeting mechanisms the company or division has to inform employees are effective settings for raising awareness. They are tribal in the best sense of the word: get-togethers about important events that create a sense of shared experience. They help personalize the open-book initiative, lessening the potential of roadblocks developing should employees in middle management and on the front line perceive another top-down mandate. And brown-baggers are cost-effective.

The Planning Retreat

Crafting a plan that maps the way for others to follow requires uninterrupted focus. The implementation team needs to set aside time, preferably two days, for an off-site retreat to assemble the core plan. The uninterrupted time allows the team to concentrate in the right environment for grappling with the usually tough issues surrounding implementation.

The planning process during the two-day off-site session culminates all the previous work. The specifics of the plan will flow rather naturally and with a higher level of confidence than if the plan had been attempted earlier in the journey. Quite literally, the team members have become craftspeople. Their confidence and enthusiasm will be evident; their approach to the plan will be bold and targeted because the preparation has been thorough and the direction is clear.

Here are the core pieces that need to be spelled out by the team:

■ Define the specifics of what the organization is trying to achieve and why. What does the direction set by management look like in each of the functional areas of the company?

■ Define milestones for 3 years: What practices, know-how, and capabilities will be in place that indicate to the managers and employees that the effort is on target (a sample set of milestones is provided at the end of the chapter to stimulate your thinking).

■ Identify the barriers inside the company and in the external business environment that need to be carefully handled.

❆ ❆ ❆ ❆

Open Books at Work: 6. Fun Training for 500 People at Once

The Scanlon Plan Associates were holding their annual meeting in Grand Rapids, Michigan. Nearly 500 people from member companies like Herman Miller, Xaloy, and Donnelley—from frontliners to CEOs—were present for a day of idea exchange on how to make their high-participation companies more effective.

This year, the meeting planners were looking for a way to learn financials, involving everyone in a fun manner to understand these basic business scorecards. They wanted an interactive game to show how the numbers can be fun—for 500 people.

No Problem!

One of the Scanlon companies makes signs (the Huron Sign Company). That helped, because they reproduced the Chutes and Ladders board game, with the creator's approval, from a standard-size board to a 30- by 30-foot square that people could walk on. The life-size pawns, in this instance the executives of the companies looking a little ridiculous (which was clearly the intent), could prance around the game squares to the cheers of the crowd on the floor of the college gymnasium where the meeting was to take place.

The financial score sheets and game rules were handed to each person as they entered the gym. The "chips" representing business transactions were plastic picnic plates big enough to see from the top row. They signified the cash, assets, and debt in the game, appropriately colored: black for accounts receivable, white for hard assets, green for cash, and red for debt.

Each team had its own grandstand section in the gym. The six teams wore colored shirts, Sunshine Yellow, Deep Red, Rich Brown, Dark Blue, Royal Blue and an outlandish Bright Orange, a veritable rainbow of business learners crammed into the gym. A pair a gargantuan *Guinness Book of World Records* dice, 3 feet to a side, were tossed and bounced around the gym floor by the different teams when it was their turn to move their executive pawn.

As the game began, a chip person moved the various chips on and off the board, to and from the bank, so everyone could

❂ *Continued*

─── ❄❄❄❄ ───

❄ Continued

see how the business was doing with cash flow, debt to equity, and profit. Volunteer employees stepped out of the stands to toss the megadice, getting applause when someone landed on the "make a sale" square, and jeers when the "pay expense" square came into play. The designated score-sheet person used a huge overhead screen to keep track of the numbers on the financial statements, and even the many folks who didn't know a debt-to-equity ratio from a net profit percentage started calculating the numbers.

The excitement rose as the game proceeded and taking loans became necessary to fund the growth in sales. Landing on the "draw a card" square raised 500 people's anxiety at once—like the chance card in Monopoly®, something either real good or real bad could happen. Often the cards called for a group decision, and 500 thumbs up or down, as in the Roman coliseum with the gladiators, indicated whether the team wanted to take on more debt, buy some new equipment, or hire a new accounts receivable clerk to collect that cash.

In 90 minutes, with the last calculation of the balance sheet, the game came to an end. Their decisions had been a bit too conservative that day in the gym. They didn't take on enough debt to meet their cash goal. But in spite of being cash poor, they were profitable and the balance sheet was strong.

The Scanlon companies, true to their heritage, had offered a unique accelerated learning event to their members. As the crowd filed out of the gym, their comments, confirmed by the formal evaluations, indicated that people had experienced some genuine learning fun, and the relationship between cash flow, profits, and the balance sheet had never been so clear. As one participant said, "I never saw how running out of cash and making a profit could be so easy to do. Now I see what all those banks are for."

This includes predicting where resistance is likely to kick up once implementation effects are beginning to be felt.

■ Create strategies that support the open-book management direction and milestones, and several that address the barriers most in need of attention.

■ Articulate how the open-book management philosophy and approach is linked to other initiatives and programs.

■ Prioritize clear actions for each strategy. These actions should be specific and lead directly to results. Each needs to have an action driver, or an owner, to carry the action through. The owners can be design team members, senior managers, or any other persons with the knowledge and influence to be effective. Owners need to coordinate their efforts to prevent overlap and create the synergistic benefits.

■ Select a mix of actions: some with a high likelihood of immediate impact and success and others that will take longer to show results.

■ Specify the resources—time, people, money—to successfully accomplish Year-1 actions.

■ Determine whether subteams are needed to customize the financial and business education, tailor the huddle system, revise the reward and compensation systems, or set up Player-Coach training.

■ Create an implementation schedule. First steps should be a natural extension of what already exists. Carefully linking the first steps of open-book to your quality or reengineering or gain-sharing plan helps co-workers see the good sense of the new practices. Changes are more easily accepted and assimilated if an awareness series, like the brown-bag briefings, has taken place.

The following example of a part of a plan is a mixture of actual plans that companies have created. The plan itself looks simple when complete; it should be doable, understandable, and not overly complex. The thinking that goes into the plan, however, is never as simple as the final result.

In this example, the strategy in the implementation plan is to minimize the perception of the open-book initiative being another "program of the month." The first action step supporting this strategy is to start financial and business education with a fun team learning event. Extending the brown-bag lunch into 2 hours and introducing a board game (like *Profit & Cash*™)* will provide a good mix of serious financial learning and fun.

The implementation schedule then lists the rollout of the activities and answers the necessary who, what, when, where, why, and how questions. The fun introduction, having piqued interest and showing some promise, is linked to the next education session which is 1 or 2 days' concentration on the company's critical numbers and ratios and on financial scorekeeping.

This in turn is followed by individual 2-hour work group sessions to create local scorecards that develop "line of sight" linkage of their daily activities to the financial statements.

Sample: *Partial Output from the Planning Retreat*

Strategy: Minimize program-of-the-month perceptions.
Action: Business education.

Implementation Schedule	Coach-Teacher	Coordinator	Time Table and Participants
Extended Brown-Bag Lunches: Profit & Cash™ (2 hours)	Mary—Finance Joe—Implementation Team Sarah—Implementation Team Tom—H.R.	George	Cross-Functional Groups 8/96—Mon & Wed •Tech Ops•Admin •Engineers 4 groups—12 ea. 9/96—Tue & Thr •Sales•Cust. Serv. •Legal 4 groups—12 ea.

* Call Capital Connections, 816-561-6622 for more information.

Implementation Schedule	Coach-Teacher	Coordinator	Time Table and Participants
Training: How ACME makes Money and Keeps Score (2 days)		Patty	7/96
Design & Development	Sue—Training Bill—Finance		10/96—1st week •Sr. Mgs. (short version)
Deliver	Gerry—Ops Gail—Sales Mary—Financial Joe—Implementation Team Mary—Financial Sarah—Implementation Team Bill—Financial Gerry—Ops		10/96—3rd week •Dept. Heads 11/96—1st week •Frontline Team Leaders
Create Team Scorecards (1½ hours)	All involved in effort assigned to guide specific work groups. Support by manager and supervisor who participated in 2-day Business Education.	Mark	Request extension of regular staff meetings. Start 12/96—complete by 2/1/97 •All Employees
Huddle Leaders Prep (½ day)	Rick—Champion Phil—H.R. Nancy—H.R. Kerri—Champion	Helen	3/97 •All managers and team leaders 4 groups

Keep On Rollin': Plan B's Can Help

After the implementation schedule is a work-in-process, the implementation team should convene every 2 weeks to evaluate progress, make minor adjustments, and begin to devise backup plans. "If-I-had-it-to-do-over-again" stories all include the regret that a worst-case scenario hadn't been planned for. To be ready for surprises, always create a Plan B or, for particularly chaotic environments, Plans C and D. Building flexibility in the plan—over headquarter's demanding changes, or potential reengineering—is a useful discipline. Then when the unexpected hits, the ability to move ahead is already a mental habit.

Dwight Eisenhower's statement—"Plans are worthless, planning is priceless"—emphasizes the notion that planning ahead and thinking things through allow for flexibility and eventual success. The design team's ongoing contingency planning is especially important for the first 12 to 18 months of implementation, while practices are in the formative stages.

Planting open-book management in an enterprise has parallels to seeding and growing a lawn. You need to water your new grass seed, and monitor closely where the seed is sprouting and where the bare spots are. If a big storm causes a runoff before the seeds have taken root, you need to respond quickly with more effort. If open-book management is to weather the storms of change, it needs protection and extra effort in the early stages, so the roots can take hold in the minds and the practices of the company.

These evaluation meetings are a great opportunity to prepare and anticipate the next level of learning. The best way to do this is to start each meeting with the same "thoughts and learnings" practice started in the intensive study section of building the team. During this exercise, each team member shares for 2 to 3 minutes any thoughts, ideas, principles, or new insights gained while assisting and listening to their co-workers since the previous meeting. The "thoughts and learnings" practice is one all employees benefit from in their huddles as more sophisticated levels of business thinking develop. It provides a period for thinking, for consideration of what's needed, in fast-paced, slightly mad work environments. Business literacy demands business thinking, a benefit of open-book practices that starts with training, continues with ongoing learning, and makes for far less rework and backtracking.

Creating Milestones for the Plan

An important goal of open-book management is to have all employees in the enterprise forecasting, with accountability, the output of their various functions. Depending on the company's current levels of business literacy and participation, however, this goal may range from an obvious next step for already empowered teams and business units, to a seemingly unimaginable leap beyond the bounds of current company practices.

Don't be discouraged if your organization falls into the latter category. You may be far from attaining the level of communication and ownership process that advanced open-book companies practice as a habit. But acquiring even the first degrees of new business capability is worth the effort and fun to celebrate. It takes a long time to train to become an Alvin Ailey dancer, or an accomplished pianist, but every day of practice brings new advances worthy of celebration.

As long as open-book systems are developing and being implemented, as long as employees are learning, you and your enterprise are on track and making headway.

Think of the following milestones as sample targets to shoot for. Some are for beginners; others, the very advanced. They are drawn from real examples in real companies developing business literacy. The milestones indicate skill levels to shoot for with open-book practices. While some are common, others are unique to each company and stem from the direction set by management. What is a future milestone for one company will not be on the list for another, or may be something the company long ago mastered. Improvement toward the next level is what milestones are all about. Companies make sensible progress toward the goal of business literacy by targeting sequential milestones, and moving to the next level with patience and persistence. Making maximum use of the newly attained capabilities while striving for the next level is a delicate balancing act for all companies.

No company progresses like clockwork in even steps through identical proficiency levels in each of the four systems of business literacy. Enterprises experience change in fits and starts, three steps forward/two steps back. And they start in different places—a company with a great set of no-kidding ownership practices may lack financial know-how. The descriptors should be taken as guidelines, not requirements. Your milestones are the ones that are important.

Here's one more advisory note. If you can't really picture or imagine your company shooting for these milestones, give yourself time. You're still too early into the process to give it form. So set your milestones later, as you gain more knowledge, get some practice and training, and your imagination can "picture" the practices.

Open-Book Management Sample Milestones

NOTE: While the following list is anything but exhaustive, more suggestions are offered here than most single companies choose. They should stimulate your thoughts.

Training and Learning Milestones

■ All employees participate in training on financial statements to develop line of sight to the income statement; can pass the company financial quiz.

■ All managers trained in leading huddles as a teaching and forecasting process.

■ Team members spend designated periods in other departments learning their work.

■ Regular cross-training and rotations are in place so all employees see the big picture.

■ Managers switch roles so they can learn more than one specialty.

Business Know-How Milestones

■ All managers can explain the business plan and how each member of their teams contributes to meeting the plan.

- All employees can explain the company's strategy, competitive advantages, and customer service commitments.
- All employees know how their work impacts the financial outcomes of the company. They understand cost system and how they affect costs.

Huddle Milestones

- All teams hold monthly huddles to stay informed and inform management and co-workers on their projected performance outcomes.
- All teams hold weekly huddles to alert themselves to problems and to track specific progress. Teams coordinate with other teams, suppliers, and customers to get accurate data and meet the plan.
- Senior managers' weekly huddles specify changes in business environment, customer requirements, articulate the challenges, and educate about needed business practice adjustments.

Scorecard Milestones

- Initial scorecards are developed with focus on key common measures across the company and specific measures for departments.
- Pilot scorecards are in use that integrate key operating and quality numbers with key financial targets.
- Accurate and comprehensive scorecards are in use across the company, shared electronically and in real time, acting as valuable tools in decision-making and problem-solving.

Innovation Milestones

- With newly acquired financial knowledge, teams take action to harvest the "low-hanging fruit," the easiest changes to get cost reductions.
- Teams regularly develop new ideas and pass them on to management for improving customer service, quality, and the financial performance of products and services.

- Teams develop new ideas, with financial cost-benefit measures, implement those within their power while coordinating with other teams, and propose fresh strategies for management in product and service development that reallocates resources or has impact beyond their scope.

Pride-in-Work Milestones

- Many employees take pride in their efforts and in serving customers as evidenced by enthusiastic and positive conversations about getting the job done.
- Most employees have pride in the company, take initiative, and want to do a better job.
- Employees regularly refer friends and family for employment, serve as a company representative on community boards, and participate in Junior Achievement or similar community activities. Many take training on their own time to improve skills.

Financial Incentive Milestones

- Rewards and incentives that divide functions or favor some teams over others are eliminated.
- Bonuses are in place based on financial outcomes that all understand.
- Bonuses in place, developed with employee input, drive energetic, concerted effort because they are tied to a company achievement that matters.

Recognition/Attitude Milestones

- Managers regularly provide feedback on work and effort.
- Recognition and celebration are more frequent than the baseline identified in the assessment. People report on having more fun than before open-book practices started.
- Managers and employees balance concerns about upward promotions with the benefits of learning, fun, and personal satisfaction in worthwhile work achievements. Financial gain through bonuses and variable pay lessens the need to climb a fixed career ladder that no longer exists anyway.

Teamwork Milestones

- Business communication across functions increases as need to coordinate for managing the big picture grows.
- Less finger-pointing and blaming occur; Teams and individuals are taking initiative.
- Teams thank and recognize each other spontaneously.
- Teams meet to analyze the quality of work processes and to improve financial and customer outcomes.

Selection Milestones

- Human resources department provides information to all job prospects on the company's requirement that all employees learn the business. It sets a new standard for employees: to think like businesspeople.
- Teams conduct thorough selection process for new team members, interviewing for skills, team orientation, and interest and aptitude for learning about the business.

Participation Milestones

- Employees are asked at huddles for their numbers and what they are doing to make the plan.
- Teams are given choices on what minicelebrations they want to have as they meet monthly goals.
- The overall bonus is put in place using employee inputs on what customers want, such as on-time delivery, what financial goals make the most sense, such as needed capital expenditures, what profit margins can be achieved, given the economic expansion or contraction cycle of the industry.
- Managers have input into the operating plan put in place at the beginning of the year, commenting on sales figures, expense items, product improvements, new work processes, and standards.
- All employees have input into the operating plan through team meetings with their managers.

Chapter 10

꯭ ꯭ ꯭ ꯭

Business Education: Designing Open-Book Training

If you think training costs a lot, try estimating the cost of igno-rance, lack of teamwork, and lack of business know-how.

Anonymous

Effective training jump-starts open-book management prac-tices. Educating managers on their new responsibilities and employees on what the numbers mean and how they will be forecasting them is the final stage of "Getting It Going." It sets the foundation for the huddles, so business literacy will be-come pervasive and lasting.

Most people find this phase of the implementation exciting and challenging. It offers them an opportunity to move a couple notches forward on the learning curve. This is when the estab-lished direction and the business plan start to take hold. The training stimulates higher levels of business thinking, which is the underpinning for the new practices starting shortly after the training.

The training in Phase 4 will be more visible than anything done thus far for all employees—more so than the low-key, brown-bag series of awareness events—and will stimulate varied reactions: interest, concerns, hope, and skepticism. An enthusiastic and confidently prepared team, and a senior management that knows the plan, can respond to these reactions with information and educational programs.

Training in open-book management practices moves close to the everyday action in the workplace—how people think and act. The goals set by the implementation team in their plan mold and shape the training activities. Companies wanting to improve inventory turns will train accordingly, and those wanting to improve customer service will show what better service does to the top and the bottom line.

Many organizations form subteams to create a full training process, including:

■ Business learning events.
■ Customized huddle systems.
■ A huddle leadership format.
■ Ways to highlight no-kidding ownership practices.

Others use the original implementation team, or bring in an external coach to work with and provide assistance for the development of the needed educational workshops.

While the implementation team coordinates the training program to get open-book management started, other employees with "subject matter expertise" often have much to contribute. These experts in finance, sales, or operations can inject their knowledge into the training modules with the help of the implementation team. And senior management's know-how and sponsorship of the training are vital.

Employees about to begin open-book practices very often lack a solid understanding of business and financial basics. All managers, especially those conducting the huddles that send the numbers up to management, need this base of understanding to be conversant in financial terms. Attacking this learning deprivation is a good place to start the training design, but it doesn't end there.

The four business literacy systems require the following core practices for individuals and teams. The assessment measured these practices and now the design team uses them as learning objectives for the training.

Critical Numbers Know-How Practices

■ Think regularly about and analyze your own work through a financial and big-picture lens.

■ Make decisions based on the needs of the entire company versus individual- and department-specific goals.

■ Learn how to analyze the company's financial performance and status using critical ratios and financial statements.

■ Plan and act to reduce variances between current and expected performance.

■ Make judgments on how to add value for customers that are justified financially.

Intensive Huddle System Practices

■ Hold consistent and frequent information meetings that send pertinent and accurate business and performance information throughout the company.

■ Expect all participants to account for their individual contributions by tracking current activities and outcomes to the business plan and department/team indicators, using the common language of financials.

■ Huddle leaders account for the company's performance and teach others about the business. Rehearse the financial know-how necessary to understand how to think, make decisions, and act as responsible daily contributors.

■ Using the system of meetings, forecast future performance with factual explanations of positive or negative variance from the original plan.

■ Using information provided in the huddle system, individuals and teams take initiative to solve problems and seize opportunities.

■ Involve all employees in developing a yearly plan, creating broad buy-in for the numbers, and deep and detailed knowledge of costs, sales goals, and specifically targeted critical numbers.

No-Kidding Ownership Practices

■ Seize opportunities for problem solving and decision making. Own your job, your team's outputs, and your part in results of the company, good and bad.

■ Set up financial reward systems beyond base compensation and tie them to results. Design these systems and teach all employee/stakeholders to understand how their actions impact customers, colleagues, and financial results. Share equity when possible.

■ Publicly celebrate the payout of rewards as victories.

■ Frequently and genuinely recognize and celebrate individual employee and team contributions and efforts even if results are initially unfavorable.

■ Perceive each employee, team, and department as having a position of psychological ownership, if not financial.

■ Converse daily with employee groups concerning business performance, and how they are working to impact a positive outcome.

Player-Coach Leadership Practices

■ Use technical, operational, quality, sales and marketing, customer service, and other performance measures to teach others what the numbers and ratios represent.

■ Coach co-workers to use numbers and other business data on a daily basis to solve problems and make decisions. Share what they are learning as they learn it.

■ Communicate current information as quickly as it is available with explanations that help others understand its meaning. Animate the numbers.

■ Using business and financial know-how, encourage each employee to develop him- or herself and to:

Take initiative appropriate to the position.

Account for performance outcomes consistently and accurately.

- Consistently tell stories of employee accomplishments and contributions. The more responsibility the leader has, the more important this is. Convey values with stories, creating shared purpose, and build community.

- Use fact-based decision making, involving and empowering others to decide at the level their knowledge and experience allow. Use other decision-making processes, such as intuition, minimizing risks but describing what they are, when facts are minimal.

While each company develops its own set of training objectives, based on the direction management sets, the core practices cannot be overlooked. The training modules that most companies include, as a minimum, are:

For all employees:
The principles and systems of open-book management: How they work in general and what this company wants to achieve with open-book methods.
Critical numbers know-how: understanding the financials.
And additional training for managers:
The manager's role in open-book companies: teaching the business, huddles, rewards, and recognition.
Critical numbers know-how: understanding the financials so you can teach others.
Running the huddles with the up/down/across communication process.

Gather Training Resources

Education and training can be built using existing company documents, plans, and systems. The team members can gather many helpful internal resources to start their training work:

- The industry's profile and competitive information.
- The company's vision, mission, and management philosophies.

- The long-term strategic plan.
- The current-year business plan.
- Current financial statements and key performance indicators.
- Financial analysis methods and tools, such as trending and variance analysis and key ratios.
- Reporting methods and forms.
- Information systems and capabilities.
- Objectives and progress updates of recent leadership and team development initiatives—or quality, reengineering, and other improvement programs.
- Human resource plans, compensation philosophy, and current reward and bonus goals.
- Any other documents, company goals, and policies that might be useful, such as attitude surveys.

The best internal training resources of all are the people in the company. The implementation team members, the financial specialists, the manager, and the many gifted employees can all make the training lasting learning. The design team has to think how best to use the collective know-how already in the business.

One of the objectives of the business education plan for the Sprint Government Systems Division was, "Begin to push financial knowledge and the use of financial information into all parts of the division." So Jim Steffan, a director in the finance department, took on the task of developing a business case to address financial knowledge. He focused on a classic business problem put into their unique setting—should they grow quickly with new products or more steadily with current ones? The quick growth goal was attractive, but it jeopardized a cash flow goal of equal importance. Others on the task force worked with Jim to ensure the case linked the use of the financial lessons and facts from earlier learning modules.

Once his part was completed, Jim served in an advisory capacity to the implementation team. With a specific training plan and objectives, resource people can move in and out as needed.

Open-Book Power: Early Results through Training

Time devoted to the developing and executing the training is a worthwhile investment. In many instances, there are real and quantifiable gains even from initial stages of classroom training.

A management team that wanted to learn more about open-book management found this out. The company had already received national acclaim, the U.S. Chamber of Commerce's Blue Chip award, as an award-winning $100 million company. But, like most good companies, they knew they could do better. And, like all companies, they had a vulnerable area—tremendous fluctuation in their raw material costs. Already experiencing considerable growth, management had to be careful not to grow too fast and run out of cash. What they liked about open-book management, among other things, is its ability to draw all employees into the business so their costs can be managed more efficiently.

During the on-site briefing on how open-book management works, the CEO and the executive team focused on the intensive huddle paradigm shift, proactively managing the numbers through ongoing forecasting against the plan. Their practice had been to do the usual history lesson provided by the financial officer at their staff meetings ("Here's our summary of how we did last month . . .").

The CEO saw the possibilities immediately: "This is what we needed to get started," said the CEO. "We had some of the tools, but we needed to start using them more effectively."

In the first month of shifting from a past to a future orientation toward the numbers, the management team devised a tactic that yielded $300,000 in cost savings. All eligible employees reached their bonus.

At the Anita Springs Water Company plant in Louisville, Kentucky, Mark Gasparovich, general manager, and his management team, used their training preparation to identify costs. As they explored, they discovered that the gross profit for their different products had not been explained or understood. They acted immediately, soliciting the help of the corporate controller. Even while they were preparing for the introductory business training for their managers and supervisors, they were busy making immediate improvements.

The next step for Mark and his team was to learn how to communicate and teach what they had just learned. Armed with this new information, frontline workers could make choices, such as which line should take precedence for maintenance and repair and which operations would need productivity improvements to meet an acceptable gross margin.

While the general manager analyzed the direct product costs, the third-shift supervisor, Kevin Coffey, started to think about his own influence on labor costs. Kevin's thinking was initially stimulated in the assessment phase in the one-on-one interview. On his own initiative and using his keen understanding, he compared the time and productivity of his team when it used temporary help during labor shortages with its operations when it did not use replacement help. His decision to eliminate the rework caused by the untrained workers gained efficiency for the line. Kevin offered his new business know-how during the training as a real-time, on-the-job, as-it-happens example of thinking and acting like an owner.

The Anita Spring's example, like many others, shows the latent capability ready to be discovered in every organization even early in the training stages.

Kevin was recognized by his management and he was motivated to do more. He began to look at other problems. The more he learned about the finances and just how much it cost to produce and deliver the product, and to service the customer, the more he saw the importance of his work. The meaning of his job expanded. He could see how the value of his contribution added to the company's success.

The same phenomenon showed up on a team in a service business with less easily measured costs. An administrative assistant, Patty Peddan, in the Government Systems Division of Sprint, was part of some early practice rounds of the huddle system. Her department was responsible for training, managing several different budgets, approving vendor invoices for payment, and managing travel and other related expenses. In the training, this team explored where their activities showed on the income statement. They figured out their line of sight. They compared how they were doing against the budget and anticipated costs through the end of the year.

In addition to expense items having run considerably over budget in the previous year, they discovered a potential overrun in the current year. Patty examined her responsibilities and activities, and took ownership of how she could make a difference. She called all vendors asking for invoice details and checked for less expensive travel options, such as purchasing 7-day advance airline tickets instead of less-than-7-day tickets, and one-stop instead of non-stop flights. At her next practice department huddle, she proudly reported her research and projected savings. "It was something I could always have focused on," she said. "Open-book management helped me get that focus." Patty Peddan became an early leader in application practices, and her story was repeated often.

Training Targets: Open-Book Learning Begins

The following set of business education objectives was developed by a company intent on installing basic open-book practices and thinking into daily business decisions. *Overall Objective*: Increase the understanding of the industry and the requirements to be successful in it.

■ All employees fully understand the business:
  The need and process for expansion.
  The importance of handling each call to meet internal and external customer expectations.
  The importance of quality for securing potential business.

■ Make the financial scorecards and statements understandable and useful for all:

> Each functional team knows and understands how their daily job activity and decision-making impact on the bottom-line performance of the company.

> Each individual contributor understands how he or she is expected to specifically contribute to the company's mission and to the financial objectives of the company.

■ Focus the daily work efforts on critical numbers to achieve greater profitability.

■ Improve the decision-making of both management and workers through ongoing business education—a high level of thinking and business know-how creates an environment of challenge and fun.

■ Learn the use of the huddle system for keeping every employee current on the business activity, customer satisfaction, and financial outcomes.

Learning to Learn: Classroom Tips

Designing the modules and learning activities for the business training in the classroom is as important as tailoring the content to the specific company's business and culture. Small learning teams of three to six people, within the larger classroom setting, make an optimal learning environment in which participants can interact with each other to think, experience, and make decisions.

The goal for the classroom is for participants to engage in activities that make immediate use of the newfound knowledge. While most companies set up a 1-, 2-, or 3-day workshop for 15 to 25 participants, it is possible to include the educational modules in extended team meetings.

The design and facilitation of the modules are based on the same principles used to conduct successful huddles—action learning. Learning by doing and using experience to test theory are the keys.

The following guidelines for training designs focus on practical, usable, learning exercises.

Use Experiential Learning Techniques

To help individuals develop their own insights and conclusions, provide the participants with problems in which they immediately put the new knowledge to use. This approach allows the learners to absorb the information and is a departure from many seminars today where an entertaining lecturer simply imparts knowledge. At these latter events, the conclusions the attendees take home are the seminar leader's, not their own.

Tie All Training Material to the Daily Work

The material focuses on goal achievement and gaining personal as well as company benefit. An example would be teaching the cost system. The specific costs of each product and service can be broken out, and teams can analyze the gross margin differences between the different services and products and their influence on those.

Challenge Participants to Enter into Learning

Provide interesting financial problems to work on. Getting the financial calculations is important but assure them that the goal is not only to be able to give the "right" answers, but also to think creatively about the material to make their work more effective. This kind of activity helps participants recognize that business decisions often have no easy answers and risks and tradeoffs are common.

Returning to Kevin Coffey as an example, the tradeoffs between the cost of replacement workers and the rework they caused were real. Once he had the numbers to work with, he could calculate the outcomes of different scenarios, weighing cost and customer demands. The training helped Kevin get his "head into the game" and work the issue with his colleagues.

Repetition of Experience and Pertinent Information Allows People to Build Confidence

Emphasizing the progress made, and the successful use of what has been understood, makes it easier to learn the lessons and use them. Persistent and patient coaches repeat and encourage. In open-book training, the classroom is the foundation and the repetition and reinforcing continues in the huddles.

All Learners Benefit from Positive Feedback

The training can stretch people's abilities and at the same time be fun and build confidence. Moving into unfamiliar territory, where the learning leads to more decisions and accountability, initially requires constant feedback and guidance from those with experience.

Some People Know Too Much to Be Good at Training What They Know

They forget how they learned what they now master. This sometimes applies to financial training—the experts have to start where the learners are, not from where they'd like them to be. It takes a couple of brave souls not fully informed on finance, during the development of the training modules, to work with the financially astute. They keep asking questions until they really "get it," (understand the financials), which helps them pass on the lessons to others.

People are at their learning best when responding to a challenge and using resources to meet it. The participants will use the lessons, savor and own them, when they have invested their energy to learn and see the payoffs the learning will bring. A positive classroom experience that reveals new workable knowledge to better do their job and run the business will stimulate the courage for taking on greater on-the-job learning challenges. This generates momentum for continual improvement creating a snowball learning effect.

Training developers must not give too many answers, but rather should provide the facts and data and encourage the participants to apply this information.

The managers, as future huddle leaders and coaches, must experience the training. They need to know what all employees are being asked to do. If they don't know, or just as bad, can't teach the numbers, or facilitate a weak huddle that yields little learning, the business-literacy initiative will limp instead of spring along. Employees will be discouraged and avoid rather than seize learning opportunities.

As the managers develop their skills and head toward open-book mastery, they are poised to meet the business and the learning challenges that will emerge in the regular course of business. The know-how they start in the training can be replicated in the huddles they conduct and in the teaching moments they seize.

Lori Bartell of Excell's Agent Services tells how the training for agents at their company turned into a great example of open-book principles.

> We hired over 180 agents for our first round of training, and during our second week of training we experienced a delay in loading our database. We couldn't move forward, and in a panic, we reverted to an old management style—closed ourselves in a room and worked on a plan to present the news without losing the confidence of our new employees. We felt uneasy, though.
>
> The next day it dawned on us to use open-book management and put the entire problem in front of the agents, the numbers and the situation, and ask for their advice. The agents were impressed and offered very good solutions—which we used.
>
> . . . Although we were planning to educate the agents on Open-Book Management in a more traditional manner, . . . their involvement helped our employees learn that open-book management means sharing all information. As a company, we have a group of employees who are continually learning more about making this company—and themselves—more successful.*

Excell did the unusual thing with training and learning—they created a triumph of substance over form. They used the reality of the business to demonstrate a principle the training

---

* Lori Bartell, V.P. Operations Excell Agent Service in Phoenix, Arizona.

was trying to teach—involving employees to make the business work. So often, training gets in the way of learning because the form—nice participant manuals and a full schedule of classes—takes precedence over the live, real-time learning-filled opportunities.

Day-in and day-out business coaching like this example from Excell creates a positive employee expectancy for handling more challenges. They gain the confidence to respond to new dilemmas. Positive, repetitious personalized learning loops, started with the training and reinforced in the huddles' day-to-day usage, deepen the growth of the core open-book practices in the organization.

Over time, open-book practices will become part of the culture, a habit. Employees will use financial information as readily and comfortably as they use quality or customer service data today.

Chapter 11

❄❄ ❄❄ ❄❄ ❄❄

You Don't Have to Be at the Top: Middle Managers Open the Books

*Some are pleased to give orders and some are pleased to take.
There are a few however, who wish neither to give orders nor to
take them, but to live in the between of the world.**

Earl Shorris

Being a middle manager is a curse and a blessing. The curse
is something middle managers know too well: A middle
manager can be squeezed and made ineffective by both
the top and the bottom. The blessing is something they should
not forget: Middle managers have influence both up and down
and can take action that is felt throughout the organization.
They can either dampen or enhance the ripple effect, both mag-
nifying and blunting whatever comes their way from any
direction.

*Middle managers have many options for implementation if they are
committed to open-book management and their top management is not
yet aware, or committed to open-book empowerment.*

Open-book management can and does begin anywhere in the
organization, not just after the CEO has blessed it and started
spreading open-book religion. Middle managers who want to
improve the business permanently know that whatever they can

---

* Earl Shorris, *Scenes from Corporate Life*, New York: Penguin, 1981.

186

do to teach the business is a productive step in the direction of greater business literacy.

These active middle managers often share a small, but very powerful secret: In midsize and large businesses, top managers are too far removed from the everyday workings of the business to make the endless decisions that go into delivering services and making products. Middle managers, team leaders, and front-line supervisors bring to life the practices of the business, open-book or otherwise. This is their advantage for moving ahead.

A fundamental act for middle managers wanting to create open-book environments is sharing big-picture information. They teach the business. By installing open-book thinking, middle managers can attack the job myopia and lack of teamwork that comes with specialized work. Many employees simply get absorbed in their particular team or job activity and lose sight of their very real connection with the financial performance of their company. Even finance majors and MBAs can leave the big-picture viewpoint in their old textbooks once their job activities consume them.

A common step, for an active open-book branch manager for instance, is explaining the region's plans in detail, and how the tactics of the branch contribute to the strategy for the region. In companies with traditional management, this link to the big picture is assumed to be understood by employees and therefore not explained in detail.

WRONG!

Don't assume the big picture is clear just because employees are bright or have been around for a while. Managers are usually surprised by what people don't know about the businesses of which they are a part. And even when they know the business, don't assume that they keep a proper focus. It is shockingly easy to lose sight of the macro goals and get caught up in details that turn people and teams in the wrong direction. The remnants of bureaucratic specialization persist everywhere. Employees get "jobs" and often don't think beyond them unless a business-literate environment encourages them to do so.

How Important Is It to You to Be Open-Book?

There can be a risk for middle managers—how important is using open-book principles if they could cause you real trouble with the hierarchy? The phrase from consultant Gifford Pinchot, creator of intrapreneuring as a field and chief researcher on corporate renegades who buck the system and innovate in spite of the company, is a helpful guide: "It is better to be an unemployed intrapreneur than an unemployed bureaucrat." While this philosophy has appeal, it may not be practical for you. If you believe you might sustain serious harm or distress by being too bold, think carefully before taking risks.

Middle managers in companies with a tradition of keeping the strategic plan for managers' eyes only must make a choice about following, changing, or ignoring the tradition. Technology and market secrets must be protected from competitors, obviously, and so there is reason for caution in organizations.

But often an old practice of not trusting employees with information is the real culprit. Or, it is another carryover from the days of bureaucratic privilege—part of managers' status in the hierarchy is maintained by reserving information for certain levels. In the hands of immature managers, this privilege is reminiscent of kids taunting other kids on the playground, "I know something you don't know."

A positive trend has emerged in concert with the principles of empowerment—to share the business plan more broadly. But this practice is hardly universal. Many middle managers who share a plan reserved only for their level, or who practice and advocate other open-book practices without the support of higher-ups, track in the footsteps of intrapreneurs—those innovative souls known for creating new businesses inside companies. Intrapreneurs have always been leaders in asking for forgiveness rather than permission when it comes to sharing information.

The traditional rewards for being a good bureaucrat—security, guaranteed pensions, and predictable career ladders—are far less real than they once were. So erring on the side of openness with information, teaching the whole business, sharing what the hierarchy used to not share, may well be less risky than it appears.

So middle managers, if you want to share information that your company doesn't, don't be a martyr, but you may want to have your resume ready.

Practice the Principles

The steps to practicing open-book management for middle managers include the following:

1. Study the field so you know what you are about.
2. Assess how business-literate your department or team already is.
3. Involve your team.
4. Make a plan to train on financials and educate using the daily happenings in the business.
5. Execute and refine.

Use the overall guidelines described in Chapters 6 through 10 as your approach. It is a Demming-like think-do-check-act cycle that can be adapted to any size operation. You may do all the work with your team directly and not use an implementation team, and your plan may be very informal and flexible, but the same steps will work:

■ Thinking it through and training to get it started.
■ Implementing systems that can survive even if you are not there to keep them going.

The adoption of open-book management thinking requires a shift in self-image. You are now less of a manager and more of a business coach. You are watching process and outcomes more than you are watching people. The following five steps will help you get started:

1. *The first step to implementing from the middle is to understand what you are talking about*. Think carefully through what you've been hearing or reading about open-book management and ask yourself some questions:

> What would an information-rich, financially attuned department look like?
>
> How can I learn about it and teach my team?
>
> What open-book practices should I start with (e.g., teaching financials) and which will have to come later (e.g., pay for performance)?

While you are thinking about answers to these questions, read informative articles (listed in the Bibliography and being published regularly), watch videotapes, go to seminars, and fill in the pieces of the puzzle that are missing for you.

2. *Assess the level of business literacy in your department using the four dimensions systems as a guideline*. The systems analysis on numbers know-how, communication, rewards, and leadership will give you a baseline to work from. It is useful to get an external coach, a consultant, to help you with this stage if you have the budget. His or her analysis can help you stay objective and see what options exist for starting business-literacy practices.

Find out what information is available in your company that may not be used, or formatted so people can use it. Ask yourself, What is missing for my team, what do I need to learn more about, how can my team positively impact the critical numbers of the company?

This baseline establishing process can adapt to your style, budget, department size, and organizational culture. You can make it official through an assessment task force, or you can be informal, walk around, observe, and ask some questions.

But what you can't afford to not do is think. The assessment has the following goals:

> To gain a clear picture of your team's strengths and how to use them.

To identify the financial and business education your group needs.

To look for some business opportunities that your group can pursue to contribute to the financial health and performance of your company—accomplishments that can be measured and celebrated.

3. *Involve your immediate team early on for full education, buy-in, and the contributions only they can make.* If your team has helped with the assessment, then you are already on your way. If you've been doing most of the thinking up to this point, it is time to pass around the articles, start discussing the principles, and send your team to the seminars.

Staff meetings are a great place to educate and involve the team. Several managers report on articles that are passed around, or take the chapters of a book like this one, one chapter at a time, and discuss them over several staff meetings in succession. Have a different team member be responsible for leading the discussion at the meetings and observe what the discussions bring up:

How do these principles apply to us?

What barriers exist in our operations from doing much of this?

How do our values, systems, goals, and practices currently support going in the direction of business literacy?

Once the team gets involved in these type of discussions, it isn't long before the training question for the next step will emerge:

What do we need to know, and get trained on, about the business and the financials so we can be an open-book department?

4. *Design and deliver training that will enable the group to interpret the numbers, see the big picture, and start to have huddles.* Use the guidelines in Section II, especially Chapter 10, for this important

step. Remember, you need to set training objectives first—once you do that, then the training itself will be easy to design.

Legitimate training objectives might include:

Map your team's line of sight to the company's financial statements.

Be able to read the annual report and understand where the department makes its contributions.

Understand the cost system.

Learn the various budget categories.

Be able to construct a business case, with net present value analysis (an analytical process accountants regularly use) so that departmental requests for budget increases have a better chance of approval.

Construct scorecards that track current progress and that have a section to forecast future performance against the plan.

Prepare all employees for huddles, using scorecards that tie customer satisfaction to financial outcomes.

Use external vendors for the training where they can help, and have them customize to your business and department. And use your own in-house experts to teach what they know, including the folks not on your immediate team (e.g., experts in finance) so that the training is specific.

5. *Execute your huddles, using financial measures, and have your team forecast the numbers they own on the scorecard.* Give your team time to practice the huddles—the last part of the training can be a mock-huddle where employees get used to the idea of having numbers to forecast against a budget—and expect the need for lots of practice.

Your current staff meetings are your best huddle opportunities. Use them and incorporate the huddle principles rather than starting new meetings. These first huddles will be very important for the tone they set and the roles people play. In fact, they become crucial events for you, as a middle manager, to exercise player-coach leadership. The learning and the accountability you drive through the focus of the meetings will determine the success of the main huddle and the prehuddles your team is holding with their staffs.

As always, look for what you can celebrate, reward, and have fun with, so that the numbers come alive and stories of a department of business thinkers start to get told. These stories become the system for conveying the heart and soul of an open-book department.

Use That "Damn Budget"

Instead of the excitement of keeping score in the daily competition to perform financially, most employees in companies without business literacy don't learn the numbers of their company, don't keep score, and don't have a clue about the value they bring to their company's performance. Most often, they haven't been asked to learn financials and can't track their work to the income statement or cash flow statement they impact. This is what many middle managers can change.

More often, what these employees *do* relate to is the ever-present bastard child of the income statement—the budget, the oft-cursed, typically grueling exercise of corporate gaming and sandbagging to fight over resources. The scorekeepers for the full income statement are in upper management and finance, traditionally, and the rest of the middle managers target their work activities to some subset of the budget. Quota is the individualized budget number for salespeople to drive toward, and a set of expense categories exist for the rest.

It is no wonder departments go in different directions, especially when managers advance their individual careers by reaching their department, and not companywide, numbers. This combination of budget-specific numbers and career-climbing is a ready-made prescription for "me-only" thinking and posturing.

Middle managers can break down this dangerous blind spot that blocks good business thinking and teamwork by opening up and educating their groups on the budget. Explaining the expense categories, their makeup, their history even, helps in telling the story of the business. The budget is the primary tool to use to create initial line of sight to the company financials.

At Syncrude Canada Ltd., an oil sands mining company, managers take their budgets very seriously. The term they use to manage the resources they are accountable for is rich in meaning—"steward to the budget." As Syncrude deepened its journey into business literacy, one of their discoveries was that the budget had created too narrow a mind-set for many managers, and the missing piece was the connection of the budget to the company financials. Once employees made that connection, line of sight to the big picture was clear and business thinking took precedence over functional thinking. Figure 11.1 shows how Syncrude's line of sight could be pictured and described to the employees in the extraction plant.

Middle-Manager Open-Book Moves

A frontline supervisor at a Fortune 100 plant with 1,200 people read about open-book management when the head of human resource development handed him some articles. He got very enthused and within a few weeks became the biggest advocate for open-book management among his peers and upper managers, a team of about 25, all of whom had been handed the same articles to read. Instead of waiting for his training department and upper management to make a full commitment to open-book practices, he moved ahead with training. He knew that upper management was so busy that it would take a while for them to commit to sharing and using the numbers. "My plant manager is very committed to quality and teams," he said, "so I knew that he knew this was a step in the right direction. But corporate had us into at least 10 other initiatives in safety, quality, and everything else, so I knew he wouldn't have the time."

He asked the cost accountants to teach his 30 production people how the cost system works—in this case a standard

Figure 11.1 Syncrude Basic Literacy Model

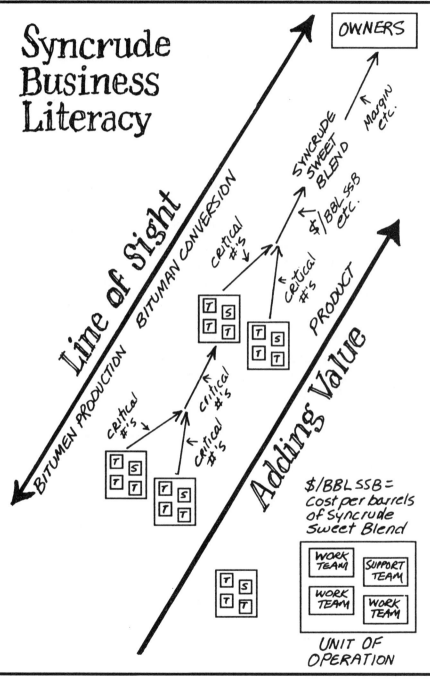

system, common in manufacturing for tracking costs and setting productivity and financial targets. One thing this middle manager didn't like about the status quo was the barrier that existed between production people and the cost accountants in finance. By asking for training for his team, he created a needed connection that would help both teams meet their goals for the companies. After the training, he turned over production forecasting to his team, coaching them with what he knew. In the first quarter, he saw cost figures better than they had ever achieved previously. And he let his team know how proud they should be of their work.

From his line supervisor job, he significantly advanced open-book management for others to emulate.

Pam Wagner, a staff manager of a training function of Sprint, was able to use opening up the budgets in a very helpful way for her peers. A midyear budget review was coinciding with the divisionwide open-book training spearheaded by her department. So, the questions arose: What are the numbers telling us and how can we positively impact the numbers?

Pam and her team found a previously unnoticed positive variance in the financials—the division was not using its allocated budget for training, so it appeared there was money going to the bottom line. At first the team was very excited at seeing thousands of dollars in profits. But then they realized these were prepaid dollars of the use-them-or-lose-them variety, based on the projections the managers had put in the plan.

Pam's team alerted the division managers to the potential waste of this resource in plenty of time to schedule and use the valuable training support they had already paid for through the remainder of the year. She ensured the lesson in open-book planning for all the managers was not lost—make your projections and watch them carefully. And they celebrated their accomplishment at the next staff huddle with some "way-to-go's" and fun storytelling of how their manager/colleagues responded.

Both of these middle managers went about applying the principles of open-book management:

■ Seek out ways to make a financial contribution to the company.

■ Learn specifically how lack of business and financial know-how limits performance.

■ Use a financial lens to set to a big picture goal, increasing line of sight.

■ Analyze "the story" behind the possible improvement and educate the team on the possibilities.

■ Take ownership with a plan of action and measurable results.

■ Involve the team early for joint ownership.

■ Look for ways to celebrate.

■ Be a player-coach, promoting learning and having fun.

Questions, Not Necessarily Answers

Throughout the implementation of open-book practices, management can expect questions. Lots of questions. They should seek out and encourage these questions, wherever they come from, about the business, the numbers, and about how and why decisions are made.

But as tempting as it may be to answer these questions immediately, it is better not to answer them all fully right away. The questions are a great way to entice employees into learning. A simple question like "Why did our costs go up this month?" can be answered with a "What do *you* think the reasons were?" And if the answer isn't immediately apparent, provide some time for people to think it over.

Once people catch on to the process, they like to do their own learning and direct their own educations. The joy of self-directed discovery fuels ongoing learning. Leaders need to support, listen, and inquire, but they need to refrain from fixing it all by themselves. Getting the whole team to offer ideas is part of the leadership role. Open-book management is all about wrestling with a reality in which not all questions have answers.

Recruit Others and Network

Once middle managers have established a base of open-book practices in their area they will likely, by way of example, already begin influencing their peers, internal customers, and supplies. Some managers will start to inquire about the success of the team's work, which is a great opportunity to discuss what you know and provide articles and books for their reading. And, people being people, others may get jealous of successes and the accolades coming to the open-book team.

At this point, open-book pioneering middle managers have several choices that revolve around risk and visibility, and the passion for improving the business through business literacy:

■ Whom, outside their area, do they want to recruit into more open-book practices?

■ What sponsors do they need higher up in their own area of the organization, or in finance, human resources, and so on, who can help spread the word and protect the experiments from corporate attacks?

■ How visible should they be—will high visibility trigger negative reactions and likely cause more resistance than help?

Here is where the art of leadership takes over, and there are no manuals with easy answers. In one Fortune 500 company, a strong early open-book advocate was a director, a middle manager, who, facing obstacles to spreading open-book practices in his immediate division, did a stellar job of "selling" business literacy to several other divisions through his network of peers. He was like water, flowing where he could and not trying to go upstream.

The best way to recruit sponsors, and to educate up, is to show them results. Nothing speaks more strongly to senior managers than measurable improvements. When the positive results are obvious, then you can tell those in need of being educated, and who are potential sponsors you need, *how* you achieved the results. Once you have their interest, pass on the article or book that you think would make the right initial impact, or invite them to a huddle where they can see the teams managing their own numbers.

Collaborating with your colleagues to spread the practices will magnify your efforts. And it can be fun. Offer your friends help, and don't set yourself up to become an easy target for naysayers. Timing and sponsorship is everything if you want to promote the practices. Don't be too eager—earn the right to toot the open-book horn.

Remember the words of Buckminster Fuller when it comes to recruiting and networking: "Never show fools unfinished work."

Use the Recognition Tools You Have and Make Up Some More

For the middle managers implementing open-book systems, no-kidding ownership recognition practices provide many options. In the setting in which you work, the compensation and incentive programs may be seriously broken. The incentives may be tearing departments apart, have built-in injustices, or are rewarding short-term results. Do you have to throw up your hands and endure if this is the case?

Maybe.

Maybe not.

The good news is that with some imagination, a degree of risk-taking, and enthusiastic follow-through on your part, you can accomplish a lot in the area of recognition that employees will really appreciate.

Books and articles on this topic are everywhere.* The key is to live the open-book principle: If people are improving performance and business results, they deserve rewards, both financial and psychological.

If you have used the budget to start teaching the business, have created a line of sight, and the team is working for the

---

* Bob Nelson, 1001 *Ways to Reward Your Employees*, New York: Workman Publishing, 1994, is a recent book on this subject.

good of the company, then set up some celebrations and rewards, from casual days to football tickets to flowers.

Whatever the team members find of value is worth a try.

Open-Book Performance Management

The traditional paradigm for managing performance for middle managers is feedback on behavior, rewards for good performance, and lots of skill training. The peak, or maybe it's more of a trough, of this performance paradigm for bureaucratic, top-down, management-control-less-than-able-employees, was a kind of effectiveness training, quite popular in the 1970s and 1980s and still around today. *Based on models of parenting—controlling the behavior of children in a caring and respectful way—this training*

Open Books at Work: 7. Yellow Roses and Pay Increases

At a travel agency that was anything but open-book in its approaches, a middle manager who knew about no-kidding ownership principles and hoped to increase business literacy wanted to reward her hard-working group. They had just gotten through their busiest month, had no idea how much profit they had created for the company, but knew they had done well.

The pay raises they had received 3 months ago had the usual short-term effect, appreciated for a check or two and then forgotten. And even the appreciation wasn't universal because the pay was still slightly behind the other agencies in their city.

The manager took a little cash out of her spending budget, went to a flower shop, bought 8 dozen long-stem yellow roses for her all-female team, and wrote each a personal note of appreciation for making the month go so well. Her business literacy lesson was fundamental—when the customers win, we win.

In her words, "I was hearing about those long-stem roses for a long, long time. It did more for morale with my little group than the pay raises just a few months earlier. I think it was the surprise of it all that had such an impact, and the personal touch."

promoted communication techniques for middle managers that resembled the approach an ideal parent would use with a child. Many middle managers approach performance problems with this kind of background still in mind. This was the ultimate benevolent paternalism of the hierarchy, and the direct polar opposite of business literacy.

Good middle managers understand the limits in this approach—while feedback is a learning requirement, appraisals and ranking are an insult. And how many classes on communication skill training can someone go to? Skill training is always important, but the permanent changes in thinking and attitude evoked by business literacy take a different tack. It assumes adulthood and partnership with all employees. It addresses many less than optimal behaviors that may have looked like lack of skill but are actually symptoms of specialist thinking, by changing the employees' mind-set about what their work entails. Poor communication with another department may be more the result of employees not seeing the business importance of coordinating efforts with the department than a communication skill deficiency that employees need to get "fixed."

Open-book performance management is not opposed to the best skill-building models of enriching human performance, but it *is* opposed to the worst, such as benevolent parenting. Middle managers using open-book practices work with people as equals, and manage performance, including their own, through the systems they put in place to create business thinking.

Keep Cool and Other Ways to Avoid Pitfalls

The initiators of open-book management, middle managers and others, often will get frustrated and impatient. It's natural and normal to want to move fast, bring people on board quickly, and remove all the roadblocks to making all the systems work well from the beginning. Some roadblocks will not, in fact, be quickly overcome. But roadblocks don't prevent creative and persistent action. In the ongoing drama of everyday business life, there are wins and losses, achievements, and disappointments. Only persistence will win out.

So stay at it and set a reasonable pace—too fast and there are no roots, too slow and there is no momentum. See your work as experimentation. The business literacy initiators at Syncrude don't like the phrase "pilots," which can fail. They prefer "garden" projects, which can grow for a while, be uprooted, and planted elsewhere in another season. This is a healthy perspective when introducing open-book management into an uncertain or risky environment.

Don't underestimate the political arena that you, as a middle manager, operate in. Each person, including you, has an investment in things being a certain way, with systems and relationships being stable. Use the "stay connected" principle (see Chapter 8) to relate to others so they feel less threatened by the changes you advocate. Allow those who *are* threatened and defensive to provide advice and input so they can be part of the project: People support what they help create. Ask your senior managers to teach what they know about the business to you and your team. Help them become mentors in spite of themselves, if necessary.

Open-book practices tip the scale in the direction of business victories.

People achieve. Performance improves. The whole operation continues to get better with time. But business literacy does not promise or provide a panacea. It is hard work, and there will be trying times. As one manager put it, "All change efforts, if they are really trying to make significant changes, look like a complete failure at least once."

With constant effort to reach the goals and consistent repetition of open-book practices, a competitive edge of empowered, business-smart employees will be realized. It takes real professionals to keep at it, and to get back up when they are down because the progress isn't apparent. Some days, holding onto the vision is all there is to do. Most days, for middle managers who have become leaders, that's enough.

Section III

❦ ❦ ❦ ❦

Keeping It Going

Most companies don't fail for lack of talent or strategic vision. They fail for lack of execution—the routine blocking and tackling that great companies consistently do well and always strive to do better.

T. J. Rogers
Cypress Semiconductor

The rollout of open-book management relies totally on the preparation and education developed throughout the first four phases described in the previous section and chapters. The last two phases—implementation and on-going improvement—are covered in this section.

Four phases are devoted to preparation and planning and two to implementation for a simple reason: The enormous shift in employees and management thinking that open-book practices require demands preparation and thoroughness. Open-book companies, like Rome and even Dubuque, it is rumored, were not built in a day.

In reality, the rollout and implementation phase, phase 5, (see Figure 6.1) is joined at the hip with the on-going improvement specified in phase 6. The rollout will come to a dead stop, and business literacy will become another program-of-the-month archived in the "do-you-remember-when?" company memory if a lack of commitment to keeping it going occurs.

As cited earlier, the six phases are meant to assist in the thinking and the preparation for intelligently introducing open-book management so companies can experience more predictable and positive outcomes. But executing the six phases won't happen in a neat and linear fashion. You can be smart implementing open-book practices, and then smart leaves off and true grit takes over. As is the case with doing anything worthwhile, from creating a new line of services to changing the billing system, determination to carry it through salvages most efforts when the setbacks and discouragement occur.

Sticking to a clear vision of the end result and using that vision to encourage and support the entire company, as has been stressed throughout, is the sine qua non for the development of a business literate company.

During a planning session in Dublin, Ohio, at Schrock Cabinet Company, its wise and visionary president Merv Plank, addressed his implementation team when they hit the roadblock called "too little time and too many priorities." The team had been moving along with some excitement in their planning when the reality of additional work on top of already very busy schedules dampened their enthusiasm.

Merv did not deny or make light of the issue, but just as importantly he did not accept that current priorities should stop the effort. Instead, he calmly laid out, again, the vision of the future of the company, its growth challenges and how the company would need to respond. He articulated how open-book management, by mobilizing peoples' intelligence, would be key in helping the company achieve its objectives.

> We are aware of the challenge that needs to be met in achieving our aggressive growth goals. We'll need everyone to be pulling in the same direction.
>
> First, we want everyone to focus on the customer. Second, I ask that each of you personally assess the use of your time. Third, don't lose faith. The challenges are tough, but keep the goal in mind and believe in our ability to get there. Fourth, I need you to be real champions, to be ready to lead the way.

By inviting the team to take a fresh look at some of the activities they were already pursuing, Merv was raising the level of thinking in a player-coach leader fashion. By asking for some ROI thinking, he suggested that some pet projects and activities may not be that important in light of Big Picture goals.

Merv did not belittle or lecture. He listened and posed a challenge, setting the stage for further learning. His tone was one of respect and care, and his message was honest and put forth a call to think and do at a higher level.

The remainder of this section deals with the "sticky wickets" of implementation, like resistance, and the culture-changing power of participative planning (Chapter 12), information-sharing (Chapter 13), and rewards (Chapter 14). This section returns us to the two power systems that drive open-book management, once leadership and financial knowledge are in place—Intensive Huddles for communication and No-kidding Ownership for motivation.

The phrase "It's tough to get to the top and it is tougher to stay there" holds true for open-book systems. It is tough to get them started and it is tougher to keep improving them.

Open-book management is a philosophy. It is a set of practices. Like any professional practice, it needs constant, relentless improvement, honing, adjusting, and gobs of attention, often when the people who started it don't feel like giving gobs of anything. This holds true for planning, huddles and rewards, and leadership.

But what will make business literacy thrive in spite of the difficulties is our capacity to learn, to risk, and to achieve. Put something at risk that holds importance to employees at any level, show them how they can affect the outcome, and watch attitudes and energy shift in the direction of accountability. Humans are wired for open-book challenges.

Doing What Will Keep It Going

Anyone who leads an open-book effort needs to understand the many factors that make for targeted and knowledgeable work by all employees. Business literacy operates at many levels with numerous ingredients. Lots of things can happen or not happen to hinder or even negate the effort. Business literacy is about managing the real business of the business, with all its ups and downs. So every person at every level in the company or division needs to stay alert, with their informed brains turned on and fully functioning, to create more wins than losses.

Figure SIII.1 provides a summary with which managers and teams can assess whether they have the right mix of ingredients to make business literacy work for all employees. Business literacy ranges from microlevel job-specific know-how to macrolevel industry knowledge and technology strategy. The ideal is for player-coach leaders to provide all the ingredients to create a lavish, stimulating learning and communication environment, so entrepreneurial teams know:

■ What to do and why within the context of their business and its goals.

■ How to do it.

Figure SIII.1   Business Literacy Ingredients

Business Literacy Ingredient	Related Dimension	Barrier if the Ingredient Is Missing
Vision and Values The why of it all–the purpose and meaning of the company and the principles that guide it.	Player-coach leadership	Confusion, lack of ideals, no tie to customer or environment
Goals and Plans The what and the how—specific targets and strategies and tactics for achieving them.	Critical numbers know-how	Energetic chaos
Business Knowledge The fundamental understanding of the business—how and what it sells, the competition, drivers and re-strainers, understanding the financials.		Anxiety and ignorance
Job Skill The know-how and capacity to carry out the specific tasks on team, be it marketing, machining, service customers, or programming		Motivated incompetence
Measures and Feedback The lavish communication of com-pany data on the big picture (market share, competitive data) and at the team and individual job level (stan-dards, budgets, costing, sales and service) with good scorecards to measure progress	Intensive huddle system	Lack of learning and improvement Decisions made from out-dated assumptions
Teams and Teamwork Small group synergy for problem-solving, and across-group coordina-tion for process improvements.		Lack of synergy and innovation
Recognition and Rewards The intrinsic and extrinsic rewards that create psychological ownership, fun, and motivation.	No-kidding ownership	Who cares attitude
Participation and Shared Decisions Decision making at large and small scales to bring the best ideas to bear and to tap and nurture team and individual intelligence.		Lack of buy-in and limited learning

■ How to access the necessary resources.

■ How to coordinate with other teams.

■ What they'll get out of it.

■ What the risks are for doing it, and not doing it.

As open-book companies forge the mold for the new business paradigms, eight ingredients for ongoing business literacy will be fundamental. Look at Figure SIII.1 closely; it tells you what happens when a company has seven ingredients, but lacks one. When all eight are present, a company of businesspeople will flourish. The old saw "If the only tool you have is a hammer, you tend to treat everything like a nail" contains much wisdom. Business literacy implementers need at least eight tools, or ingredients, in the four open-book systems, to get the results they want.

Dealing with Resistance

The discussion of maintaining open-book management would not be realistic without addressing the almost ever-present factor of resistance. Even if a management team is moving ahead on all or several of the fronts listed in Figure SIII.1, they can and will meet resistance.

This phenomenon—at best a reluctance to embrace change, and at worst a colossal digging in of the heels—is often both easy to see and to understand. Resistance to anything new and to any additional work is common in many businesses where new programs get introduced and fade away and in the many companies where downsizing has instilled fear or numbness. In these settings, employees at all levels are cynical and tired of feeling used.

In relatively small work systems, veteran employees and managers with high awareness can predict where the resistance will come from based on past experience. But in all environments, more subtle, disguised forms of resistances may surface and take on energy when certain conditions are right. Going-through-the-motions compliance, covert resistance by sticking with old behavior, or complaining to peers but not to management are just a few of the subtle behaviors that mask reluctance to change.

Jack Knuth, retired CEO of the Allied Signal plant in Kansas City, became a student of resistance as he changed the culture at the large manufacturing facility he managed. "People don't want to appear resistant, especially to upper management, and they don't want to admit they are scared or just feeling put upon by the demands of what the work ahead will bring. So what they get very good at is creating fairly accurate intellectual arguments against the change. Knowing what to accept as valid and where to sense the fear or even laziness, is a big part of managing resistance."

In most cases, when managers introduce open-book methods, they should expect and plan for some resistance. And with some skill and finesse, it is possible to minimize the impact of the resistance. In most cases, the rule of thumb is that if you attack or meet resistance head-on, you'll get creamed and be overpowered, as well as diverted from your original goal. So instead of going head-on, go with the resistance and see what it teaches you.

Resistance is natural and in many cases can be useful. Listening to instead of countering negative comments shines light on legitimate concerns that weren't noticed by those who saw only benefits to business literacy. A good salesperson will use resistance, even surface it, to get to the real issues of the customer and increase the chance of a real buying decision. Similarly, managers can use resistance to learn about the underlying, perhaps more subtle issues that are nonetheless real and important to recognize. When Patagonia management got going too fast with its open-book efforts, they took a good look at its process, and started over. The resistance they met taught them to slow down and let the process take root.

Resistance will generally come from the parts of enterprise that are most vulnerable emotionally:

- Those who are most tired and see no upside.
- Those most likely to lose people.
- Those who are targets to gain the most work and the most pressure.

■ Those with the least effective leaders, including bosses who spray their problems and headaches all over the team.

In general, this vulnerability is apparent in people or teams who have, or think they have, the most to lose. This is why middle managers often resist empowerment or reengineering that takes out overhead, them included. If the company does not have enough growth to absorb people, is there any wonder enthusiasm wanes?

Pride and Status

Some employees in the Fortune 1000 companies look at the smaller companies that have adopted open-book management practices, and they initially reject the lessons there:

"Oh, those small companies may be able to share financials, but *we* can't. Our systems are too messed up," or "We are too big," or "We have too much going on."

Companies in one industry will look at another industry and think: "Well of course business literacy works in manufacturing, but not in a service companies with all these degreed people running around."

While some of this is honest intellectual questioning, usually, more than a small amount of the refusal to see what can be learned from smaller companies and other industries is the sense of emotional loss and the admission that others have been doing something very worthwhile a lot better. The felt loss is one of self-esteem that comes with false pride and complacency.

At one Baldrige-winning big company, the company president relates how the humbling experience for the senior team came when they realized they were part of the problem. The emotional downer, however, released a positive energy that had been blocked in defensive resistance, and the real learning kicked in at the moment they could see the truth of the situation. By dropping their resistance, they had created a collective "teachable moment."

Managers who have been responsible for interpreting variances relied on by others may react to the loss of status and importance that open-book management brings when everyone can interpret variances. They may not recognize their own resistance for what it is and put some rationale on it such as: "We must be careful about how much information we give to people who don't know how to use it."

The tricky part is that there is a portion of truth in these rationales. It takes both agreeing with this truth and showing managers that the benefits outweigh the risks to help them think more and resist less. Loss of status is the real issue here, not open-book management. Going with the resistance can replace the status of "you are the only one who knows this, therefore you are special,"—a fundamental, not negative, human need—with the status of "you are the best one to *help teach* this, therefore you are still special." Countering resistance with lectures on why status is not important cannot accomplish this goal.

If most employees accept the current company existence as good, or at least adequate, in fulfilling their work expectations, then a new *anything*, open-book management included, is usually perceived as threatening and is met with some degree of resistance by most managers, or employees, or both. To counteract this process, many organizations in the 1980s (especially in the area of quality) experimented with employee involvement techniques—adopting the theory that if employees are involved in the change initiative, they can more readily see the value at the end of the change and can figure out for themselves how they can benefit.

A critical benefit of involving employees at all levels, including the union if there is one, is their truly becoming a part of something rather than being on the receiving end of management mandates. When people are dictated to, they experience a form of being helpless. That feeling state results in several responses:

■ *Outright anger:* "Oh, yeah? See if open-books are going to make a difference."
■ *Energyless, compliant behavior without real commitment:* "Sure, I'll go to this huddle and pretend I'm on top of my numbers."

■ *Lip service with no behavior change*: "Maybe if I go on vacation, management will have forgotten all about this stuff when I return."

This helpless experience has happened enough times in some companies that even when management involves employees early on in the change, the resistance response is so automatic that employees can't and won't detect the benefits or opportunity in the change. In this kind of environment, the dependency of the helpless now has real power and the rollout of any new program or initiative will be rocky and unpleasant. The leader's task at this point is to keep recruiting a few at a time until a critical mass of positive response and experience can be built up.

In some companies, employees have jumped in quickly and often to participate and make necessary adaptations, only to see the programs or initiatives peter out. The programs have faltered because they likely met some resistance after the initial "honeymoon" period, or because they were more fluff than substance. As the fun wore off, the consultant moved on, the boss retired, and the promised benefits didn't accumulate, it became too challenging to uproot the old familiar pattern and to continue to be energetic in pursuing the new. Often, some managers and employees experienced a loss of status or recognition as the new program shifted attention to a different part of the organization. When that happens, the change is not just to be avoided, but ignored to death.

Managing Resistance

Determined managers create their own ways of managing in and through resistance. Instead of going head-on, which has to be done occasionally, they generally outflank, outlast, and outsmart the resistance until it withers away. Preparing yourself by anticipating the expected spots and forms of resistance is an absolute necessity. Remember the following how-to's as you consider your options when encountering open-book resistance.

Revisit the Vision

To those who see the business value of business literacy, there usually isn't much resistance. Likewise for those who can see how they will personally and professionally benefit. These employees will adapt to the changes that open-book practices bring to their environment.

If people are resisting, it is often because they do not see the vision or understand the big picture. Review the open-book vision that you and your colleagues have created for the future of your company. Is it specific? practical? compelling?

If the answers to these questions are yes, then evaluate not just how you have communicated the vision but how employees have heard it. Has there been so much other "noise" in the work environment—rumors, bad news, politics, mistrust, other initiatives—that others haven't really paid attention to the open-book promise for the company? If that is the case, craft another communication effort to capture attention, involve the key players, and get past the resistance.

Start Small with Discrete Business Literacy Challenges

You needn't go after the winner's purse right out of the gate. One tactic for dealing with resistance is to work with a department, or with a team. Give them a goal to shoot for—one expense or cost item perhaps—and show them how their work impacts the bottom line. Then challenge them to meet the goal and watch what happens. If they respond, be ready with another goal for the original team and go enlist another group, educating as you go.

Listen and Let People Vent

Listening to those who see the downside, like the work ahead, can help to take some of the steam out of the emotional load behind the stated concern and it can bring new insight to the project. Preaching or arguing can create more resistance because people search for even more evidence to support their views, often creating fanciful anecdotal evidence: "and I heard of this company in New Mexico and they tried open-book and all the employees quit and the competitors got all the information and stole the patents and . . ."

Listening takes time and work but usually pays off in the long run. Its power is consistently undervalued by managers, perhaps because listening demands skill, patience, and sincerity to do it well. And the payoff to the listener can also be considerable. In one open-book company where there was middle manager resistance to an aggressive sales plan, top management decided there was substance in the argument they were listening to. They lowered the goal by 15%, cut expenses, and weathered the downturn in sales that came much more easily.

Create "What If " Scenarios

Begin informal conversations with the resisters that focus on better results of all kinds for the future. Such conversations get people out of the "ain't it awful . . . look what they are doing to me" mind-set and create a sense of possibility and positive influence on the future. The intent is to stir up some "just suppose" thinking.

It isn't necessary, at the beginning, to tie these speculative conversations directly to open-book management. If the CFO, Charlie, is resisting, speak in his terms: "What if we were able to respond to a competitor's move in less than 2 weeks with a well-thought-through cost-effective response? What if we could do that, Charlie? What would that be worth to you, and to the company?"

After Charlie has started to articulate this "just suppose" scenario, picturing the benefits of the new capability in the organization, it's possible to make the tie to open-book management.

If the company has a recent history of poor follow-through on new approaches, then the employees have something real to resist when open-book management shows up. Leaders will have to ride out the history with persistence. And when they eventually create an environment, the died-in-the-wool resisters may have to leave—they won't be able to adapt to a company of businesspeople.

Chapter 12

❦ ❦ ❦ ❦

Open-Book
Participative Planning

Business lives and breathes the cycle of financial months, quarters, and years. Budgets are monthly expense and revenue tracking devices that roll up into quarters and years. A rotation of the sun becomes a fiscal year, a moonspin a financial month, and the four seasons are the four quarters that drive Wall Street's eagerly anticipated earnings reports. Commercial humanity and fiscal cycles mimic tribal humanity and lunar/solar rhythms (see Figure 12.1).

Businesses tuned into the deep currents of open-book management make the most out of the repetition of the weekly, monthly, quarterly, and yearly business cycles. They put the plan and company goals in front of everyone continuously. As employees participate in the cycles by tracking the numbers, they learn the nuances of the business and the importance of their numbers, even those that at first look insignificant. Open-book management regularly and repetitively exposes employees to the many and varied influences that affect the business.

With this exposure, employees closely follow the action of the business and make better business judgments by getting at those "devils in the details." This level of know-how cannot be sustained without systems that ensure the discipline that comes with repetition.

Madison Avenue knows the power of repetition. Why does Wendy's advertise more than once a month? So you will unconsciously turn your car into a Wendy's for one of Dave Thomas's latest creations (and you don't even like burgers). The jingles we

Figure 12.1

DILBERT reprinted by permission of United Features Syndicate, Inc.

have heard over and over are stuck forever in the neurological chemistry of memory, keeping even the earliest of TV ads still fresh in our minds. Early boomers can stump younger colleagues by asking them what "LSMFT" means.

Finish these sentences:

A stitch in time saves _____.

A penny saved is a penny _____.

Filling in the blanks is easy because you've heard the phrases so many times.

Business-literate companies know that people without finance and costing backgrounds need lots of repetition to "get it"—to learn the financial language and its meaning for the company's business. Open-book management employs the same simple but effective technique of repetition to focus all employees on the business of the business. Repetition is a gift of structure and reinforcement for employees so that the common language necessary for the business to run can be spoken and understood by all.

The repetition stems naturally from the planning cycle, itself repetitious because business years follow business years follow business years.

Using the Plan for Involvement and Deep Learning

Companies can and often do get early gains from opening their books and bonuses, but sustaining the effort over the long haul means using the planning cycle of a business to engage employees evermore deeply in creating the future of the business.

In a pattern that is all too typical of most companies, the results of a large company survey by an open-book design team showed that less than 10 percent of all employees saw the business plan document, and even fewer used it for decision making. And the problems with planning stretch much beyond that. Many employees resent the planning process because it ties up valuable time needed to do "the real work." They have come to believe that whatever input they do have, if any, to the plan, is not really heard, or that politics between the top managers has more to do with the plan than employee input.

Advanced open-book companies reverse these realities by using the tools of planning to involve all employees in creating the blueprint for the future. Since most employees don't touch or see the business plan, participative planning opens up new possibilities for real employee contribution. Planning creates the sense of obligation and responsibility for short- and long-term financial and customer results.

Asking all employees to develop opinions and contribute them engages employees' intelligence and sends them the all-important messages—your thoughts matter; everyone participates, has a stake, and takes both wins and losses in the course of business. But it's more than a message. Without using participative planning to tap the local intelligence throughout the organization, those closest to the customer and operational and administrative problems can't seize the opportunities to make major improvements.

Participative planning also creates enormous potential for learning the big picture. This is one reason it takes more than a single business year to do open-book management well. *There is so much for everyone formerly out of the planning and learning loops to learn about the business.* The yearly business planning cycle allows everyone to step back from the intense action orientation of the job and to reflect on accomplishments, problems, opportunities—to think more strategically *about* the system rather than taking action *in* it.

The us/them mentality that has plagued companies since the beginning—the boss/subordinate, owner/worker, management/nonmanagement, sales/operations splits—will never go away. But it can take its proper place in the background while the main business of the business—serving customers and making money, and creating jobs and improving the quality of life for a society—can stay in the foreground. A sound participative planning process starts and maintains the learning and communication that drives the lack of understanding and big-picture business perspectives out of a company.

Steps in Open-Book Participative Planning

Participative open-book business planning follows a process similar to this:

1. The Sales Forecast
   The sales team put together the forecast using their best information and intuition on customers, new products, competition, and history. Some companies can poll their customers' needs to verify upcoming trends.

   All employees comment and have input into the sales numbers using their best judgment from their all-important and different vantage points. Yes, it is a radical notion that others besides the president and sales and marketing might have good input into a sales and revenue projection.

2. The Budget and Expense Forecast
   This is put together by all the departments and functions to support the sales forecast.

--- ❄ ❄ ❄ ❄ ---

Ode to the Genesis of Traditional Bureaucratic Planning

In the beginning was the Plan
and then came the assumptions
and the assumptions were without form
and the plan was completely without substance
and darkness was upon the faces of the workers.

And they spoke among themselves saying,
"It is a Crock, and it stinketh."
And the workers went to their Supervisors and sayeth,
"It is a pail of dung and none can abide the odor."
And the supervisors went to their managers and sayeth,
"It is a container of excrement, and it is very strong,
such that none may abide it."
And the managers went to their directors and sayeth,
"It is a vessel of fertilizer, and none may abide its strength."

And the directors spoke amongst themselves, saying one to
    another,
"It contains that which aids plant growth, and it is very
    strong."
And the directors went unto the Vice Presidents and sayeth to
    them,
"It promotes growth and is very powerful."
And the Vice Presidents went unto the President and sayeth
    unto him,
"The new plan will actively promote the growth and efficiency
    of this company, and these areas in particular."
And the President looked upon the Plan,
and saw that it was good, and the Plan became policy.

These forecasts are also spread around for comment so that
everyone who has a considered and informed opinion can
make his or her thoughts known. A capital plan is also put
in place at this time for those companies or those years
when capital outlay is necessary.

3. The Final Plan: Management puts the final plan together
   having heard all points of view, agreements, arguments, and
   debates, and makes their best informed collective guess.

The Sales Forecast

All business plans start with a sales and marketing plan, with accompanying revenue streams projected by months and the associated expenses for delivering those products and services that make up the streams.

Accordingly, the place to start with participative planning is with the sales forecast, which will be made by the sales team. But an important open-book principle has to be activated *early* in the forecasting cycle: Others who are impacted by and have informed opinions on sales need to have input. The key word is early; the week before Christmas, just as people are ready to rest and enjoy the holidays before the beginning of another fiscal and calendar year, is not a good time for a major disagreement to emerge between sales and customer service over which products to push and service.

Thorough participative planning can take from 3 to 6 months for companies doing annual plans. Longer than that and the process is a bureaucratic burden; shorter than that and important steps and judgments can be missed. An ample amount of time gives people time to dialogue, question assumptions, think and think again, so the sales projections can take in all the factors that affect customers' buying decisions.

The procedure to get the input from appropriate departments depends greatly on the company and its practices. Each company has its own decision-making style, and planning cycles take on the personality of company management. Whatever the style, *open-book planning creates involvement and democratizes the planning process.* That doesn't mean everything goes to a vote—this is not totally representative democracy necessarily—although on the right issues that can be a good idea. (A manager of a Chicago title office faced downsizing as the only option in a real estate downturn, and he had the employees vote on what measures to take to stay in the black. Through voluntary layoffs, going back to school, and part-time work, the employees voted themselves into the decisions that got them through the slump until business picked back up.)

Some companies, very much into democracy, take the route of full consensus. More commonly, management makes the final planning calls. If the managers have been true player-coach leaders, demonstrating stewardship and a concern for the long-term viability of the enterprise, frontline employees gladly give over the responsibility for the final calls on planning to upper management, knowing that this is why the leaders get paid.

Manco, the world-famous duct tape manufacturer, a value-added distributor and converter of adhesives and other retail products, has gone to a 6-month planning cycle to handle the shifts in their marketplace. Diego Perez-Stable, Manco's chief financial officer, describes how the 12-month outlook at this open-book company was just too long and became obsolete for their business: "We could be pretty accurate for the first 90 days out, and not too bad for the next 90 after that, but after 6 months the forecasts were just a crapshoot. . . . We used to be fortunate to get our budget together by the beginning of the fiscal year. We're working long and hard at planning and we're doing better, but we still have a long way to go for us to feel more on top of planning."

Manco has been vendor of the year for both Wal-Mart and K mart, and their aggressive growth strategies depended on everyone thinking entrepreneurially. "The last thing we needed was to have a real opportunity to move ahead on," reports Perez-Stable, "and then not have a team pursue it because it wasn't in the budget. That's one reason we went to a shorter planning cycle."

At Manco, the marketing team, those closest to the products, create a sales forecast, and the sales team, those closest to the customers, follow up with one of their own. Then they meet and reconcile their views, hash out the differences and come up with a set of revenue numbers for the next 6 months.

Then operations kicks in. "Our operations team plans the quickest of all," Perez-Stable says, "because they have to respond to promotions at our customers, ensure the right levels of inventory, or do the private label runs. They forecast expenses monthly against the plan." As point-of-sale information is collected instantaneously and across more products and customers, planning at Manco becomes more precise and quicker still. "That's where it's headed in our business," says Perez-Stable, "planning will come straight from our customers' data."

Every open-book company does it their way.

Springfield Remanufacturing Company (SRC) sends draft documents throughout the company for input. Their approach is to ask employees to focus on the company's weaknesses. Jack Stack and his team will make a plan to attack weaknesses identified and agreed on by SRC employees and board of directors. An open-book division of a large company emphasizes customer service goals that will distinguish them from the competition. They ask all employees yearly for strategies on customer service, in addition to the continuous improvement ideas generated throughout the year, as their means of creating a marketing advantage.

The point in open-book planning is clear: Encourage everyone to think about the whole business. Allow input and dialogue. Tap everyone's intelligence. Connect all different viewpoints to common unifying goals. With participative planning, a key principle of no-kidding ownership kicks in long before rewards and recognition: *People support that which they help create.* Participative planning creates psychological ownership long before an employee-owner, in a company with an ESOP, sees his or her stock value go up.

The Budget and Expense Forecast

While the dialogue on sales continues, each department has to put together its own budget. This is where middle managers throughout the companies take over. They and other veteran player-coach leaders teach the less experienced troops the nuances of the cost and expense process they "own" in the budget. Whatever number they settle on as a team for the year, they have to live with, so they take care and do their best thinking. And their number has to be approved by others as reasonable and fitting with the percentage of their expenses to gross sales.

Here are a few examples of what occurs in open-book planning:

- If delivery costs are double what they were last year because of a new customer service promise, then everyone will know why and what they will do to make up that expense elsewhere.
- Human resources may know that a training program in safety they have to support will cost 25 percent more than last year—they have to put in the number, explain it, and defend it. And they need to be prepared to cut back if other plans are considered more important.
- In manufacturing, engineering will put forth a capital budget (primarily impacting the balance sheet, and the need for cash) having listened to their customers on the floor, and will prioritize against the sales plan they got to know intimately. The emphasized products indicate where the greatest need will be.
- Customer service will put in for increased head count, for higher salaries, for more equipment to electronically tie to customers, again to serve the sales plan.
- The intrapreneurial team in research and development or marketing will ask for set-aside money to pursue two new product ideas that have promise in future years.

There always will be competing needs for the limited budget, just as what you would like differs from what you need and can afford in your household budget. Open-book planning, however, offers some distinct advantages over the usual power plays in corporate boardrooms for more money:

- With open books, no hidden line items and squirreled-away secret cash for extra boondoggles and perks are possible.
- With everyone on a unifying bonus plan, any department padding expenses is seen as taking away profits. Lean and mean builds status, not the usual empire building.

■ Previous years' performances are widely known. Those departments that delivered and added value earn their right to a hearing when they need to add expense.

■ The sales forecast informs everyone about direction and initiatives they have to support.

■ Increased business literacy has everyone thinking like businesspeople, like CEOs, wanting to increase profit and return on assets and not fatten departmental budgets.

The planning process also includes putting the projected bonus plans into place. The business strategy, with the educational and motivational opportunity inherent in the bonus, informs the discussion about which results to target for a unifying bonus plan.

If improved quality is a strategy, then the bonus will include quality measures. If financial results, such as increased profitability, are also a goal, then bonuses will be in part dependent on profit margins. (More on this aspect of planning in Chapter 13.)

The Final Plan

With the dialogue and feedback complete, it's time for final commitment to the plan. Management has the responsibility to take the plan, explain it, discuss the risks, the opportunities, assumptions, and of course, the critical numbers.

During the planning process, the organization is in a deliberation and dialogue mode. The final plan shifts to declaration. Now management makes a statement of intent, done with conviction, that sets the energy of the company in motion.

Most companies do well at declaration time to perform a start-off ritual. The meeting, or series of meetings, thanks employees for all their work, discusses final questions, and celebrates the start of the new year. Management has facilitated the required planning and now managers, as player-coach leaders, spark the energy to go for the plan, to exceed the goals, serve the customers, make the numbers, and become a better company in the process.

Again, open-book management helps player-coach leaders transform the ordinary tools of management, like planning and budgeting, into participative tools that create motivation and commitment.

High-involvement planning in open-book management leads to a document that captures the collective aspirations of all employees. The numbers in the plan and the budgets are promises the employees make to each other and customers about their future. Instead of that thing that collects dust on the credenza, created at an executive retreat, the plan lives in the hearts and minds of managers and employees.

Open-book planning creates the foundation for the necessary connections in all employees' minds between what is going on outside the company with what they need to be doing inside the company. Without this connection, intellectual capital is left on the table and opportunities are missed. With a few iterations of open-book planning behind a company, the plan becomes a powerful strategic advantage for unifying and engaging the workforce. The first year takes some work and has rough edges, but with each year, practice will smooth out the process and deliver a better planning product.

Chapter 13

꧁꧂꧁꧂꧁꧂꧁꧂

Information as the Company's Lifeblood: Intensive Huddling Works the Plan

If I could have only two measurements, the two I would choose would be customer satisfaction and cash flow.
> —Dennis Dammerman
> CFO
> General Electric

A s numerous surveys have shown, employees rank the feeling of being "in the know," of being informed, as one of the highest, if not the number one, factor important to their work satisfaction. But as important as it is to employees, the surveys also indicate that communication is somewhere between ineffective and woefully bad across much of the corporate landscape. In a recent *Training* magazine's cover article, "Obfuscation Resounding," the issue is defined as two-pronged: "What (managers) are saying, or meaning to say, often doesn't seem to get through to employees. . . . Or maybe it is getting through, but the employees don't believe it."*

Putting aside the credibility issue, the frustration of not getting sufficient information is most often expressed by that oft-repeated question echoing through the halls of corporate America:

"Why do you think management is doing *that*?"

---

* Bob Filipczak, "Obfuscation Resounding," *Training*, July 1995, pp. 19–36.

This question generates the usual employee theories as to what went through the minds of management when they decided to move headquarters, or merge with a competitor, or drop a product line. The theories, often slightly tinged with a mild sarcasm, include things like:

> Perhaps McKinsey was in here again, and the usual executive lobotomy occurred while the strategy experts, making fees that could jump-start the economies of small third world countries, worked their decision magic.

or

> After analyzing the conclusions in a special report (several months of work by a cross-functional team of the company's best and most experienced minds), the executives, who didn't like the report they had commissioned because it meant they would have to change their own behavior and do things like listen to middle manager ideas, pitched it. As an alternative, they brainstormed for a half hour, dug up some old memos with some good-sounding decisions on them, and updated the old decisions with new, timely sounding jargon and imperatives like "customer-obsessed" and "organizational agility."

The employee frustration doesn't end there. It usually turns into criticism of what is wrong with the decision, and how unnecessary work or pain resulted from similar actions in the past: "We did a similar move back in 1986 and it cost us our bonuses for three years, not to mention that we halved our market share and they took away our afternoon cookie break."

Management generally offers three powerful reasons for the normal information breakdown—time, time, and time. Managers just don't have the time, in their view, to do all that communicating and explaining. With the downsizing that has left large spans of control for middle managers, some companies are near the danger zone of burned-out, frenetic, lots-of-heat-but-no-light effort. Managers don't have an efficient system to bring other levels of the organization up to speed on the events that they observe. More often than many want to admit, managers make bureaucratic, blind-sided decisions without the knowledge of those on their extended team.

From management's vantage point, a shift in the marketplace, a threat of new technology, an initiative that is necessary to keep the customers, can all combine to make a call for new action logical and necessary. But employees left out of the plan and the information flow, or buried in data bits that lead to no real information, see little reason for the actions and less reason for working hard to support them.

If downward communication is difficult, faulty upward communication from employees to management is no less a problem. The requests for more information or resources from the front line are routinely watered down, lost, given politically correct spins, and otherwise distorted until even the most well-meaning managers are hard pressed to know what they are being asked to communicate or support.

The system of open-book management that addresses the time shortage/information shortage, and distortion problems that plague companies is the Intensive Huddle System. Why management, upper, middle and lower, does what it does is better understood in open-book companies than elsewhere. Business literacy creates a learning and communication-intense environment where what happens and why it happens are a normal part of the environment, not the exception, and the language of finance unifies and clarifies. Huddle systems help the business information that executives acquire saturate the company while simultaneously bringing frontline employee information up or over to levels and functions it needs to reach.

Here's how they work, in some detail.

Huddles: Meetings with a Difference

Imagine a smooth-running conveyor connected to intelligent work cells and robots allowing specific inputs in assembling a customized, mass-produced deluxe car. Calibrations happen automatically to accommodate customer requirements, like the beige interior with leather seats and four, not two, cup holders for coffee. Attention to detail is automatic and built into the system.

The huddle system is the social equivalent of the mechanics of flexible manufacturing. Precise and timely relays of accurate information engage teams to make the necessary calibrations to accomplish the small goals in pursuit of the big picture goal. The huddle system is a series of meetings (weekly, semiweekly, or monthly—rhythmical in any case) in departments or natural work groups throughout the company focused on their key performance factors. Data are accumulated, summarized, and rolled up into line items on the cash flow statement, the income statement, or the balance sheet that represents the performance. With *a background of business and financial knowledge*, each individual and all teams account for their activity with a clear understanding of how they impact the company outcomes and which line items represent their performance and contributions.

Patagonia's Huddle Helps the Environment

Most companies would like this problem: too much growth potential. Leadership at Patagonia for years worried about what fast growth would do to quality, the customer, the culture. As the premier provider of sportswear and active outdoor wear for climbing, skiing, camping, Patagonia, located in Ventura, California, is the Harley-Davidson of clothes—in a class by itself with a brand name known the world over as the best.

Like some other companies, Patagonia had perceived quality as competing with financials. Customer and quality obsessed, along with a huge commitment to the environment, describe the values around which Patagonia's culture was built. Patagonia pays 1 percent of sales or 10 percent of profits, whichever is *greater*, as a match to employee contributions to environmental or charity groups.

Employee empowerment was a natural for the clothes maker, but that was a problem: "Things went crazy," said CEO Alison

May. "People grabbed hold of what they thought of as power and started saying, 'I'm empowered here. I'm going to do things my way.' Pretty soon I saw that things were out of control."*

When May took over the reins in 1992, the financials were as casually presented as one of their plaid outdoorsy shirts. Worse, they lacked precision and were in disarray, so her financial background told her to clean them up as a first-things-first act. When she then learned about open-book management, she explored the notion that teaching financials could help the company get focused and have empowered employees based in reality. "We used to look at financials as kind of a pain," she reflected. "Now they are a legitimate tool we use to achieve our ends. Money's not the only goal, it's a tool we use to reach our goals."

And she realized huddles are a tool that turn the financial learning and the information into action.

Patagonia's first huddles were more for financial education than for information. They were voluntary, except for management, and 75 percent of the employees took the classes. The education led to a greater sense of teamwork and better communication between departments. Informal huddling and cooperation expanded greatly.

To share information effectively, planning at Patagonia needed to be transformed. "We've turned everything upside down," says quality director Randy Harward. "Always before, our goals were set according to whatever dollars could be budgeted. Now our planning means goals first, budgets set accordingly."

Besides management-driven huddles, Patagonia's ongoing main huddle is a weekly voluntary all-employee meeting that covers financials, major programs, and strategies, and whatever else is on people's minds. It's a give-and-take format that makes the big picture available to everyone.

For Patagonia, business literacy is a means and an end. Says Hayward, "As we attain more knowledge about communicating

---

* "No One Told Us the Game Process Could Take So Long," *Playing the Great Game of Business,*® (first quarter 1995, pp. 4–5).

with the financials, we move closer to our main goal of gelling quality, the financials, and our environmental focus into one."

Huddle Components: The Closed Loop

Huddles have two primary subjects:

1. Accounting for what's happened in the past week or month, especially compared against the plan numbers. This practice drives understanding the business by analyzing variances.
2. Forecasting what the future will hold and explaining why it is over or under the planned performance.

Participants analyze past performance for lessons learned and practices worth improving and repeating. Forecasting is not meant to be a prediction, punished if not totally accurate, but is the collective best guess, and a commitment to do everything humanly possible to achieve the target. Expressed in three familiar categories from the income statement, the team or department communicates to their business colleagues:

1. The revenue numbers generated by buying customers because they found value in the company offerings.
2. The expense or capital employed numbers that measure how efficiently that value was created.
3. The profit or loss, or other EVA (economic value added) cash flow or balance sheet numbers measuring the overall company staying power to grow and add more value and jobs (or to shrink, drop product lines, or go out of business, if the numbers are bad enough).

Like Patagonia, every company creates a format for huddles that work in their operation. The huddle system is a communications and thinking discipline that calls for precision, regularity, and commitment. Huddles are the lubricant for open-book management. Just as a car runs better and keeps its value with regular oil changes and tune-ups, the company operates more efficiently with huddle-based information tune-ups.

Three types of meetings make up the huddle system:

1. *Prehuddles*. Team meetings analyzing team performance in quality, production, service, or financial terms.
2. *Main huddles*. Manager meetings reporting on the team information that is rolled up to create the current income statement, cash flow statement, and balance sheet.
3. *Posthuddles*. Team meetings where every employee sees the whole financial picture and is briefed on key company happenings.

The Prehuddles: Going into the Details

The prehuddles consist of teams and departments gathering their information for the week so they can do a variance analysis on their current performance and forecast how their future performance will measure up to the plan and the budget. Sales teams project their numbers for several months out, since the sales number drives the volume of work and the sales forecast provides a longer horizon into the future. The other departments manage their cost center numbers to their monthly budget or plan goal.

Prehuddles send numbers and information up.

With employees knowing their number, they can tell the story of the activities that put the company performance over or under the planned number. The leaders in positions not as close to the work or to the customer rely on accurate prehuddle information and the analysis of those that do the day-to-day work. Without it, they will not understand the fluctuations in the business or financial numbers. They will make decisions about improving processes and customer initiatives not based on the most current facts. An airplane crew needs the instrument panel to make its decisions: A good huddle system is the instrument panel (see Figure 13.1).

Figure 13.1 Huddle System Information Flow Chart—Closed-Loop System

PREHUDDLE
Team Information
Flows Up, Is Compiled
and Explained

MAIN HUDDLE
Financial Information
Flows Across

POSTHUDDLE
Company Information
Flows Down, Is Clarified
and Taught

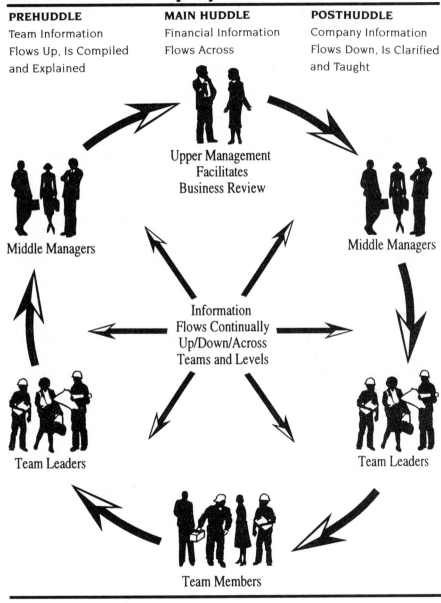

Upper Management
Facilitates
Business Review

Middle Managers

Middle Managers

Information
Flows Continually
Up/Down/Across
Teams and Levels

Team Leaders

Team Leaders

Team Members

The Main Huddle: Building the Real-Time Big Picture

This is a gathering of all the functions, staff, line, business units, or other configurations in less hierarchical companies. The numbers and activities that the teams and departments reported in the prehuddles are rolled up into financial numbers and financial reports. All functions see all the performance numbers using the income and cash flow statements, and the balance sheet if useful, as tools that pull together the big picture. This is the unifying process at work. The backdrop for all these forecasts is the original plan, so all employees are getting a picture of how well they planned and are executing.

Main huddles send information and numbers across.

The "owner" of each line item on the financial statements forecasts his or her number for the month and gives the current business reason for the variances from the planned outcome (see Figure 13.2). Here is the paradigm shift at work again. In non-open-book companies, department heads wait for the financial department to get them the cost and margin data, taking an extra time-consuming step and looking at financial history *after* their decisions, without the all important stories behind the numbers. If, on the other hand, the financial team's role in an open-book environment has been to teach their peers to manage their own numbers, they attend the main huddle as a support team. They accumulate the numbers from the department leaders who own the lines on the statements. In this way, finance computes the as-it-happens, useful set of financial statements that provide direction for all to follow.

For example, if sales for the current period is projected to come in $10,000 above plan, then the vice president of sales is reporting the reason—say, an increase in volume from XYZ customer. In the sales team's prehuddles, there likely was some celebration, anticipation of the additional costs for the bigger sale, and discussions about increasing the customer's order further. The vice president of sales knows her peer vice presidents will

Figure 13.2 Line Owner

Sales	Line Owner
Product X	Mary
Product Y	Allison
New Venture	Paul
Expenses	
Contractors	Helena
Supplies	Miguel
Utilities	Latitia
Engineering	Wilma
Delivery	Joe
Overtime	Rodney
Research & Development	Axel
Total	**Finance**
P(L)	**Computers**

want advance warning of this increase to modify their plans to deliver the extra service to this customer.

At a manufacturing company with a just-in-time inventory program, an increased sale will require purchasing to order additional materials. The material may cost more when it is purchased without a long lead time, or in smaller quantity or with additional freight costs for the needed delivery date. In an open-book company, purchasing communicates the increased costs to sales, which has anticipated this factor. Additionally, the operations team informs sales of any overtime associated with the sale, so gross margins are instantly computed.

The Posthuddle: Top-Down Accountability

All the thinking, communicating, and sweat that has gone into operating the huddle system to this point will make the business

---

Main Huddles and Tribal Togetherness

While the main huddle itself is a forum for forecasting and giving an account of the different parts of the business, important business activities and communications happen before, after, and around it. This forum keeps everyone on track with real-time data, emotionally connected to each other with the stories and listening that is at the heart of communication, and focused on the targeted business results by constantly forecasting the future.

The main huddle also features customer- or employee-related announcements, such as customers' on-site visits, or important personal events, or some departmental thank-you/way-to-go, or warning about a negative trend to be aware of. In other words, after the numbers are delivered, news and information that connect the big team and put a human face on the business take over.

This human feature in the main huddle is enormously important. Often when numbers junkies first see the financial part of a main huddle in action, they think they have died and gone to accounting heaven: "A perfect meeting, with numbers everywhere, everyone talking in the real language of business, and no messy human interactions and personalities and politics."

They often are tempted to take it farther, "Skip the meeting . . . we'll put all the data on E-mail. That way we can all keep working!"

While E-mailing the data may be a good thing to do, it is not a substitute for the tribal nature of group meetings, with face-to-face contact. E-mail cannot generate the emotional energy that main huddles spark. Electrons lighting up a computer screen provide a secondary media.

Player-coach leaders have a huge opportunity at the main huddles to lead and use this event for the emotional and unifying possibilities that exist. They don't have to be showstopping performances, but it takes practice to orchestrate a meeting that lets the employees and teams tell their stories, brag a little, squirm at the shortfalls, or laugh at themselves. The main huddle is an executive art form: compressing the financial and the human outlook of a company into a meeting of reasonable length that educates and motivates all who attend.

≈ Continued

─ ❧ ❧ ❧ ❧ ─

❧ *Continued* ˛

At the beginning of the meeting, the leader sets the tone with an opening remark, a business lesson, or an update. At the end, he or she takes a few minutes to summarize the important real-time concerns and needs of the business and focuses the participants' attention on the challenges at hand. The bonus is always a focal point for a comment, a way-to-go, or a call for action.

During the meeting, the leader asks questions about the numbers to evoke the stories that need to be understood:

"How did that expense go so far above the plan?"

"What accounts for the warranty cost going down?"

"How's the customer reacting to our price increase?"

Gentle probes, and sometimes not-so-gentle ones if a number is a big problem, keep the learning levels high and the participants alert and prepared.

hum. Yet a crucial piece remains. What about all the employees who gathered in prehuddles to project their outcomes for the coming period, those who couldn't be at the main huddle but who made it possible for the high level main huddles to be substantive and real-time? What do they receive?

The numbers gathered on the financial statements built at the main huddle, now go to all employees. These posthuddles occur shortly, within 24 hours preferably, after the main huddle, in the same groups that prehuddled. Employees see the big picture, what the score is, who and what departments are having victories or problems. The communication loop—up-over-down—completes its cycle.

Posthuddles send numbers and information down.

Department and team leaders need to give an account of the big-picture performance to all the players that made it happen.

It will contain the good and bad news. Posthuddles are a walk-through, line by line, of the current performance with the same variance explanations that were given in the main huddle. The goal is twofold:

1. Have every employee gain the same information.
2. Educate employees about the business using current, real events and results.

The teams use the data, like the increased sales example, to make smart decisions, to redirect resources, to adjust a process.

Companies working with the huddle system for the first time can expect a 6-month practice and debugging period. Rather than expecting to achieve perfection, open-book starter companies can shift the expectations of success to what people are learning about the business and about the problems in making it run well.

The 6-month practice period for the huddle system works best when it follows soon after the base business and financial training, and after preparing managers and supervisors to become sound huddle coaches. If it's not soon, some of the training is lost.

The point here is simple but profound: Give yourself time to institute huddles. Getting just the managers comfortable and skillful with the numbers, let alone all employees, can take time.

If your division or company is organized in a network configuration rather than hierarchically, which is increasingly the case, then the various business units determine appropriate flow and rollup of information accordingly. Best methods for the huddle disciplines and practices need to be tailored to the communication and business needs of your operation.

Diebold, the market leader in ATMs in the United States, began pushing the high-level numbers it had been generating into the hands of the operating units responsible for them. CFO Jerry Morris reported in the March 1995 issue of CFO magazine that it took 2 years to implement a system that gave income statements or expense budgets to individual departments and

Huddles? We Already Have Too Many Meetings!

One concern often arises about the huddle system: "How long does all this take? We've got more meetings than we can handle already!"

For the main huddle, most teams target 90 minutes. In the early stages of developing open-book practices, huddles will be cumbersome and have kinks. But with practice, they will become automatic and will be the source of time-saving coordination.

One company's first main huddle, which they held to get started and practice, was a discouraging 2 hours and 45 minutes. To the open-book coaches, it was a triumph, albeit a slow one, like watching an 11-month-old take those first baby steps.

But a few months later, they had the "main huddle from hell"—a 4-hour marathon that never did get finished because they broke a rule of main huddling: The leader tried to solve problems. *Main huddles are for information-sharing only, not problem-solving.* When problems come up at a main huddle, and they will—that's one of the purposes of these meetings— the leaders note it, probe quickly, and move on. If attention is needed to solve the problem, the concerned parties hold another meeting with fewer participants.

After another quarter's practice, this team's main huddles conveyed lots of information and averaged less than 2 hours.

Since the huddle system uses the language of numbers and is built on the knowledge of the employees using it, this system is a great time-saver. It takes less time to give the account of activities and results using key performance indicators and financial numbers because everyone knows what they mean in relationship to the business goals. And when questions are asked, it usually takes but a few minutes to respond satisfactorily.

As the huddle system matures, the employees who usually spend the most time tracking down others—and this is often the task of middle managers—to bring themselves up to speed on various events soon find that most of what they need comes through to them in the huddle system. Problem-solving and planning meetings get focused more quickly and actions are easier to implement because the thinking of all those whose help and cooperation is needed comes to the fore.

cost centers. They call it responsibility accounting at Diebold and it has kept their results on target: from $476 million to $760 million in sales from 1990 to 1994 and a stock price that more than tripled, adding more than a billion dollars to market value.

Was there resistance by managers to the new accountability for the numbers? How long did it take to get the managers to embrace the numbers and the huddles?

"You bet [there was resistance]," says Morris. "Suddenly, managers had to stand up each month before a roomful of senior executives and explain why they weren't meeting their targets. That could be painful, and embarrassing. But *halfway through the second year* [italics added], when it was evident it was here to stay, responsibility accounting kicked in."

"Our ability to run the business has improved . . . and I think the managers are happier: They get more satisfaction from their jobs—and they get paid more too."

A Huddle System at Work

The following scenario is how a huddle system in an open-book company might work. The first perspective is from a branch manager's office in an imaginary company, Acme Products, the company that supplied gadgets to Wiley Coyote in his quest for the Road Runner. We'll start at the beginning of the year, which is the calendar and fiscal year. An open-book planning process has already created the plan.

Sue, the branch manager in Memphis selling for Acme, leads and manages to her sales plan. In thousands of dollars, it looks like this:

	JAN	FEB	MAR	APR	MAY	JUN	JUL	AUG
Plan	98	79	91	101	69	80	85	90
Forecast	86	87	103	101	69	80		
Actual								

Here's how she gets to the all-important forecast line. There are four Acme prehuddles in January, the four Friday staff meetings when Sue sends her projections for the months to her Regional Director. Sue concentrates on January, but keeps her forecasting eye out for changes in the upcoming months. Her communication with her reps and the sales administration team is crucial and constant. On Thursdays, she gathers her final numbers from her team for the Friday huddle with her boss.

The huddle meeting in the first week of January is the "longest" forecast, as in every month, because the fewest workdays have passed. On the phone call with her boss and peers from the other sales branch offices, Sue sends along the following opinion numbers during the month. The plan never changes: The forecast changes every week with better and more current information coming in.

Week 1	January forecast—92 . . . a customer just postponed an order for gears she was counting on. "Damn, lousy way to start the year," she thinks. No change for the rest of the 6 months.
Week 2	January forecast creeps up to 93 . . . one order will be a little bigger and she adds 8,000 to February because one of her guys finally got a new customer he had been courting. "Whew, we recovered the loss in January and added a little more."
Week 3	"Terrible news! A big cancellation, not just because of a slowdown, but a competitor, Acme Plus, got the order." January slips farther, to 86. Now she is in deep yogurt. No change in the rest of the year.
Week 4	Only one week to make it happen. Good news for March . . . increase in order takes forecast up to 103, a great month. She makes that change and keeps January opinion at 86, 12 below the original plan.

In the first week of February, the cycle starts over. She makes her first projection against plan for February. And the actual for January is recorded. The 86 goes in the books. As it's a rolling forecast, she now includes the July number—no change at 85.

Meanwhile, back at headquarters, other departments are also taking care of business. As the numbers from sales come in weekly, the numbers for January expenses are also projected weekly at the main huddle meetings.

The first week of January, the top management team gets together at their weekly huddle to see how the company is going. Different numbers come from different managers. The sales manager gives the sales number; the purchasing manager, the materials number. Labor and overhead comes from operations. Engineering comes from engineering, and the head of administration owns the "admin" number for human resources, information services, and legal. (This is a much simplified actual cost version of an income statement. In manufacturing, standard costs and variances against the standard are often used. For those not in manufacturing and used to variance tracking, the following example is an approximation of how the huddles and the learning work.)

The huddle for Week 1 bears these income statement results:

Sales	3.60	
January Plan		3.6 million in sales projected (the compiled sales number of Sue and her 24 branch manager peers).
Direct Expenses:		
Materials	2.12	Line owner: Fred, head of purchasing
Labor	.49	Line owner: Bill, head of operations
Overhead	.29	Line owner: Bill's assistant, Kelly
Gross Profit	.70	
General Administrative Expenses:		
Engineering	.17	Owner: Karen, head of engineering
Administrative	.29	Owner: Ernestine, head of admin.
Net Profit	.24	

As the year rolls on, the guesses or forecasts get even more interesting because Acme's plan, unlike the 6-month planning cycle at Manco, was put together for the whole year. Early in the fiscal year, forecasts should be easier to predict than later in the year, when many months have passed between the time the plan was made and the actual sales and production of goods and services.

All the planning and forecasting against the original plan is engaging in and of itself, focusing energy and attention on the business as it is happening. The repetition breeds familiarity, even intimacy with the numbers. The learning goes deep as the teams work to make plan and deliver their numbers by gaining control over everything they can.

The stories behind increased or lost sales for Sue and her peers, and increased or decreased expenses of production and delivery unfold continually. Karen in engineering is proud of the redesign job that went so smoothly with such minimal down-time, and Fred in purchasing is sweating because a 10 percent price increase on some parts is hurting profits. The whole business—all the people—participates in and watches the drama of the business year unfold in the weekly or biweekly increments of the huddles. Different teams take particular ownership in doing their part to bring home a performance better than the plan projected. Humans like goals, and like to exceed them, and Acme's entire team is pulling in the same direction for the thrill of the accomplishment.

Acme's bonus, a profit before-tax formula, intensifies the interest in monthly results. The bonus is now paid monthly versus at the end of the year, because the feedback loop is so immediate and the learning and corrective action take place in the needed tight time frames to make a difference. The balance sheet and cash flow scorecards are continual reminders not to be so focused on short-term goals that long-term ones are sacrificed, and that profits are great but cash runs the business.

Scorecards: Basic Huddle Tools

Once the design of the entire huddle system is customized, managers, often with the help of the design team, or open-book coach, must give attention to the content and quality of learning in each huddle. If the financial statements are the basic scorecards for the entire company, each team needs a set of scorecards for their activity. Just as a football team will watch the scoreboard for the overall game outcome, the coaches keep separate scorecards for the offensive line, special teams, and every other player. The learning is in the specific feedback.

The idea of the scorecard is to be able to follow the action, hold teams and team members accountable, and keep team performance totals. The scorecard is a chart that allows all team members to post their contributions for specific periods. It provides a sum of the team's current output against the key measures and goals. The goals are carefully selected because they act as key performance areas for meeting financial outcome.

All contributors, whether they are involved in a high-level negotiation with a perspective supplier or taking customer orders over the phone, need feedback about how effective their work is in reaching the open-book goals.

Here are some questions the developers of scorecards need to ask:

- What is the expected output—sales, number of widgets produced, number of hours and amount of resources to create a draft proposal, a training manual, or new market strategy?
- What is the cost of these activities?
- What is the value of the outputs compared with the cost of the inputs?
- How much do we need to produce or accomplish in each period?
- How is this goal tied to overall financial goals?

The endless measures tracked by scorecards, unique to companies and processes, stem from a few fundamental measuring categories, called forth by four basic questions:

1. How much (quantity)?
2. How well (quality)?
3. How soon (timeliness)?
4. How much spent (cost)?

When a lot of work is done well, quickly, and at low cost, the enterprise and the customer are well served.

The managers and the design team's work is to help teams create a scorecard that is practical, representative of the work, and tied to the goals of the company. The aim is to have all scorecards represent team contributions, to "tell" the story of what's behind the numbers on the big three financial scorecards. With good scorecards, line of sight becomes precise and each employee can name the lines on the budgets and financial statements, and customer and quality indicators, that they most influence and own.

A sample scorecard for a service and operations team looking at the vital signs of its critical numbers might look like this one, slightly modified from a real service contracting firm (see Figure 13.3).

Some work in companies can be long term and not show up in the financial statements as normal get-the-service-delivered operations. For example, the research and development group in a bio-tech firm or pharmaceutical company will likely have a success ratio they are targeting along with a set of budgets they manage. Their scorecards are made accordingly, to accommodate the lengthy time cycles of their work.

A sound huddle system depends on creative and accurate scorecarding. Scorecards establish the strong connections between the immediate performance microactivities of the teams and the big-picture companywide macroperformance of financial

Figure 13.3 Sample Scorecard—Service Contracting Division of Large Company

December   YTD Team Award ____%

Scorecard Indicators

Sales

Proposals   *Contract*

Submitted month   ____   ____   Submitted month
YTD   ____   ____   YTD
Wins   ____   ____   Approved
Losses   ____
Active   ____   ____   Active

Operations   *Order Processing*

Current month   ____   # Disconnects   ____
Prior month   ____   % Orders keyed
                               within 24 hours   ____
Routine adjustment ____
                               Average installation
Other adjustments ____   intervals   ____

Administrative   *Customer Satisfaction*

Head count   ____   Disputes   ____
Contractor $ ____   Service
                               Availability   ____
Average YTD employee
training hours   ____   Quantity of service
                               interruptions   ____
Capital expenditures ____
                               Due rates
Revenue/Head   ____   renegotiated   ____
Expense/Head   ____

results and market share and customer satisfaction. Scorecards promote the sense of shared ownership for the present and future.

TransAlta, an Alberta Utility, saw scorecarding as central to its work in business literacy. They knew the right scorecards integrate the efforts of levels and teams and tie financial outcomes to operating realities. TransAlta's Tom Janzon cited the business literacy opportunity:

> With TransAlta's move to having the area offices act as business units, we didn't know what the effect would be. Those reporting to me had been far removed from the financial data. . . . [With practice] we learned how to focus on what can provide the greatest gain, like in our production vehicles. We found we could provide a $100,000 gain by working a truck differently. And for 10 units that's a million dollars.
>
> The biggest challenge has been getting the employees to take ownership for the things they can change. To accomplish this, we are providing basic graphical scorecards so that particular persons or teams can start to interpret what they can do to make improvements. The scorecards chart what they do in the day-to-day work. We are going to design more scorecards to go after waste or increase revenue.
>
> —Tom Janzon

As the open-book practices in a company mature, so do the scorecards that represent key performance areas. Each iteration symbolizes new insight and the capability to better use the system and practices. It is like learning software—the more you use it, the more skillful you become. You find shortcuts and new applications. Scorecard practice makes perfect.

There are many ways to broadcast the key numbers: posting the scorecards on bulletin boards, building giant thermometers like the United Way campaign, graphing progress, having a number to call so employees can get the measures, posting the stock price, putting the measure on their desktop PC. Multiple communication channels create the information-rich environment for learning that business literacy fosters, and leave lots of room for fun.

Huddle Leaders Make It All Happen

For a huddle system to work well, managers and team leaders need to be prepared and trained. Part of the preparation is acquiring critical numbers know-how; part is creating a scorecard for their work team. The final preparation step is learning the purpose of the huddle, presenting an overview of the huddle system to their team, and *rehearsing the information flow of the prehuddle and posthuddle meetings*. Rehearsing and practice are critical to build skill levels and confidence.

When huddle leaders are not confident in their ability to plan and teach the financial and business information, the open-book system breaks down. Generic or brush-off answers to specific employee questions can hurt the whole process: "Oh, that expense there? That's a general expense that comes from the general operations of things, in general."

First-time huddle leaders need the help of business coaches from different parts of the company: finance, senior managers, or any employee with the knowledge and capability to explain and answer questions. A huddle leader may find it helpful to arrange for a business coach to attend a series of team meetings and to teach certain business lessons at each huddle period.

Especially during the first 6 months, huddle leaders will find it useful to have an external open-book coach observe the pre- and posthuddles to give feedback and tips on how to improve their leadership and team participation. One of the more common shortfalls of new huddle leaders is not seeing all the opportunities for learning that the huddles create. They'll concentrate on the number, not the story behind the number that people need to hear. Or they give too many answers before the team has developed curiosity and is eager to learn.

One measurement of early huddle system success is using helpful internal and external coaching resources. A coach helps the leader create learning and accountability and fun, and prevents the process from being mechanical. This time period is like spring training for the huddle leaders as well as the participants.

At the end of each huddle meeting, the team does a brief evaluation by listing the pluses and minuses of that session and ideas for improvement.

It is important to encourage employees to ask questions at huddles because fundamental learning about the business is taking place. The huddle is the key learning cell in the enterprise. It is the local learning laboratory that drives organizational intelligence. Generating questions is the key.

Remember, the status for leaders in open-book companies comes from how much you learn and share, not how much you have and hoard.

The Joys That Come with Huddle Discipline

As the business year unfolds, a company needs to reconcile the reality of its current performance against the aspirations expressed in the business plan. Financial performance and other indicators provide a steady, sometimes chaotic flow of feedback from the marketplace to the company. As the marketplace changes, companies need to comprehend what the changes mean and act quickly. The changes won't come on cue, but in fits and starts, and employees equipped with business knowledge and a set of practices for moving information and decisions quickly increase the chances of meeting the challenges and executing or exceeding the plan successfully.

Along with rewards that matter and leadership that understands open-book principles, the huddle system and its ample and intricate flow of information sustain business literacy. With open books, high-involvement planning, and intensive huddles, the organization avoids the oh-so-frequent "why did management do that" syndrome. All employees are tuned into the why, are encouraged to ask questions as the months flow by and the numbers are or aren't met. The story of the business year unfolds with the little, and not-so-little stories, of the frontline teams rolling up into the big story. Like a sports announcer at pregame analyzing the matchups of the opposing players and the little contests within the big game, the huddle system captures all the effort. The small sales and service challenges met and not met, the mistakes, the good and bad luck, the day-to-day triumphs and tragedies of work told and retold in the huddles let the human and financial drama of business unfold in front of all those in the contest.

In addition to saving time and providing the big picture, the closed loop of the huddle system as an information-sharing process:

- Involves and spreads accountability.
- Coordinates action and enhances teamwork.
- Accelerates and reinforces learning.
- Alerts everyone to the emerging problems.
- Makes emotional tribal connections for the people side of the business.
- Alerts teams to opportunities to serve customers and improve quality.

Huddles do all this because, in the hands of player-coach leaders, they promote what every company needs—they turn data and information into knowledge and wisdom.

Chapter 14

❈❈❈❈

Carrots and More: Bonuses, Fun Work, Recognition, and Ownership

(The) H.H. Brown (Company) had a very unique compensation system that, according to (Warren) Buffett, "warmed my heart." Each year, the key managers of H.H. Brown are paid a base salary of $7,800 plus a percentage of profits calculated after capital investment. This, noted Buffett, makes the mangers acutely aware that the equity capital is not cost-free. . . . At H.H. Brown, the managers truly walk in the same shoes as the owners. *

Robert G. Hagstrom, Jr.
The Warren Buffett Way

The sad truth is employees of modern corporations have little reason to feel satisfied, much less fulfilled. Companies do not have the time or the interest to listen to them, and lack the resources or the inclination to train them for advancement. These companies make a series of demands, for which they compensate employees with salaries that are often considered inadequate. †

Ricardo Semler
CEO, Semco

---

* Robert G. Hagstrom, Jr., *The Warren Buffett Way*, New York: John Wiley & Sons, 1994.
† Ricardo Semler, *Maverick*, New York: Warner Books, 1993.

Picture a manager looking dreamily out the window to a green pasture with a pond, a white picket fence around a yard, and some beautiful aspens and maple trees surrounding a beautiful garden. "The land is simply gorgeous," he sighs, as he gazes across the field from his office. He's so touched by the sight that he pulls his five-member management team into his office with him. In a gesture of team-building and unity, he draws them to the window and has them view the land with him. With a warm look in his eye, he intones to his team his most motivating message: "Team, you see that beautiful land out there, do you see how peaceful and inviting it is? Well, some day, if we all work real hard, that will all be . . . MINE." (Thanks to Steven Covey for the inspiration on this vignette.)*

What's wrong with this picture?

Employees don't mind the owner getting his dream property with its beautiful pasture and white picket fence and pond. But employees have every right to ask, "What's in it for me? Where's my pond? I don't want a pond, but I sure would like a little house in the 'burbs. Can I have my stake in the action as well?"

Open-book management companies don't educate on the numbers and intensively huddle for nothing. They do it to meet the needs of their companies—and the needs of their employees with No-Kidding Ownership practices. They want good business financial decisions being made by everyone in the company. And they want all these decision-makers to be rewarded psychologically and financially, regularly and frequently, so that when they perform well they get their rewards, and when they don't, they don't.

Avoiding the mistakes from past common practices is a good place to begin thinking about financial incentives in open-book companies. A mistaken practice that is taking years to undo is rewarding people for the number of people reporting to them, or the level of responsibility they have, as indicated by the scope of their decisions and whom they dealt with.

---

* Steven Covey, *The Seven Habits of Highly Effective People*, New York: Simon & Schuster, 1989.

This practice in compensating professionals led to ridiculous empire-building bureaucracy bloat, with so-called managers all over not managing people but functions. The old position descriptions provide a chuckle but also are a sad commentary, as managers would throw everything they could at the human resources department to get the pay level up—"This position facilitates, budgets, coordinates, leads, manages, analyzes, and coordinates with vice presidents, presidents, prime ministers,

---

Open Books Not Yet at Work: 2. Speed over Service

At a large motel chain 800-number incoming call office, the staff has the job of making accurate reservations for the customers wanting to stay in the national chain of hotels. The reservationists are bonused as a team average on how fast they can process the calls, have a 110-second target rate, and their calls are monitored for quality factors like product information, courteous response, and selling more rooms and dates for travelers.

The young male reservationist has a call. He rapidfires the questions so he can beat the 110-second call rate:

"What night is that, Ma'am?

"One room or two?

"Do you need a cot?

He is a more than a little staccato as he pushes out the phrases with real efficiency and near-zero warmth.

His final statement is telling.

"No, Ma'am, this *isn't* a computer."

He apparently has gotten this question before and hasn't made the connection. His supervisor has given him feedback before about getting too monotone, and he hasn't made that connection either.

When he gets in a hurry and works toward the bonus number, his task voice overtakes his service voice. Who knows how many bad impressions he left, or how much business he's lost, because of a timed goal that pushed him to be less than helpful in his tone. Skill training may help.

A review of the bonus is also due.

saints, the cherubim, and occasionally, but not often, God, in order to ensure the product is satisfactory."

Another typical past practice is that managers have one set of financial bonuses, like return on assets, or profit before tax, and employees another, like increasing claim accuracy, or improving customer service. How are employees supposed to get the big picture of the business when this happens? What if they improve the accuracy of the claims, but slow down output to the point that volume is off and profits are threatened?

Design Tips for Incentive Pay

Incentive and variable pay programs are on the upswing, with business-literate companies among the leaders. Studies by the consulting firms specializing in this work all show increased numbers of companies for variable pay. Robert Half International Inc., cited in a 1995 study, that nearly 80 percent of the executives surveyed think performance-based pay practices for most employees will become more common.

While the bonus/variable pay programs increase, some cautionary articles are appearing. CFO *Magazine's* recent cover article was entitled the "Myth of Incentive Pay."* The take-it-easy, not-so-fast group—spearheaded by Alfie Kohn, a consultant who made a name out of trying to show why financial reward systems ruin human motivation—primarily point out that too high a set of expectations for a perfect variable pay plan are bound to create disappointment.

Bonus systems are not easy to design, admittedly. But when designed well, they are value-added for all employees. *And when variable pay links to the many other factors of human motivation that open-book practices elicit, then the company can expect a charged-up, business-thinking workforce with the smarts to make a difference and the desire to make it happen.*

---

* "The Myth of Incentive Pay," CFO *Magazine,* July 1995.

Here are some ideas for getting beneficial results from the bonus process.

Change Your Reward Systems to Keep Them Fresh

Don't let people, including management, get so used to a bonus that they start seeing it as an entitlement. Business conditions change and incentives can change with them. Sometimes sales growth is more important than growing profit margins, sometimes not. If bonus plans are built to deliver real financial goals, re-designing won't be viewed as manipulative, but as seriously working on behalf of strengthening the business.

Put Management and Employees on Similar Bonus Systems

It builds trust, just as it reassures all of us to know that Congress is finally obeying the same laws as the rest of the country. The closer the reward systems are, the more they will align levels and functions, and create teamwork and concerted effort. Management wants the bonus and the profit sharing as much as the employee, so why would they build a bad one? This does not mean there is no room for distinctions: Sales may get additional bonuses for increasing sales while the whole company is on a cash flow goal, and managers with more responsibility than individual contributors may get higher percentages. But have as much unity as possible in the goal.

Be Prepared for Bad Quarters and Months

The first half of a great business year can be followed by a miserable second half. And the money that goes out in profit sharing to employees in the first half through monthly bonuses could be badly needed for other, more basic things, like meeting payroll. There are many ways to hedge against the cycles in the business year. One way is to simply bank part of the bonus and pay out the rest. At the end of the year when the final numbers have been put together, then employees can get the rest of the bonus they have earned.

Another way companies work against this end-of-the-year problem is by ratcheting the bonus up. The first three quarters could be 20 and 20 and 20 percent, the fourth quarter could be 40 percent of the bonus. People like an end-of-the-year bonus around December because of the holiday expenses.

Match Bonuses to Your Employees' Business Knowledge Level

As you enter open-book practices and many employees have little financial know-how, design a simple bonus with a direct line of sight. Profit before tax is a common candidate, but it also could be a line item in the budget that employees can control and see their impact. Service warranty costs, delivery costs, and productivity measures that easily equate to identifiable cost are all candidates for bonuses.

Making half the bonus quality or service driven, and the other half financial is common. As employees progress in their knowledge, an ROA (return on assets) bonus will both be understood by some and stretch employees to new understanding.

Companywide Bonus Systems Don't Eliminate Other Team or Individual Bonuses

When individuals or teams make special contributions, management can reward them without destroying the common destiny that a companywide bonus creates. The point is to emphasize the team goal.

There are as many ways to put together a bonus program as there are companies. The main ideas are not to be afraid to experiment, don't pay out bonuses when the company hasn't made money (the professional term for this feature is "self-funding"), and don't bonus behavior in individuals or departments if it doesn't help the whole organization.

If you want to speed up volume, don't put time limits on the bonus. A Midwestern firm selling engineering services devised a system to go for profitability. Instead of putting quarterly or month-end numbers on the bonus, management set a profit

Open Books at Work: 8. $2,900 in the Trash Teaches a Lesson

David Hanson, president of SynchroFlo in Norcross, Georgia, called his bank one day in early 1994 and asked for a lot of dollar bills, 10,000 of them to be exact. He picked up the bucks, took them back to his office, piled them on a table and covered them with a tablecloth. He then called in his 30-person production staff, the ones responsible for the $30 million in annual sales of the packaged pumping systems SynchroFlo sells to irrigation and high-rise building customers. The company's gain-sharing program had proven successful and it was time for the first big payoff. The gain for the first quarter had been impressive and the employees were getting their share.

Imagine the "oohs, aahs, and wows" when he pulled the tablecloth off that pile of money and said, more or less: "Here you go. It's yours. Well most of it." Hanson shared the good news about the improvement, but went on to make one other point—about quality and productivity. "Unfortunately," he continued, "I've got some bad news too."

"Two production errors cost us in the first quarter. Remember," he asked his production staff, "the job we had the wire on the wrong terminal when we turned on the process and it went caput?" Hanson counted out $400 and threw it in a trash can. "That was $400."

Then he continued, with a second question: "Remember the station we loaded in the container, and as it was being loaded there was a place we bent the skid a little, and the skid is now in Indonesia? . . . another $2,500."

Another trip to the trash can.

"Don't worry about this now. There is nothing we can do about it. But the remaining money will be split in half, and you'll see it in this paycheck," said Hanson. Paychecks were handed out, on the spot, with an additional $100 plus in them. The other half accrued and was paid out at the end of the year.

In that one little episode, Hanson taught, and motivated, by illustrating and by giving feedback that created accountability. Psychological ownership of quality intensified in the next quarter.

⮑ *Continued*

❧ **Continued**

By the way, Hanson did not really throw the money out. He retrieved it from the trash can and put it back in the bank. Money is, after all, money, and he still had to pay the bills. He'd taught his lesson.*

---

* "Throwing Money Away Helps Workers Appreciate the Cost of Mistakes," *Bottom Line*, Spring 1994.

---

amount bonus. In this instance, every time the company makes $75,000, there's a payout to the employees. If they get to $75,000 in 6 months, that's when the payout is. If they get there in 6 days, that's when the payout is. The message is quite clear to all employees. Everybody figures it out. The faster people work toward profitability, the more bonus people will get.

Chesapeake Packaging has a monthly profit goal of $85,000. For every $11,000 above that, employees get a 1 percent bonus. The system has everyone's attention and generates excitement in big sales months—as the volume comes in, the employees work to keep margins high. This is just one more example of clever bonus and profit-sharing systems that open-book companies use.

Good Work Is Its Own Reward

Business literacy motivation does not end with financial rewards. A telling line from a not so well-known 1950s movie starring William Holden, *The Executive Suite*, points to the deeper human need for work—"You can't make men work for money alone," says Holden, playing the young executive preaching to his uninspired board, "you starve their souls when you try it." Variable pay is just one ingredient in a very rich stew. Researchers have established that people like to work—that work can be rewarding—in and of itself. And most people don't need researchers to tell them when they have a good job, one that is actually fun.

Most of us engage in work naturally and enjoy it, when it meets certain easily identified criteria. Just ask people to tell you about the best job they've ever had. They'll say:

■ "I had a sense of accomplishment. I could see when I finished the job that it was something that was done right."

■ "I made lots of decisions. They let me use my brain. Nobody was hanging over me all the time, watching my every move."

■ "I never knew what was going to happen. It was different every day. I never got bored."

■ "I felt like I was doing something worthwhile. I could see that I was making a difference to people and that was neat."

What they're describing are characteristics the experts label "intrinsic motivation factors." Unlike extrinsic motivators such as money and praise, which come from outside the person when the work is done, these factors emerge from the work itself. They include, in more psychological terms:

■ *Feedback* that provides a sense of accomplishment.

■ *Autonomy* to make your own decisions.

■ *Variety* to alleviate the boredom of repetitive work.

■ *Task significance* to give the worker a sense of making a difference for the customer, the team, or the company.*

Open-book companies provide feedback with critical numbers that are known and understood by all. Their intensive huddles disseminate that feedback in an environment fostering autonomy where teams forecast the outcomes they are responsible for. No-kidding ownership in these enterprises generates decision-making, accountability for results, and rewards that foster a sense of accomplishment and attach personal significance to the task at hand.

---

* Richard Hackman, Greg Oldham, and E. E. Lawler III, in the early 1970s, did most of this research.

Even the most boring jobs in open-book management companies can take on meaning and purpose. The scorekeeping, feedback, seeing your individual impact directly through the line of sight on the financials, and the customers' willingness to buy are all intrinsically motivating.

In sports, prominently displayed scoreboards provide team members and fans alike with immediate feedback. But in business, the scoreboards are too often concealed. No wonder motivation is lost and people wind up just going through the motions.

Take bowling, for example.

A regular guy is out with his friends and decides to go bowling for a couple of lines. He has a beer or two, warms up a little bit, feels like he's going to have a good score, and rolls that first ball down the alley. As the ball heads for the pocket, making that familiar hard-rubber-on-hard-wood rolling sound of a 16-pound ball spinning over the wood slats, a little piece of canvas cloth comes down in front of the pins. The ball shoots through the canvas, hits a bunch of pins, which the guy hears because there is the usual rumble, but he can't see his score because the cloth is in the way.

In outrage and surprise, the bowler runs up to the manager at the bowling shop. "What kind of a deal is this?" he shouts. "I just bowled a line and heard all this noise but I can't see my score."

"Now relax," says the bowling manager, putting his hand on the bowler's shoulder for calming effect. *"Around here we don't keep score, we just bowl for the fun of the game!"*

The story, unlikely to happen, makes its point: What makes a sport engaging, or anything else with skill and accomplishment at stake, is keeping score. How can we have a game without keeping score?

Yet our work systems put people in settings regularly without providing a score. There are pieces of cloth up all over the workplace that prevent people from rapidly learning, from using their brains, from feeling the true significance in their work, or from creating variety by continually improving. One of the gifts of business literacy, by involving people in the big picture and encouraging rich cross-functional communication and connections in the huddles, is work without pieces of cloth. Open-book management, with team-based design, attacks bureaucratic specialization and the mind-numbing boredom past generations accepted.

Monetary Incentives Don't Work without Recognition

Picture this. A first-day employee, Anita, is excited about demonstrating to management that they made a great decision in hiring her. She is motivated to the hilt and is going to demonstrate that they hired the right person.

She gets her first assignment, Project A, from her boss. Anita pours herself into Project A, works hard on all the details and gets it looking perfect, handing it in with much satisfaction. With a look of anticipation toward her boss, waiting for feedback, Anita instead gets handed Project B.

She works hard on Project B, and another job of near perfection comes together. Like most new employees, Anita wants to make sure that this employer knows how well she can do. As she delivers the project, she eagerly awaits, with the look of a professional adult but the anticipation of a fourth grader who has a new teacher, a sign of approval and affirmation. No feedback still.

Here comes Project C. Anita still has lots of energy, and does a good job. She gets it done right and hands in the work with more than a little bit of doubt. "Am I starting to notice a pattern here that looks all too familiar?" goes through her mind. Sure enough, no feedback; here comes Project D.

Before doing Project D, Anita decides to see how much vacation she accumulated her first week on the job. Her breaks get a little longer, her quality slips a little and she hands in Project D with something nearing indifference.

Project E shows up . . . and so on . . . and so on. By the time Project R shows up, Anita is conditioned into average performance, going through the motions with a who-cares attitude.

This pattern is far too common in the workplace. Spirited and enthused people turn into people biding their time. Anita's hopes are not uncommon and her desire for recognition is not a sign of weakness. It is a near universal trait that people seek affirmation for their work. Remember this telling phrase: "Scratch an adult, and you find an adolescent." Right under the surface of our adult selves is an emotional being who needs recognition, who is emotional and shouldn't be ashamed of it.

This is what Demming was attacking in the schools when he said they grade and compare students and destroy their motivation. Our workplaces have been motivated by fear and by lousy recognition and rewards.

Implementers of open-book management must not make the mistake of thinking that monetary incentives are everything. *Monetary incentives won't work optimally unless a personalized and sincere set of person-to-person recognition accompanies the financial payouts.* Any company, open-book or not, that overrelies on incentives doesn't understand people. There are managers who can give out a thousand-dollar reward, and in doing so, they insult the recipient. Other managers, with a heartfelt thank-you and a deep look in the eye, can encourage people to freely give 110 percent of their best.

Some psychologists call thank-yous and praise "at-a-boys and at-a-girls." Such a label shows a clinical attitude with no real heart or passion about human endeavor. Real recognition, however, whether in the form of T-shirts, pats on the back, thank-yous, or casual days at the office, when done artfully by true player-coach leaders in the workplace, is heart-enriching and priceless. Authentic recognition is not about "at-a-anything." It is about human dignity in the workplace. It is about acknowledgment and human pride in making a difference.

Open-book management companies keep the effort going when they combine the power of recognition programs, the so-called "soft" nonmonetary rewards, with the power of financial incentives.

―――― ❄❄❄❄ ――――

Open-Book Management at Work: 9. Ice Cream and Stock Certificates

An employee-owned company had been using open-book management for a few years. The company's profits and financial health had greatly improved, most markedly in paying down a serious debt. As in many employee-owned companies, management found that the practices of opening the books and raising business literacy made sense. But many of the younger employees, not fully vested in the ownership plan, more tuned to bonuses now than ownership later, still did not feel excited about the yearly notice quantifying the value of their stock.

The employee-ownership committee knew something about both financial and nonfinancial reward systems. July was the month to give out the certificates. Instead of sending the notice in the mail, or enclosing it with the paychecks, which were handed to employees by supervisors, the committee concocted an employee-owner ice cream social. The stock value notice could be a time for celebrating and recognizing.

The vice president of Human Resources rented a small freezer truck to pull up to the docks at the company's several factories for a spontaneous celebration. On a hot July day, about break time, he'd pull up to deliver the notices and to dish out bowls and cones of ice cream, with lots of flavors to choose from, as a simple way to surprise and delight his employee-owner teammates with a financial and a social reward. Some employees remember the peppermint ice cream more than the notice. That's the way people are.

Employees in the factory 90 miles from the home office well remember the trip the vice president made to their plant. The freezer truck broke down so he had to pack his own family van with dry ice, turn on the air conditioner full blast, and drive the 90 miles wearing two sweaters and a scarf in 95-degree summer heat.

When he opened the van door and popped out with an arctic blast—like the beer commercials with snow drifting to the sand desert and covering the cactus when the beer is opened—the frost built up on his glasses to supply just the right touch. Everybody enjoyed the ice cream, the stock notice, and the memory of one frozen executive risking pneumonia in July.

The Equity Question: To Own or Not to Own

Open-book management companies are not necessarily, or even primarily, employee-owned. But once open-book management is going, a way to keep it thriving for the long term is to create widespread ownership. Equity is, and has been, a powerful motivator. If you are not convinced, ask yourself—when was the last time that you washed a rent-a-car?

And it is often a delicate topic as well. Widespread ownership sounds like communism to some. And those with wealth tire of those who want to make them feel guilty for having it. Stock options in Silicon Valley drove a whole industry for years. The hunger for equity not just across the Western world, but across the planet, is heating up. As free-market economies have burst into parts of the world formerly disavowing the power of private property, the craving for stock in China and behind the former Iron Curtain is powerful to watch. (Bo Burlingham of *Inc.* magazine reports that in southern China, crowds rioted just to get the *lottery tickets* for the possibility of purchasing stock in newly privatized companies.)

Politicians generally support widespread ownership, from Hubert Humphrey on the left:

> I see these as twin pillars of our economy: full employment of our labor resources and widespread ownership of our capital resources
> . . .

to Ronald Reagan's more conservative view:

> The American experiment (can) succeed only if power is widely distributed . . . Could there be anything resembling a free enterprise economy . . . while the greatest majority own little more than the shirts on their backs? . . . the nation's steadfast policy should afford every working American . . . the ownership and control of some meaningful form of property.*

---

* Joseph Blasi, *Employee Ownership, Revolution or Rip-Off*, New York: Ballinger, 1988.

The Company Stock Exchange

With a little vision and 25 years of persistence and practice, you could institute the principles of Science Applications International Corporation (SAIC), perhaps the most successful employee-owned company in the world. With 15,000 employees and over $2 billion in sales, the scientists who develop software and technological solutions for its many customers have a high degree of motivation and business literacy, in large part because of the company's stock bonus programs.

At SAIC, management has devised several ways to get stock into employee hands. Employees can buy stock, and own stock through an ESOP, employee stock ownership plan, as well as a 401(k). The bonus comes into play when management awards teams and individuals with stock options, contingent on their performance. The performance could be anything from winning an important contract, to making a technology breakthrough, to satisfying a customer and making an excellent margin.

There is also an annual bonus based on financial performance of groups of approximately 300 employees, depending on their performance in the niche they serve. The goal is to get employees to have stock worth two to five times their annual salary—it's the "glue," as SAIC calls it, for long-term motivation, the same glue used in many companies' executive compensation packages.

Does all this work?

The wealth-generating capacity of this company is without question—in Wal-Mart-like terms, SAIC stock worth $500 in 1969 is worth $1 million today, and stock value went up 22 percent in 1994.

A feature that pulls all the stock bonuses together is SAIC's own *SEC-registered* internal stock market. That's right—it has its own market that every quarter trades only SAIC stock at a 2 percent price to the seller among the employees, the company, and the retirement plans. The liquidity this feature offers helps pay college tuitions and build houses for the employees who need cash more than stock.

If it ever occurs to you that your bonus system is getting complicated, remember SAIC. Then go back to the drawing board and use No-Kidding ownership principles to motivate yourself and others.

Some 11 or 12 million Americans own a part of the company where they work through employee stock ownership plans. Nobody knows how many are owners through stock option and stock purchase plans. In spite of this sizable number, employee ownership may be more emerging than established. Companies are often not structured financially to share equity with employees. Venture capitalists may have put up all the risk and formation capital and therefore employees can't get stock. Most often, in privately held companies, the owners simply don't think of sharing ownership as an advantage.

In public companies, employees often participate in the healthy discounts in their stock purchasing plan, becoming owners but not viewing their purchase as a venture capitalist might, to generate wealth. Rather, they view their stock as part of a benefit package, not compensation for improving their own net worth as well as the company's. This is surely a lost opportunity that too few—and Sam Walton was one of the few—seize and make work.

Among all the factors of keeping open-book management going through motivation, equity is not the sole or even primary factor in open-book management financial reward systems. *Widespread equity is, however, something that open-book management encourages.* When equity is shared, then the long-term look that a company needs—the look past this year's profit and bonus and toward next year's debt-to-equity ratio and ROA—can be naturally built into all employees' minds. Instead of employees fighting for bonuses and small raises, usually assuming that the company owners get more profit than they deserve already, they become owner-thinkers and want the business to be healthy for the long term. They want a strong balance sheet. That may mean taking out less in bonuses to improve retained earnings, and doing whatever possible to raise the value of the stock, some of which they own.

Generating Open-Book Wealth

If employees have equity, then the financial statement that measures wealth and health, the balance sheet, can be used as an incentive. Bonuses are often attached to the income statement with its revenues and expenses and the hoped-for resulting profits. In this simple profit-sharing bonus scheme, a common one, the bonus is a percentage of wages earned, tied to the amount of company profit. For example:

Company's profits 6% = bonus of 5% above salary or wage
8% = 6%
10% = 8%

The employees in these systems learn to do whatever they can to increase profits so they can receive higher compensation.

But the companies that share equity add another dimension, which is often totally missed by huge percentages of employees and owners alike.

Take this example.

In a recent discussion with 25 managers and frontline workers from six highly participative companies discussing open-book management, a feature of their incentive systems came into question. In effect, the question was, does your bonus system have a cap, or does it act as a split, with no cap? For example, does the company give 40 percent of all the profits above a certain percentage to employees, no matter how big that number is, or is 40 percent of the bonus pool capped at a certain percentage of salary, or a total dollar amount, so that the rest goes back to the company?

In this discussion, employees, including management, couldn't think of a good reason for a bonus cap. (Does this sound like a recent discussion in professional sports, baseball maybe?) Why would they want to cap the bonus given to them if they could have an unlimited cap?

Then a certain feature of ownership emerged in the discussion. A dollar in a bonus program is a dollar. A dollar going into retained earnings, when seen from a stock ownership point of view, is a lot more than a dollar.

The financial ratio indicated by the initials P/E shows up in the stock quotations every day. That P/E symbol is second nature to business-literate individuals—it means price/earnings ratio. If the P/E is 10, that means that the price of the stock is selling at 10 times the company earnings. The average P/E ratio for much of the stock market has been closer to 15/1 for some years. If a company is privately held, the stock often will be valued by an outside appraiser in the 6/1 to 12/1 range, depending on the industry and a host of other factors.

Most workers and employees and middle managers without stock, and lots of owners with stock, forget about how this ratio works and what it means. Where else is it possible to watch 1 dollar turn into 10? How else can you get 10 times your money? Las Vegas if you are lucky, maybe. On the streets peddling something illegal, maybe. But not just anywhere, that's for sure. These days, CDs, mutual funds, and bonds all exist on returns of less than 10 percent. Comparatively, the employee-owners of a company could cap their bonuses, put the dollars over the cap in retained earnings, and earn $10 for every one they put in company stock. In actuality, it is not quite that simple, since profit doesn't equate directly to earnings. But the principle holds true and employee-owners who understand what they have get the point. Is 10 dollars, for every one invested, better than the 10 cents a mutual fund would return? Can anyone wonder why ownership creates a craving for those who understand it?

But back to the bonus cap discussion with the 25 employees.

As the cap on the bonus was put in light of this feature of equity, a little hush entered the room, a pregnant capitalist pause, as it were. Not all in the room understood the ownership question clearly, for sure. They were not fully business-literate on that point. But all knew the discussion had taken a serious turn. And the silence was telling as minds churned and stretched to figure out how this return on the dollar differed from a bonus dollar. Suddenly, the power of ownership came very close to home, and everyone was struck by what they had been overlooking, that a bonus with or without a cap is not the whole discussion (see Figure 14.1).

When employees' own stock, and their company's value goes up, that one dollar of bonus not taken turns into a lot more in equity. This changes people's thinking. When employees in companies that share equity understand what that means, they welcome a bonus cap, after reasonable short-term bonuses are paid out. (The age of the employee often factors in here—the younger the employee, the employee-owned companies report, the more the bonus and short-term reward are motivating.)

Equity is the quickest and strongest way to get employees just as interested in the balance sheet and stock as they are in the income statement and bonuses.

Why Equity, by Itself, Is Not *the* Answer

If equity were *the* answer for employee motivation, then things would be simple. The problem is that there are employee-owned companies where an ownership mentality still does not exist.

More than one ESOP company has had this strikingly paradoxical experience. Some ESOP companies, even 100 percent employee-owned, have had the humiliating and perplexing experience of the employees going out on strike. *In other words, the employees struck themselves.*

If this is not an ironic example of business illiteracy, then what is? How can employees be owners and yet strike the very enterprise that they own? It is because they do not understand

Figure 14.1 The Magic of Equity

A Bonus   *Can Equal*   Equity

the power of equity, and management still has not taught employees the meaning of business and employee ownership. Perhaps it is only a management that has done so poorly at increasing business literacy that suffers a strike from their fellow owners.

The proponents of employee ownership have learned much in the last few decades. Some had thought that ownership, by itself, was going to have a magic effect, and it didn't.* What they learned is that ownership, without employee participation, was not very effective in helping a company perform. Because open-book management helps employees participate authentically and promotes business literacy so effectively, many employee-owned companies, like Webb Converting, and even the ones started for tax breaks, are turning to open-book methods.

In jobs that are designed well and are naturally engaging, ownership, bonuses, recognition, and pride combine to help employees think and act like competent businesspeople, or like no-kidding, honest-to-goodness owners. The good news is that for those companies where shared ownership is not practical, open-book management and its many levers for motivation can still work well. But the opportunity to kick in a motivator that acts like overdrive, beyond fifth gear, exists for those companies that can share ownership.

---

* Corey Rosen, Katherine J. Klein, and Karen M. Young, *Employee Ownership in America*, Lexington, MA: D.C. Heath, 1986.

Epilogue

The interval between the decay of the old and the formation and the establishment of the new, constitutes a period of transition, which must always be necessarily one of uncertainty, confusion, error, and wild and fierce fanaticism.

John C. Calhoun

On gritty 149th Street in the Bronx, a successful and long-term experiment in business literacy is in its second decade. Home Care Associates, a home health-care company competing in one of the fastest growing segments of the health-care industry, is a cooperative with 300 employee/members consisting, for the most part, of formerly underemployed and unemployed minority women. Unlike many workers in this low-paid industry, the home-health aides at Home Care Associates can make a decent living doing what they like, caring for the ill, often the elderly, who are confined to their homes.

How do they accomplish this when others struggle to survive in this industry?

Employee/members earn 10 to 20 percent more than the industry average. Home Care Associates doesn't try to be the lowest paying, low-cost provider, but a service-driven, price-competitive company that is owned and managed by the very workers who serve the clients. Rick Surpin, the founder of the cooperative, believes in business literacy, "because without it, we can't get where we need to go with employees in a workers' council managing the future of the business."

There are 300 employees at this cooperative who see the financial results of their efforts, and plans include "getting to 600

271

employees in three years and continuing to try to be a leader in the industry by providing advanced services," says Surpin.

The competitive edge at this enterprise is a committed and business-smart workforce that delivers superior service because of the inherent and the financial rewards.

It is these kinds of efforts that make up the economic and social significance of open-book management. So, as the book ends, the story just begins, because the applications are now beginning to multiply.

As companies and teams try their hand at open-book management, inventive applications will emerge and spread. The more business challenges and threats that are faced, the more innovative open-book solutions will be created.

When all is said and done, the innovations are only as lasting as the innovators who know how to repeat and surpass them. And the real significance of a better bottom line or a stronger balance sheet won't be more people rushing into patterns of conspicuous consumption. Rather, it is the pride that comes when individuals and companies contribute to community well-being by creating dignified jobs and great service.

Work at the end of the 21st century will be at least as different from work now, as work now is different from the factories of the late 19th century. Capitalism, and the work patterns it drives, will be renewed.

Capitalism Renewed

The 21st century is here.
Out of the bottle comes the capitalism genie . . .
it can't be kept in.
Russia, East Germany, all behind the rusted Iron Curtain,
and China
have all rubbed and seen it escape.

The new century brings the usual human paradox stuff:
Pushes for more democracy with local repression and ugly wars,
more employee owners in Russia than in the U.S.

Thinning ozone layers and depleted fish stocks, the result of our
    very productivity
The human race races on,
each generation creating new social patterns for the next,
to adopt or drop,
depending on their utility and the mood of the times.
If Churchill was right, that the problem with capitalism is that too
    few share in its rewards,
then maybe it hasn't been tried yet,
Let's not make that the problem of the next generation.
Let's make a breakthrough, like the elimination of smallpox or
    landing someone on the lunar dustscape.
Widespread economic opportunity, lasting business know-how,
open books for adding value.
Let our children fight a different battle
and wage war on something new.

Bibliography

Books

Block, Peter, *The Empowered Manager*, San Francisco: Jossey-Bass, 1987. Ideas and support for middle managers who do not want to wait for the organization to introduce open-book management.

Case, John, *Open-Book Management, The Coming Business Revolution*, New York: Harper Business, 1995. Clear, understandable treatment of open-book approach with examples.

DePree, Max, *Leadership Is an Art*, New York: Doubleday, 1987. Philosophy of leadership needed to lead open-book management.

Greenleaf, Robert, *Servant Leadership*, New York: Paulist Press, 1977. Wise and poetic description of leadership that sustains and grows business literacy.

McWhiter, Darren A., *Sharing Ownership, The Manager's Guide to ESOPs and Other Productivity Incentive Plans*, New York: John Wiley & Sons, 1993. Information on ownership for those considering sharing equity.

Pinchot, Gifford, and Elizabeth, *The End of Bureaucracy and the Rise of the Intelligent Organization*, San Francisco: Berrett-Koehler, 1993. A great theoretical overview of the future of open-book flexible organizations.

Schuster, John, *Hum-Drum to Hot-Diggity: Creating Everyday Greatness in the World of Work*, Steadfast Publishers, 1993.

Semler, Ricardo, *Maverick: The Success Story Behind the World's Most Unusual Workplace*, New York: Warner Books, 1993. A fun and compelling example of an open-book democratic company in Brazil.

Senge, Peter M., *The Fifth Discipline: The Art and Practice of the Learning Organization*, New York: Doubleday, 1990. A detailed description of crafting of a learning organization, fully supporting what is needed in an open-book environment.

275

Stack, Jack, *The Great Game of Business: The Only Sensible Way to Run a Company*, New York: Doubleday, 1992. One of the best case studies of open-book management; all four model dimensions are illustrated.

Tracy, John A., *How to Read a Financial Report* (4th ed.), New York: John Wiley & Sons, 1995. Get help wringing cash flow and other vital signs out of the flood of numbers.

Wheatley, Margaret J., *Leadership and the New Science*, San Francisco: Berrett-Koehler, 1992. Presents an important view of the nature of systems and the challenge for leaders in work systems. Totally congruent with open-book systems approach. Incorporates quantum physics in a poetic/scientific mix.

Articles

Birchard, Bill, "Mastering the New Metrics," CFO *Magazine*, October 1994, p. 30.

Block, Peter, "From Paternalism to Stewardship," *Training*, July 1993, p. 45.

Burlingham, Bo, "This Woman Has Changed Business Forever," *Inc.*, June 1990, p. 34.

Case, John, "A Company of Business People," *Inc.*, April 1993, p. 79.

Case, John, "The Open-Book Revolution," *Inc.*, June 1995, p. 26.

Greer, Olen L., Stevan K. Olson, & Marty Callison, "The Key to Real Teamwork: Understanding the Numbers," *Management Accounting*, May 1992, p. 39.

Henricks, Mark, "Open Book Policy," *Entrepreneur*, May 1994, p. 44.

Hyatt, Joshua, "Steal This Strategy," *Inc.*, February 1991.

Kaplan, Robert S., & David P. Norton, "The Balanced Scorecard—Measures That Drive Performance," *Harvard Business Review*, January–February 1992.

Kaplan, Robert S., & David P. Norton, "Putting the Balanced Scorecard to Work," *Harvard Business Review*, September–October 1993.

Lee, Chris, "Open-Book Management," *Training*, July 1994, p. 21.

Tully, Shawn, "The Real Key to Creating Wealth," *Fortune*, September 1993, p. 20.

Index